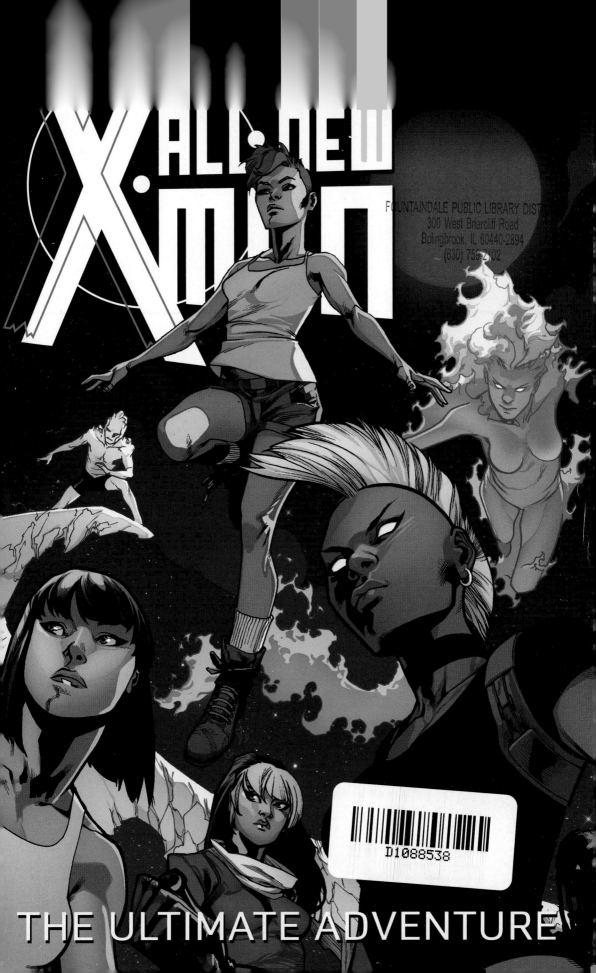

ALL·NEW X·MEN

THE ULTIMATE ADVENTURE

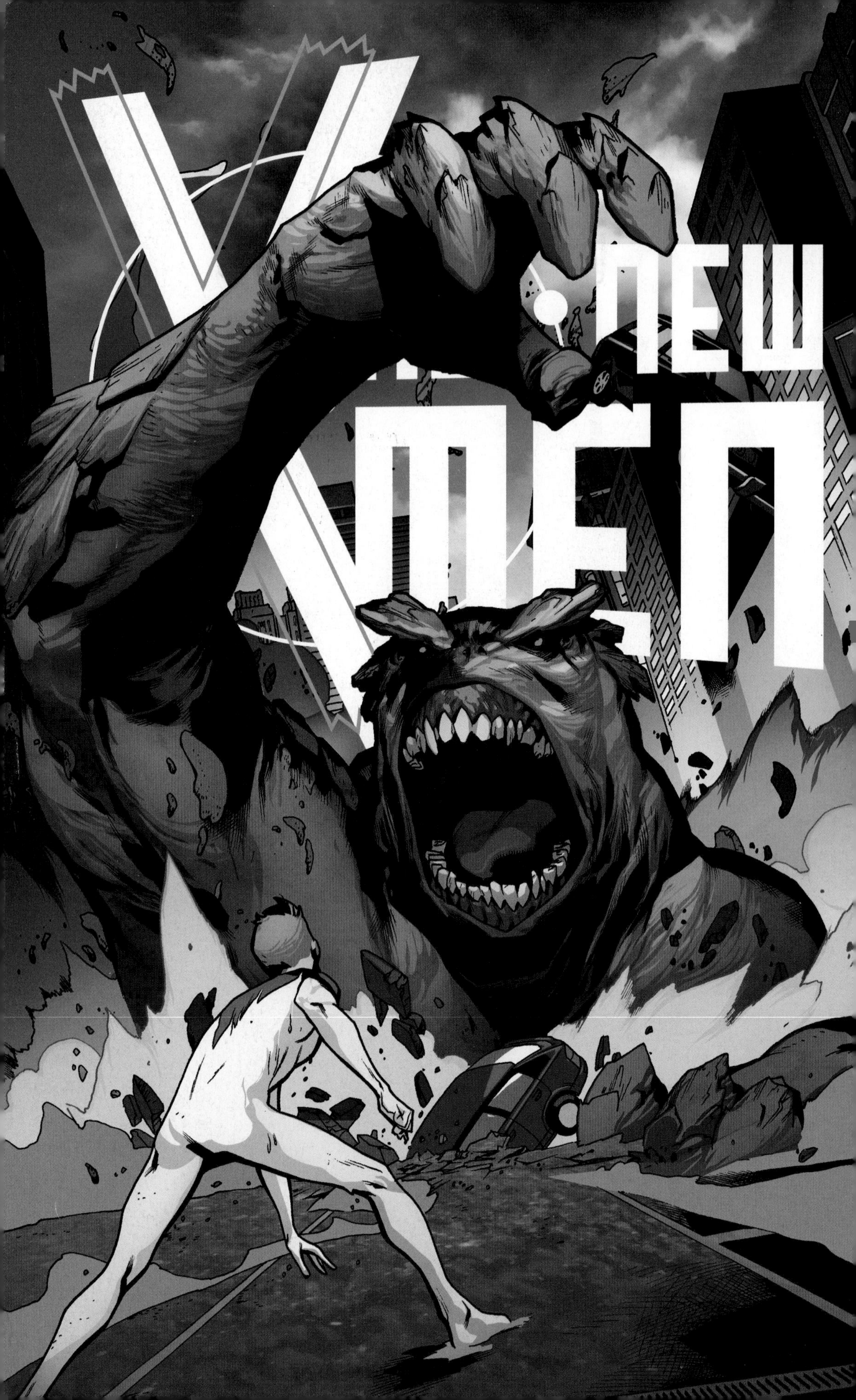
NEW
MEN

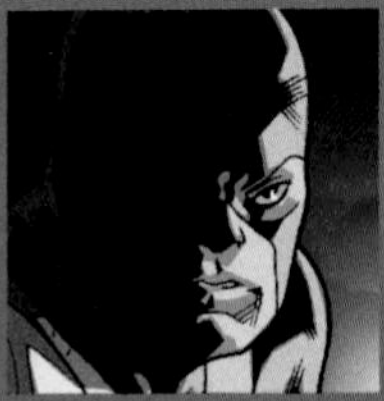

BEAST
HANK McCOY

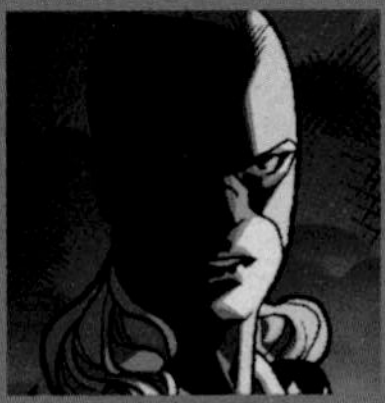

MARVEL GIRL
JEAN GREY

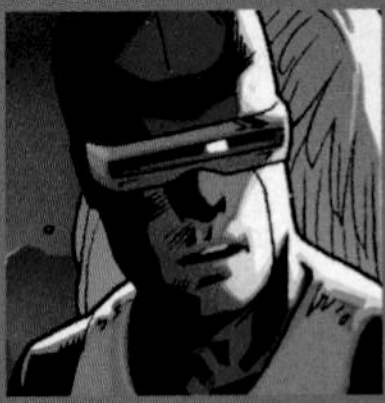

CYCLOPS
SCOTT SUMMERS

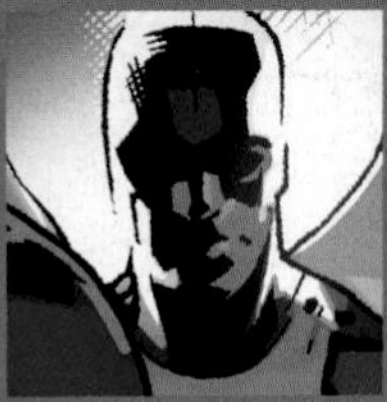

ANGEL
WARREN WORTHINGTON III

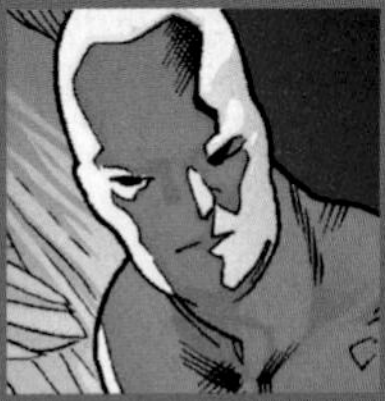

ICEMAN
BOBBY DRAKE

THE ULTIMATE ADVENTURE

BRIAN MICHAEL **BENDIS**
WRITER

MAHMUD **ASRAR**
ARTIST

MARTE **GRACIA**
WITH **JASON KEITH** (#31)
COLORISTS

CORY **PETIT**
LETTERER

XANDER **JAROWEY**
ASSISTANT EDITOR

MIKE **MARTS**
EDITOR

COVER ART: **STUART IMMONEN, WADE VON GRAWBADGER & MARTE GRACIA** (#31), **SARA PICHELLI & MARTE GRACIA** (#32 & #35) AND **MAHMUD ASRAR & MARTE GRACIA** (#33-34 & #36)

X-MEN CREATED BY **STAN LEE & JACK KIRBY**

COLLECTION EDITOR: **JENNIFER GRÜNWALD** ASSOCIATE MANAGING EDITOR: **ALEX STARBUCK**
EDITOR, SPECIAL PROJECTS: **MARK D. BEAZLEY** SENIOR EDITOR, SPECIAL PROJECTS: **JEFF YOUNGQUIST**
SVP PRINT, SALES & MARKETING: **DAVID GABRIEL** BOOK DESIGNER: **RODOLFO MURAGUCHI**

EDITOR IN CHIEF: **AXEL ALONSO** CHIEF CREATIVE OFFICER: **JOE QUESADA**
PUBLISHER: **DAN BUCKLEY** EXECUTIVE PRODUCER: **ALAN FINE**

ALL-NEW X-MEN VOL. 6: THE ULTIMATE ADVENTURE. Contains material originally published in magazine form as ALL-NEW X-MEN #31-36. First printing 2015. ISBN# 978-0-7851-8969-5. Published by MARVEL WORLDWIDE, INC., a subsidiary of MARVEL ENTERTAINMENT, LLC. OFFICE OF PUBLICATION: 135 West 50th Street, New York, NY 10020. **Printed in the U.S.A.** ALAN FINE, President, Marvel Entertainment; DAN BUCKLEY, President, TV, Publishing and Brand Management; JOE QUESADA, Chief Creative Officer; TOM BREVOORT, SVP of Publishing; DAVID BOGART, SVP of Operations & Procurement, Publishing; C.B. CEBULSKI, VP of International Development & Brand Management; DAVID GABRIEL, SVP Print, Sales & Marketing; JIM O'KEEFE, VP of Operations & Logistics; DAN CARR, Executive Director of Publishing Technology; SUSAN CRESPI, Editorial Operations Manager; ALEX MORALES, Publishing Operations Manager; STAN LEE, Chairman Emeritus. For information regarding advertising in Marvel Comics or on Marvel.com, please contact Jonathan Rheingold, VP of Custom Solutions & Ad Sales, at jrheingold@marvel.com. For Marvel subscription inquiries, please call 800-217-9158.

Born with genetic mutations that gave them abilities beyond those of normal humans, mutants are the next stage in evolution. As such, they are feared and hated by humanity. A group of mutants known as the X-Men fight for peaceful coexistence between mutants and humankind. But not all mutants see peaceful coexistence as a reality.

X-ALL-NEW X-MEN

The original X-Men — Jean Grey, Cyclops, Iceman, Angel and Beast — were brough to the present in an attempt to shine a light on the errors of the present day X-Men. Unable to return to the past, the All-New X-Men have taken up residence at the New Xavier School along with new teammate X-23, and their leader, Professor Kitty Pryde. However, the team recently lost the young Scott Summers, when he left to explore space with his father, Corsair, whom he long thought dead.

Having defeated the future Brotherhood of Mutants, the All-New X-Men have been left to lick their wounds and collect their thoughts. Seeking some rest and relaxation, Angel and X-23 took their leave of the school to spend a night out together. Meanwhile, Jean Grey began to receive training from Emma Frost in the use of her new psionic powers. Though they initially locked horns, the training process began to heal the rift between the two, bringing about a surprising revelation — Jean and Emma are becoming friends. However, Jean's training was interrupted by the arrival of Storm and the present-day versions of Iceman and Beast. And they have brought startling news — they've come to collect Scott Summers for the reading of Charles Xavier's will!

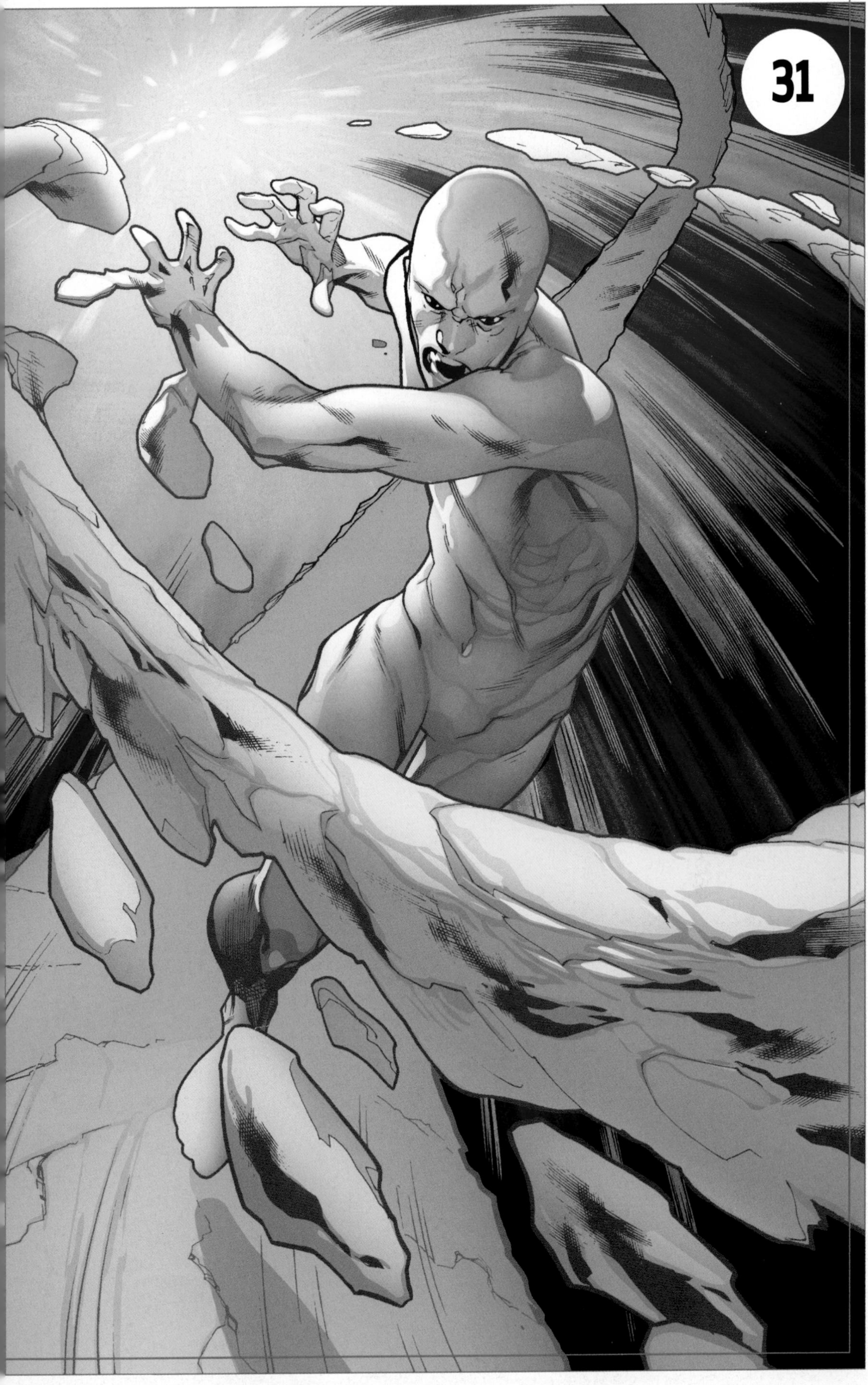
31

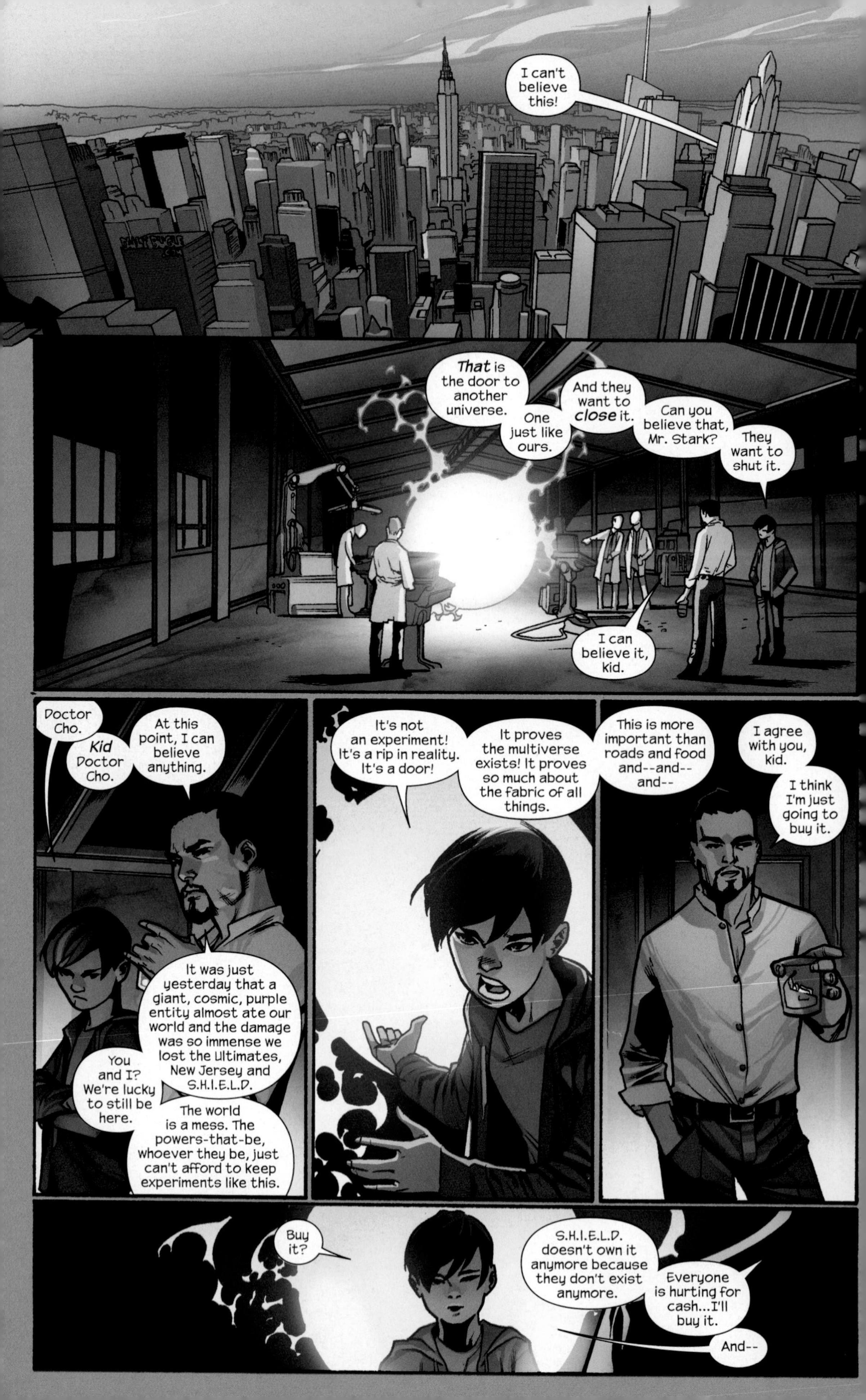

I can't believe this!
That is the door to another universe.
One just like ours.
And they want to close it.
Can you believe that, Mr. Stark?
They want to shut it.
I can believe it, kid.
Doctor Cho.
Kid Doctor Cho.
At this point, I can believe anything.
It was just yesterday that a giant, cosmic, purple entity almost ate our world and the damage was so immense we lost the Ultimates, New Jersey and S.H.I.E.L.D.
You and I? We're lucky to still be here.
The world is a mess. The powers-that-be, whoever they be, just can't afford to keep experiments like this.
It's not an experiment! It's a rip in reality. It's a door!
It proves the multiverse exists! It proves so much about the fabric of all things.
This is more important than roads and food and--and--and--
I agree with you, kid.
I think I'm just going to buy it.
Buy it?
S.H.I.E.L.D. doesn't own it anymore because they don't exist anymore.
Everyone is hurting for cash...I'll buy it.
And--

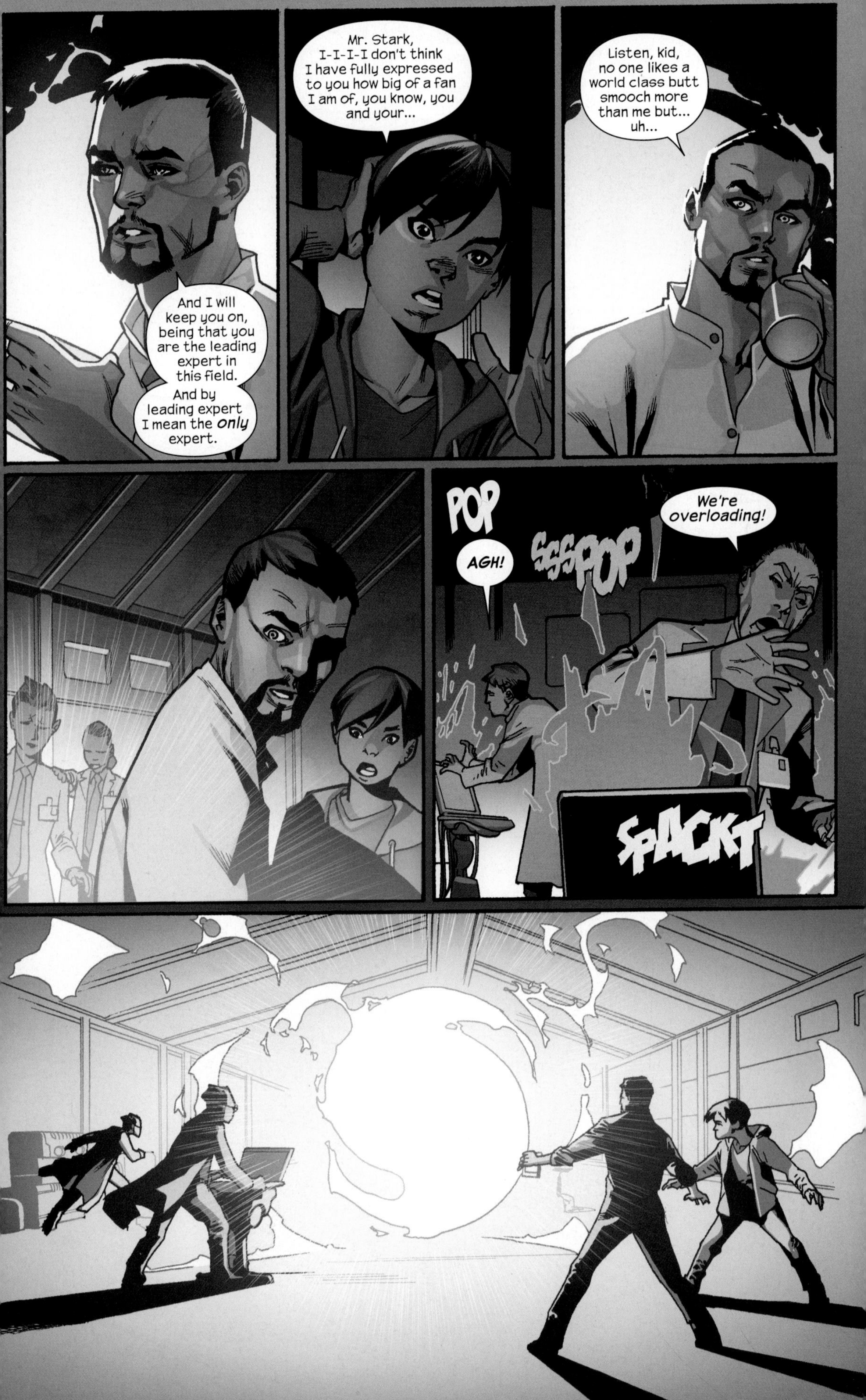
And I will keep you on, being that you are the leading expert in this field.
And by leading expert I mean the *only* expert.
Mr. Stark, I-I-I-I don't think I have fully expressed to you how big of a fan I am of, you know, you and your...
Listen, kid, no one likes a world class butt smooch more than me but... uh...
POP
AGH!
SSSPOP
We're overloading!
SPACKT

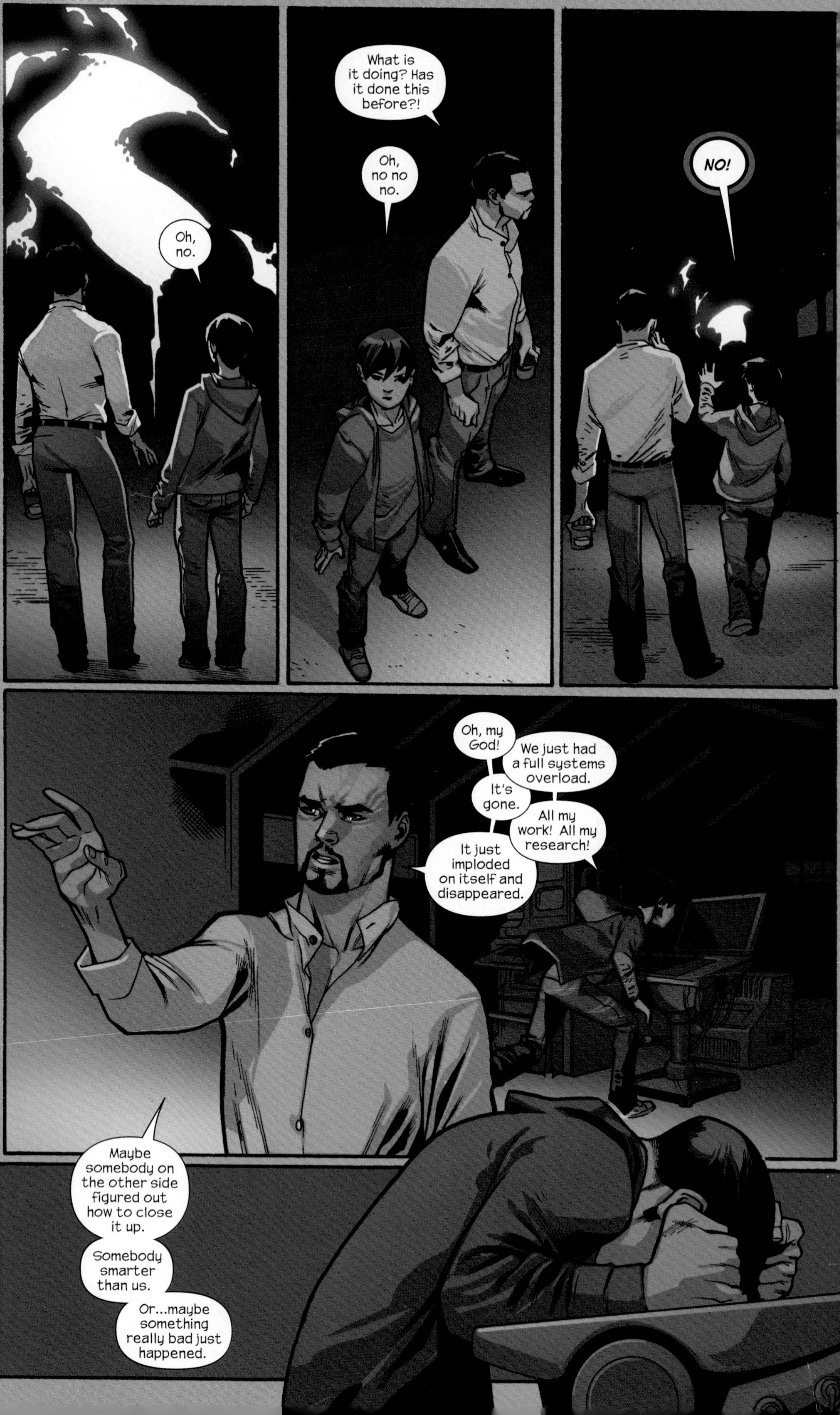
Oh, no.
What is it doing? Has it done this before?!
Oh, no no no.
NO!
Oh, my God!
We just had a full systems overload.
It's gone.
All my work! All my research!
It just imploded on itself and disappeared.
Maybe somebody on the other side figured out how to close it up.
Somebody smarter than us.
Or...maybe something really bad just happened.

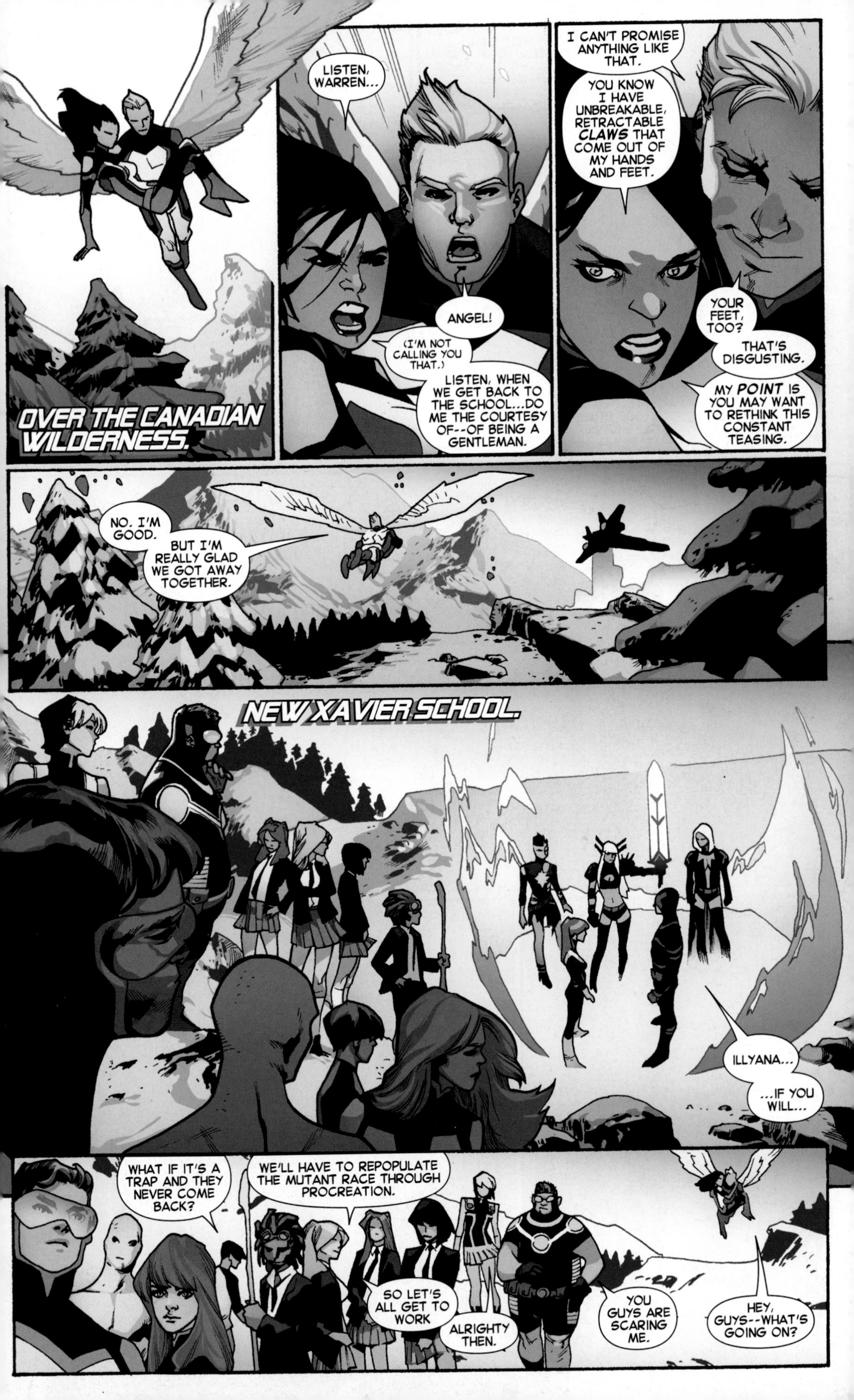

OVER THE CANADIAN WILDERNESS.
LISTEN, WARREN...
ANGEL!
(I'M NOT CALLING YOU THAT.)
LISTEN, WHEN WE GET BACK TO THE SCHOOL...DO ME THE COURTESY OF--OF BEING A GENTLEMAN.
I CAN'T PROMISE ANYTHING LIKE THAT.
YOU KNOW I HAVE UNBREAKABLE, RETRACTABLE CLAWS THAT COME OUT OF MY HANDS AND FEET.
YOUR FEET, TOO?
THAT'S DISGUSTING.
MY POINT IS YOU MAY WANT TO RETHINK THIS CONSTANT TEASING.
NO. I'M GOOD.
BUT I'M REALLY GLAD WE GOT AWAY TOGETHER.
NEW XAVIER SCHOOL.
ILLYANA...
...IF YOU WILL...
WHAT IF IT'S A TRAP AND THEY NEVER COME BACK?
WE'LL HAVE TO REPOPULATE THE MUTANT RACE THROUGH PROCREATION.
SO LET'S ALL GET TO WORK
ALRIGHTY THEN.
YOU GUYS ARE SCARING ME.
HEY, GUYS--WHAT'S GOING ON?

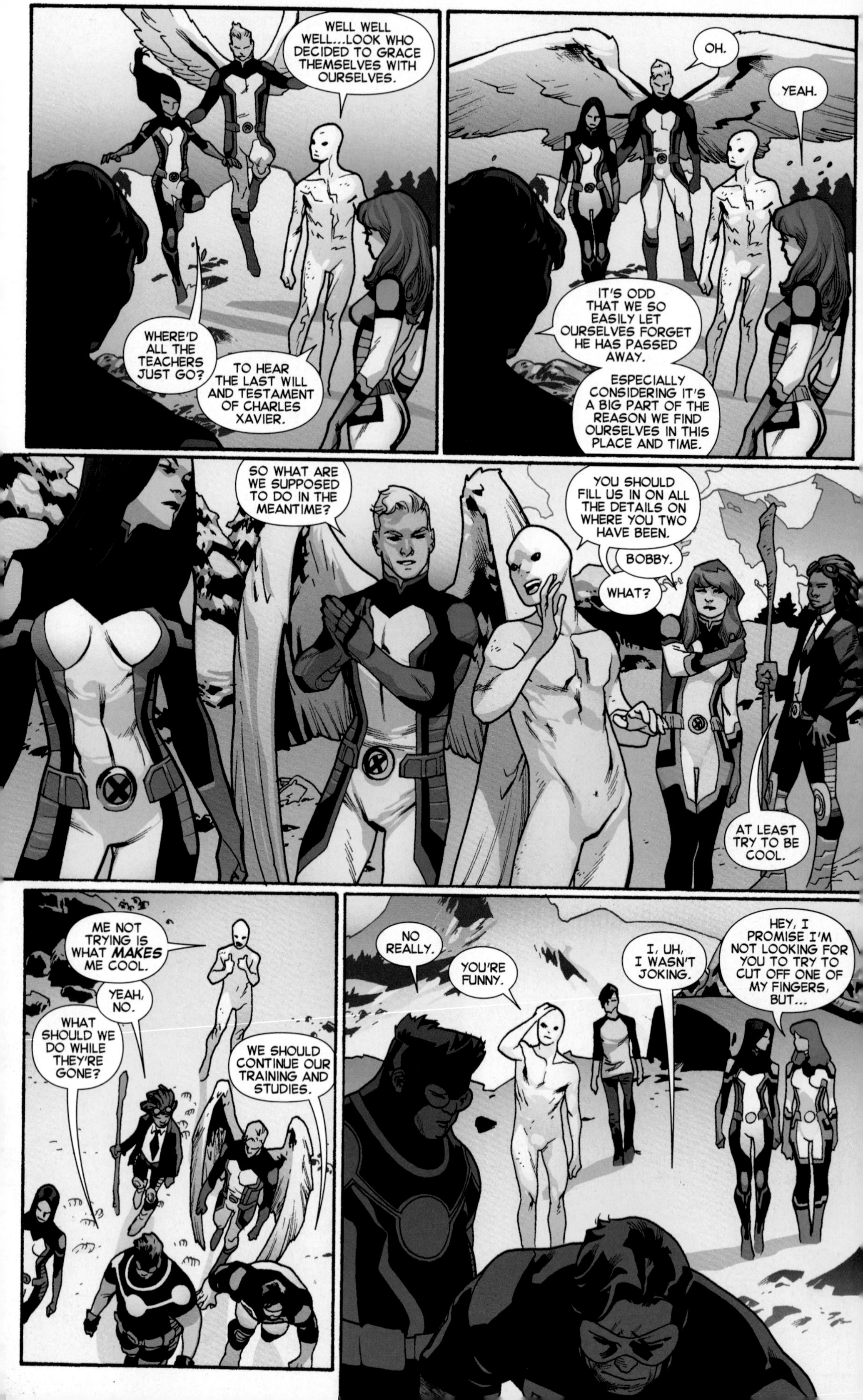
WELL WELL WELL...LOOK WHO DECIDED TO GRACE THEMSELVES WITH OURSELVES.
WHERE'D ALL THE TEACHERS JUST GO?
TO HEAR THE LAST WILL AND TESTAMENT OF CHARLES XAVIER.
OH.
YEAH.
IT'S ODD THAT WE SO EASILY LET OURSELVES FORGET HE HAS PASSED AWAY.
ESPECIALLY CONSIDERING IT'S A BIG PART OF THE REASON WE FIND OURSELVES IN THIS PLACE AND TIME.
SO WHAT ARE WE SUPPOSED TO DO IN THE MEANTIME?
YOU SHOULD FILL US IN ON ALL THE DETAILS ON WHERE YOU TWO HAVE BEEN.
BOBBY.
WHAT?
AT LEAST TRY TO BE COOL.
ME NOT TRYING IS WHAT *MAKES* ME COOL.
YEAH, NO.
WHAT SHOULD WE DO WHILE THEY'RE GONE?
WE SHOULD CONTINUE OUR TRAINING AND STUDIES.
NO REALLY.
YOU'RE FUNNY.
I, UH, I WASN'T JOKING.
HEY, I PROMISE I'M NOT LOOKING FOR YOU TO TRY TO CUT OFF ONE OF MY FINGERS, BUT...

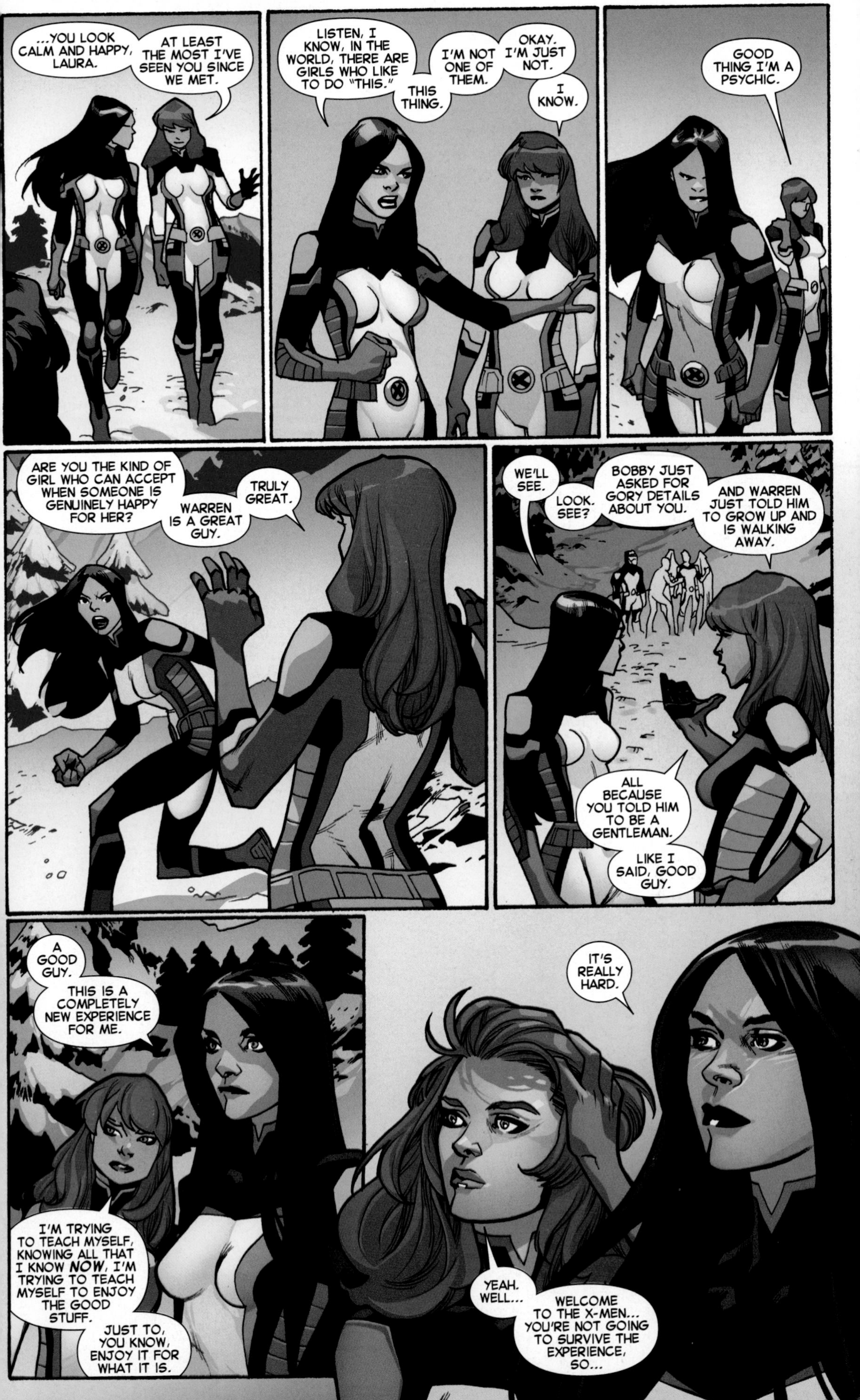

...YOU LOOK CALM AND HAPPY, LAURA.
AT LEAST THE MOST I'VE SEEN YOU SINCE WE MET.
LISTEN, I KNOW, IN THE WORLD, THERE ARE GIRLS WHO LIKE TO DO "THIS."
THIS THING.
I'M NOT ONE OF THEM.
OKAY. I'M JUST NOT.
I KNOW.
GOOD THING I'M A PSYCHIC.
ARE YOU THE KIND OF GIRL WHO CAN ACCEPT WHEN SOMEONE IS GENUINELY HAPPY FOR HER?
WARREN IS A GREAT GUY.
TRULY GREAT.
WE'LL SEE.
LOOK. SEE?
BOBBY JUST ASKED FOR GORY DETAILS ABOUT YOU.
AND WARREN JUST TOLD HIM TO GROW UP AND IS WALKING AWAY.
ALL BECAUSE YOU TOLD HIM TO BE A GENTLEMAN.
LIKE I SAID, GOOD GUY.
A GOOD GUY.
THIS IS A COMPLETELY NEW EXPERIENCE FOR ME.
I'M TRYING TO TEACH MYSELF, KNOWING ALL THAT I KNOW ***NOW***, I'M TRYING TO TEACH MYSELF TO ENJOY THE GOOD STUFF.
JUST TO, YOU KNOW, ENJOY IT FOR WHAT IT IS.
IT'S REALLY HARD.
YEAH. WELL...
WELCOME TO THE X-MEN... YOU'RE NOT GOING TO SURVIVE THE EXPERIENCE, SO...

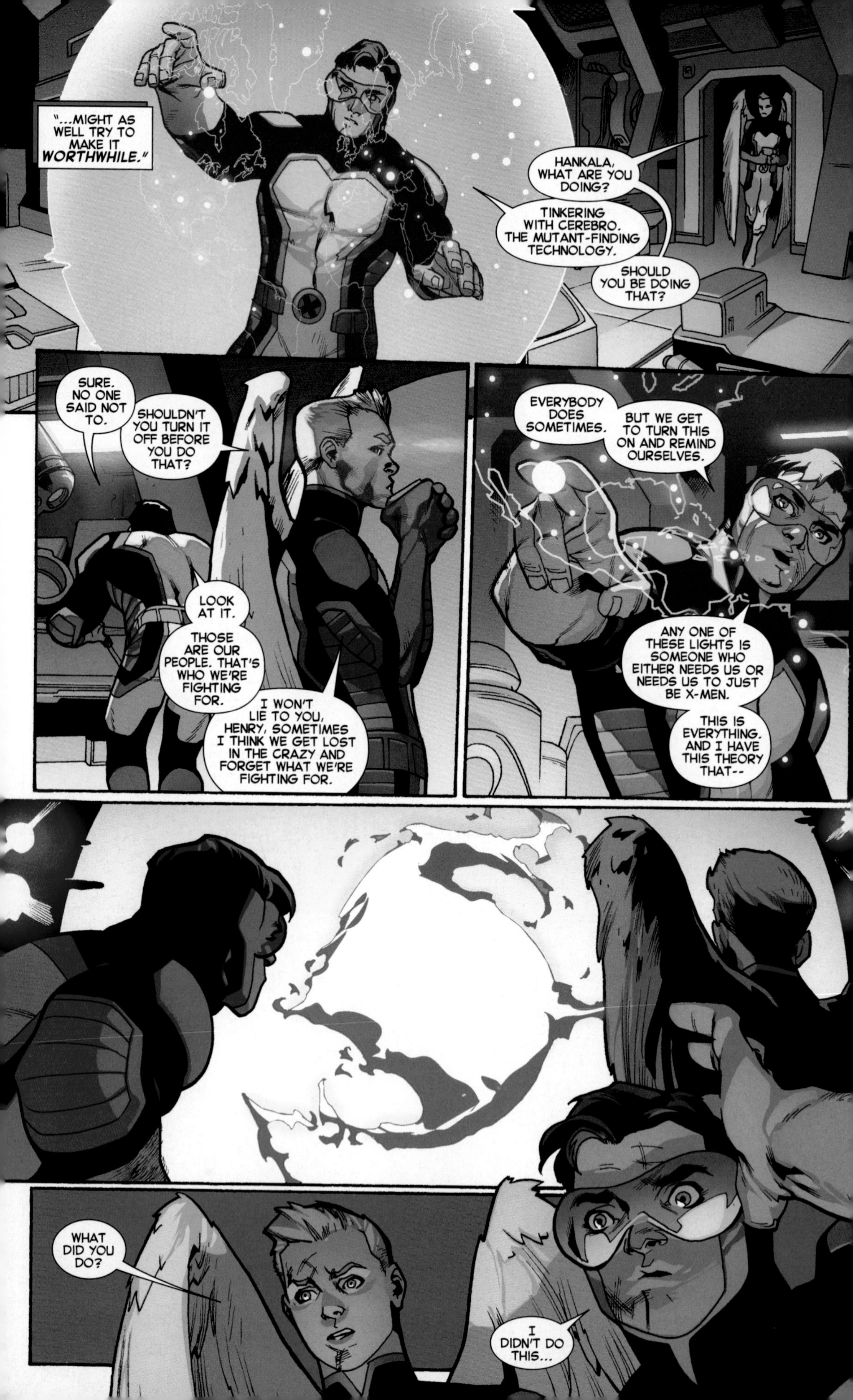
"...MIGHT AS WELL TRY TO MAKE IT *WORTHWHILE.*"
HANKALA, WHAT ARE YOU DOING?
TINKERING WITH CEREBRO. THE MUTANT-FINDING TECHNOLOGY.
SHOULD YOU BE DOING THAT?
SURE. NO ONE SAID NOT TO.
SHOULDN'T YOU TURN IT OFF BEFORE YOU DO THAT?
LOOK AT IT.
THOSE ARE OUR PEOPLE. THAT'S WHO WE'RE FIGHTING FOR.
I WON'T LIE TO YOU, HENRY, SOMETIMES I THINK WE GET LOST IN THE CRAZY AND FORGET WHAT WE'RE FIGHTING FOR.
EVERYBODY DOES SOMETIMES.
BUT WE GET TO TURN THIS ON AND REMIND OURSELVES.
ANY ONE OF THESE LIGHTS IS SOMEONE WHO EITHER NEEDS US OR NEEDS US TO JUST BE X-MEN.
THIS IS EVERYTHING. AND I HAVE THIS THEORY THAT--
WHAT DID YOU DO?
I DIDN'T DO THIS...

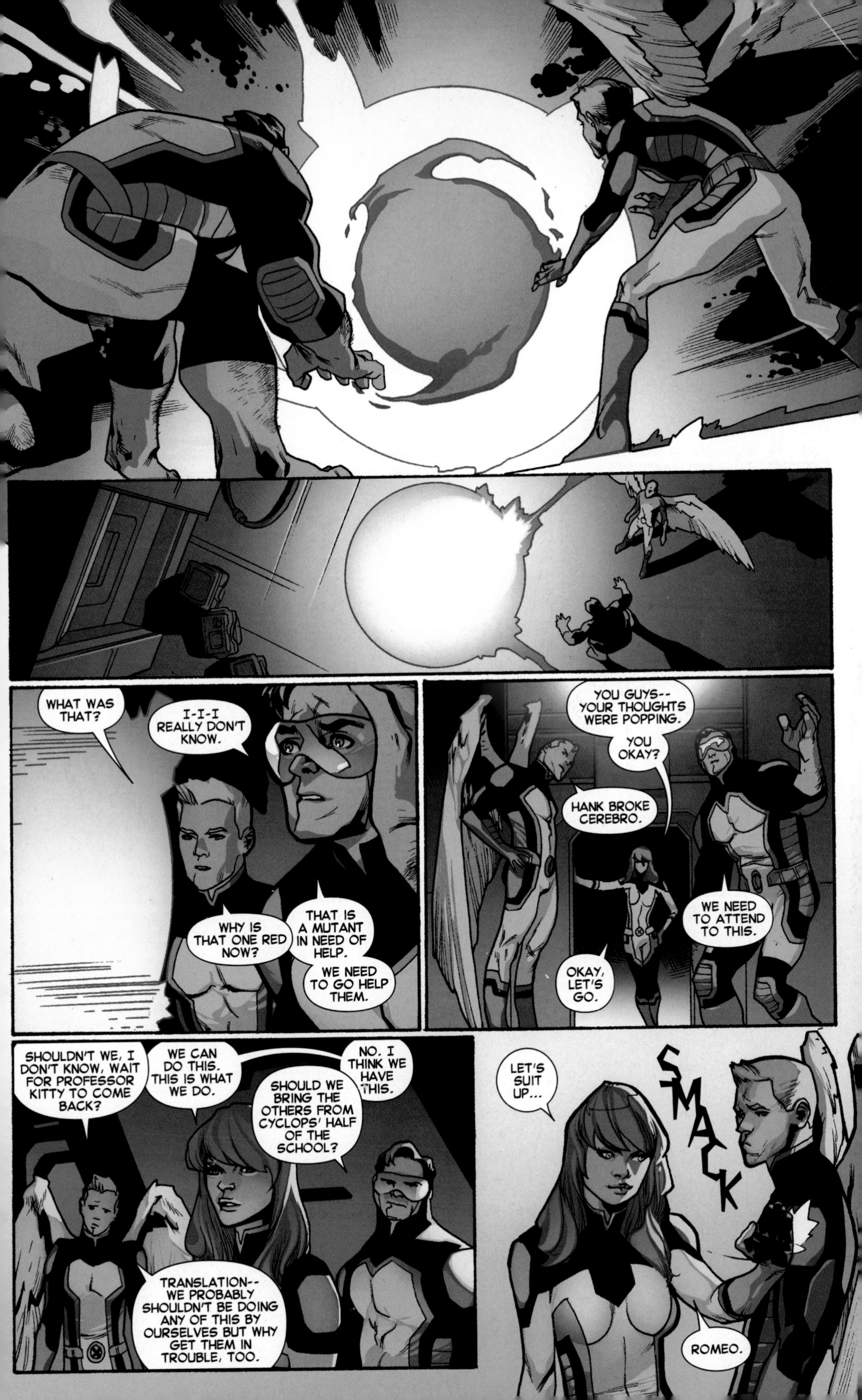
WHAT WAS THAT?
I-I-I REALLY DON'T KNOW.
WHY IS THAT ONE RED NOW?
THAT IS A MUTANT IN NEED OF HELP.
WE NEED TO GO HELP THEM.
YOU GUYS-- YOUR THOUGHTS WERE POPPING.
YOU OKAY?
HANK BROKE CEREBRO.
WE NEED TO ATTEND TO THIS.
OKAY, LET'S GO.
SHOULDN'T WE, I DON'T KNOW, WAIT FOR PROFESSOR KITTY TO COME BACK?
WE CAN DO THIS. THIS IS WHAT WE DO.
NO. I THINK WE HAVE THIS.
SHOULD WE BRING THE OTHERS FROM CYCLOPS' HALF OF THE SCHOOL?
TRANSLATION-- WE PROBABLY SHOULDN'T BE DOING ANY OF THIS BY OURSELVES BUT WHY GET THEM IN TROUBLE, TOO.
LET'S SUIT UP...
SMACK
ROMEO.

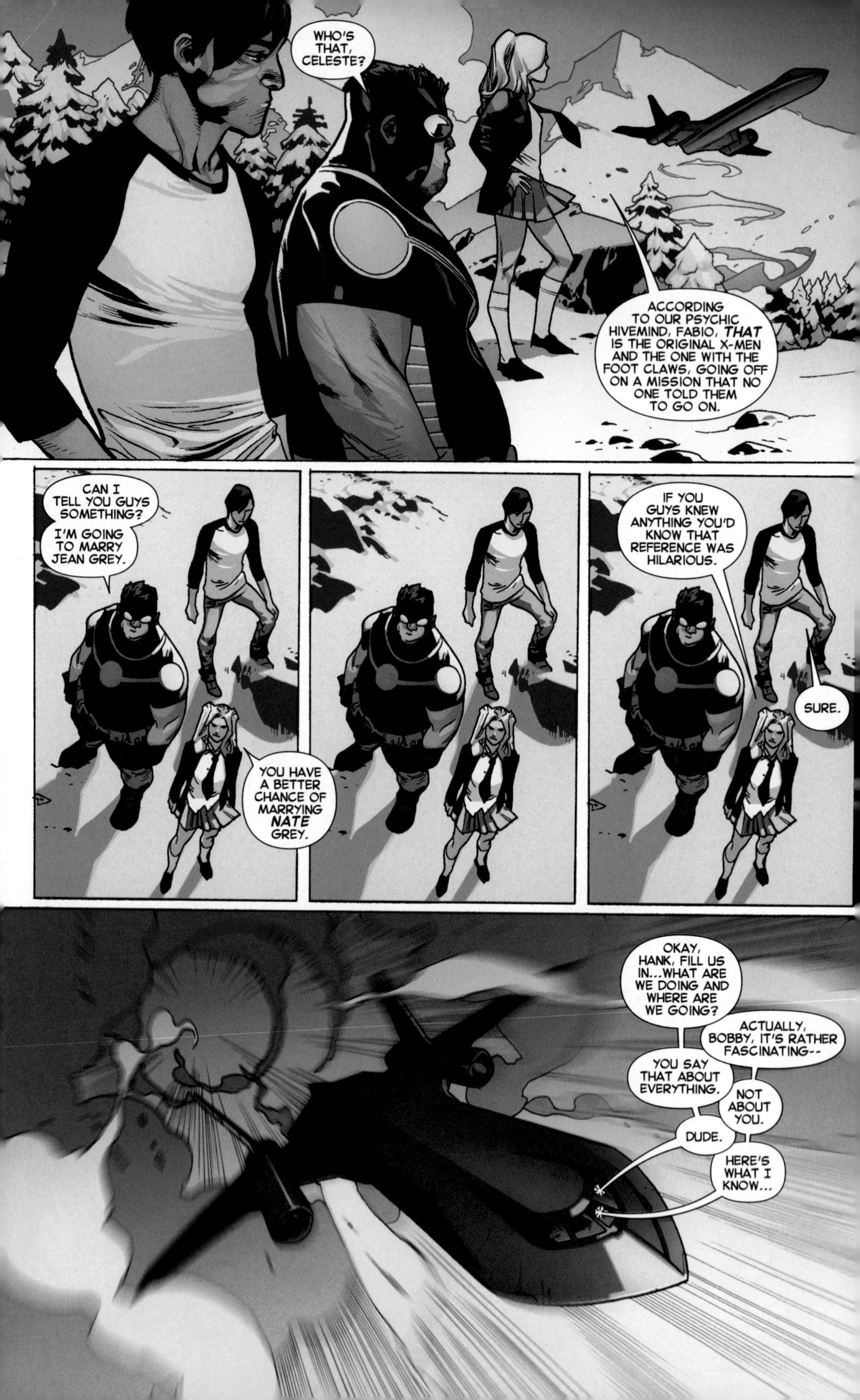
WHO'S THAT, CELESTE?
ACCORDING TO OUR PSYCHIC HIVEMIND, FABIO, *THAT* IS THE ORIGINAL X-MEN AND THE ONE WITH THE FOOT CLAWS, GOING OFF ON A MISSION THAT NO ONE TOLD THEM TO GO ON.
CAN I TELL YOU GUYS SOMETHING?
I'M GOING TO MARRY JEAN GREY.
YOU HAVE A BETTER CHANCE OF MARRYING *NATE* GREY.
IF YOU GUYS KNEW ANYTHING YOU'D KNOW THAT REFERENCE WAS HILARIOUS.
SURE.
OKAY, HANK, FILL US IN...WHAT ARE WE DOING AND WHERE ARE WE GOING?
ACTUALLY, BOBBY, IT'S RATHER FASCINATING--
YOU SAY THAT ABOUT EVERYTHING.
NOT ABOUT YOU.
DUDE.
HERE'S WHAT I KNOW...

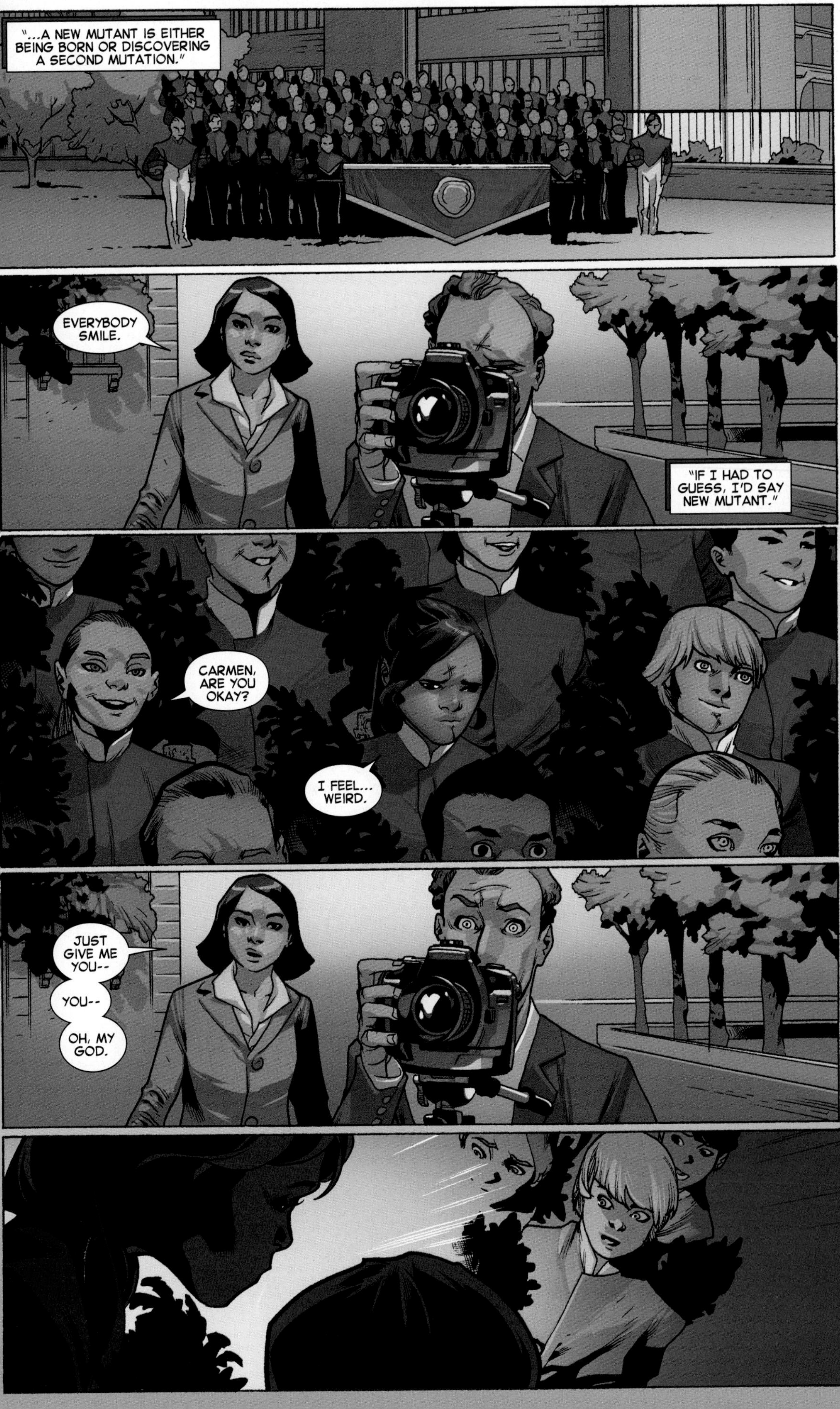
"...A NEW MUTANT IS EITHER BEING BORN OR DISCOVERING A SECOND MUTATION."
EVERYBODY SMILE.
"IF I HAD TO GUESS, I'D SAY NEW MUTANT."
CARMEN, ARE YOU OKAY?
I FEEL... WEIRD.
JUST GIVE ME YOU--
YOU--
OH, MY GOD.

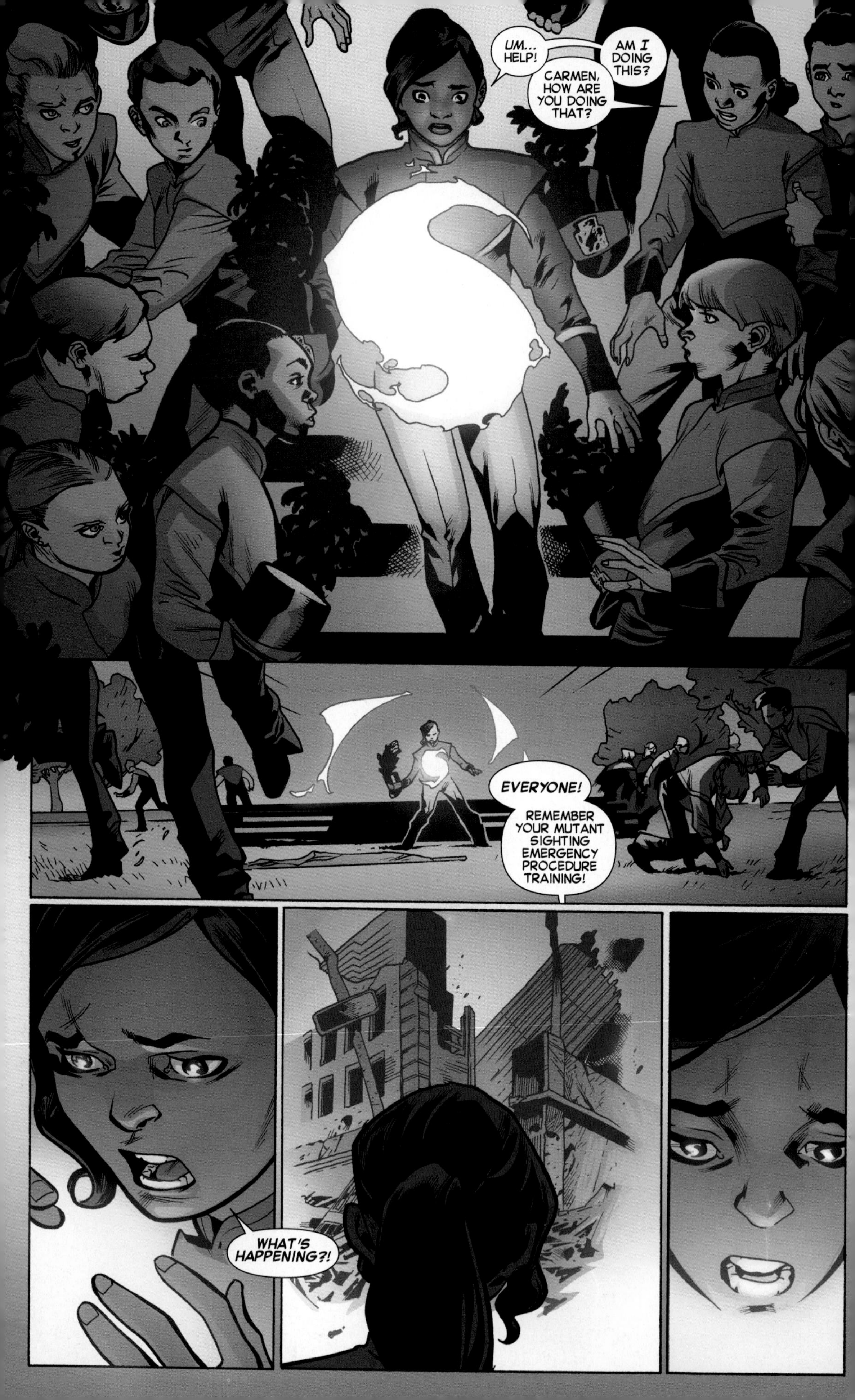
UM... HELP!
AM I DOING THIS?
CARMEN, HOW ARE YOU DOING THAT?
EVERYONE!
REMEMBER YOUR MUTANT SIGHTING EMERGENCY PROCEDURE TRAINING!
WHAT'S HAPPENING?!

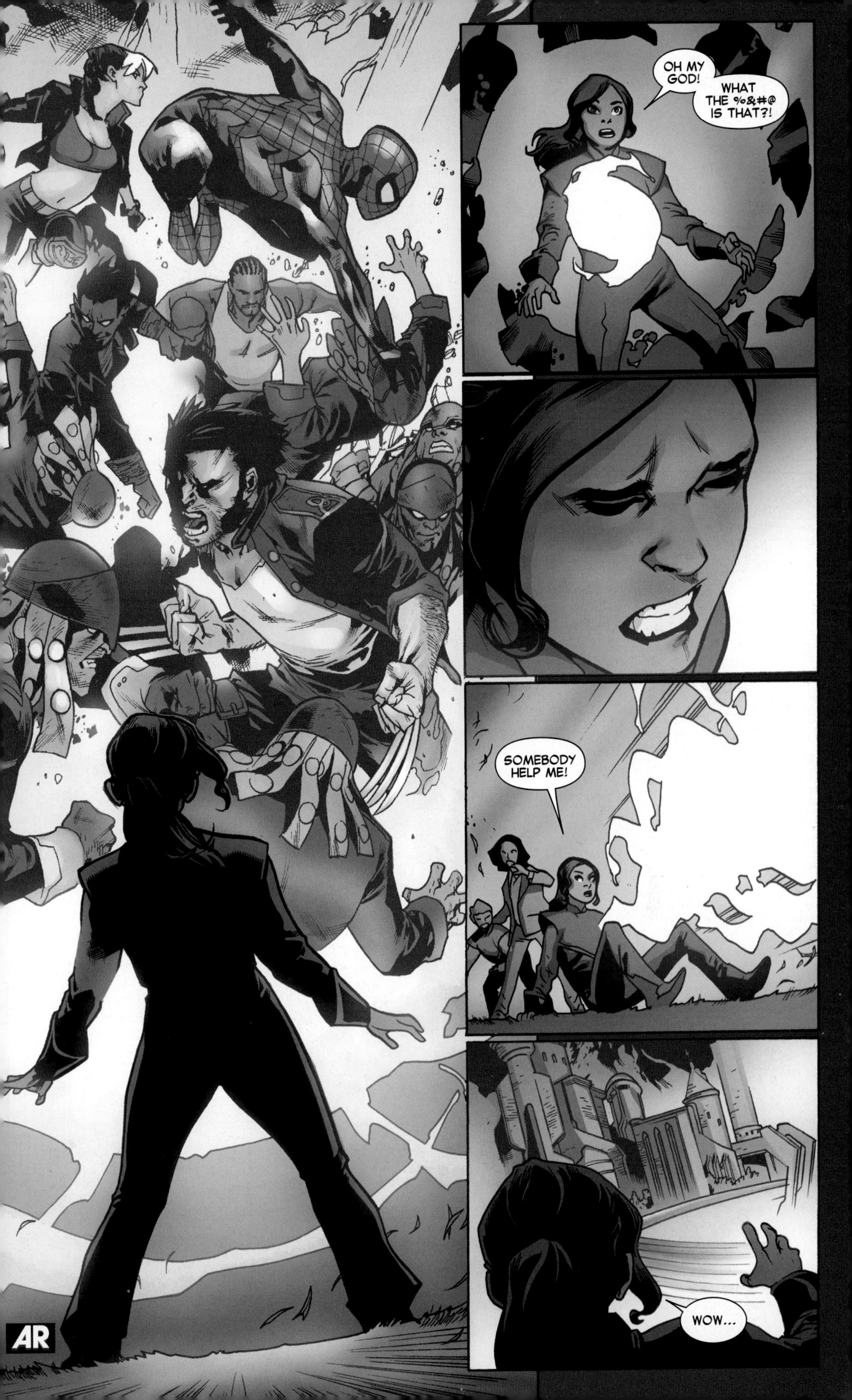
OH MY GOD!
WHAT THE %&#@ IS THAT?!
SOMEBODY HELP ME!
WOW...

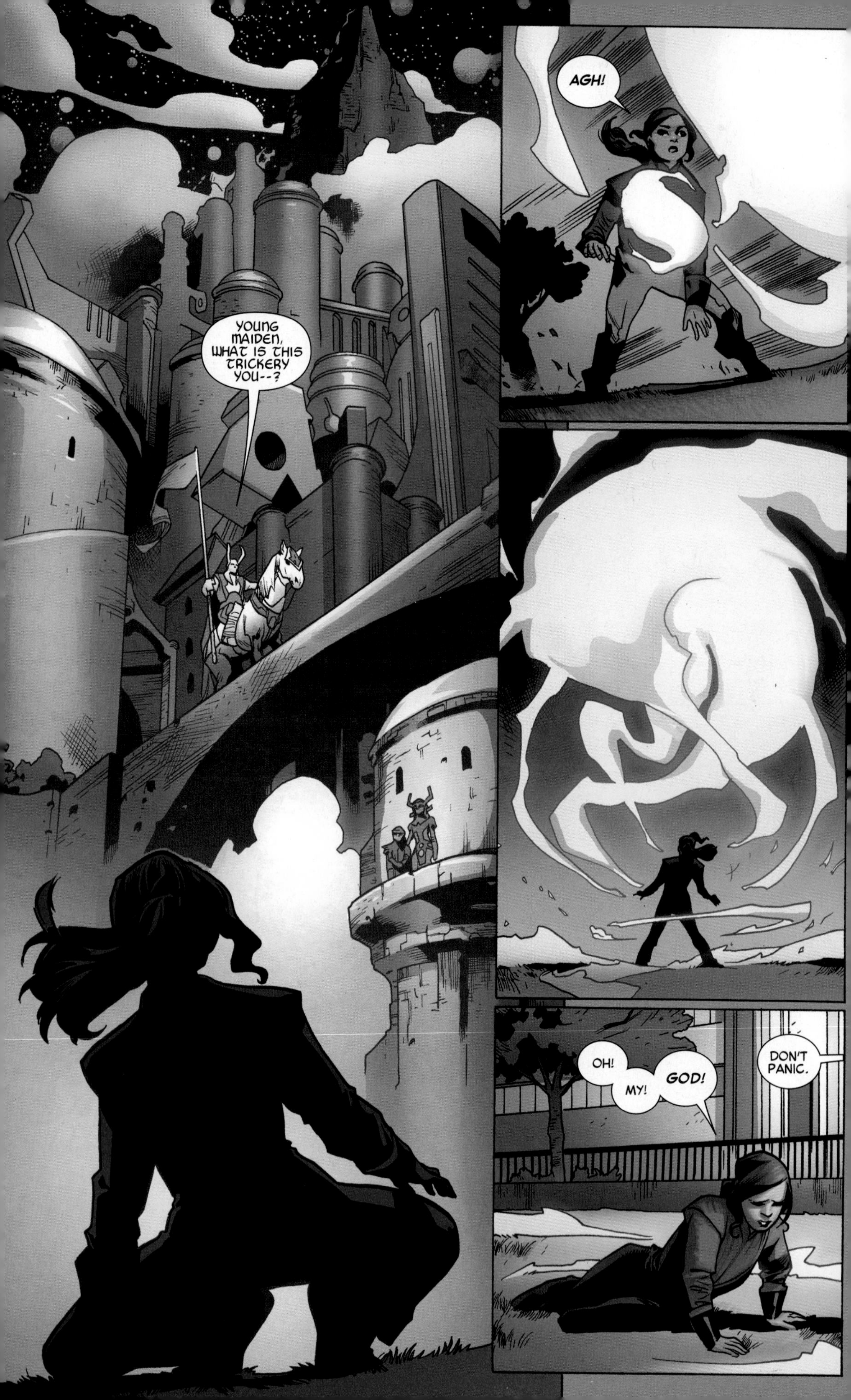
YOUNG MAIDEN, WHAT IS THIS TRICKERY YOU--?
AGH!
OH!
MY!
GOD!
DON'T PANIC.

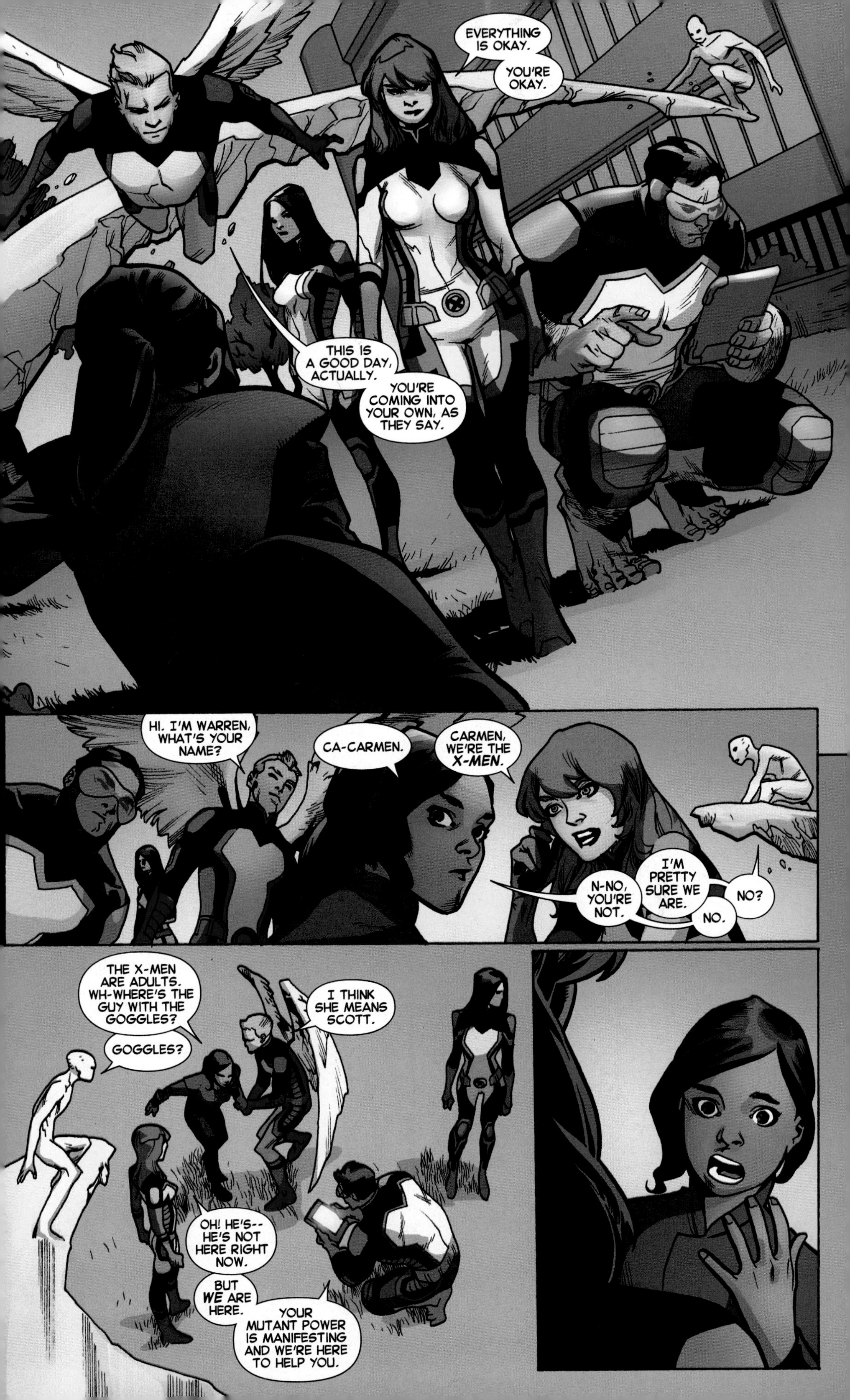
EVERYTHING IS OKAY.
YOU'RE OKAY.
THIS IS A GOOD DAY, ACTUALLY.
YOU'RE COMING INTO YOUR OWN, AS THEY SAY.
HI. I'M WARREN, WHAT'S YOUR NAME?
CA-CARMEN.
CARMEN, WE'RE THE X-MEN.
N-NO, YOU'RE NOT.
I'M PRETTY SURE WE ARE.
NO?
NO.
THE X-MEN ARE ADULTS. WH-WHERE'S THE GUY WITH THE GOGGLES?
GOGGLES?
I THINK SHE MEANS SCOTT.
OH! HE'S-- HE'S NOT HERE RIGHT NOW.
BUT WE ARE HERE.
YOUR MUTANT POWER IS MANIFESTING AND WE'RE HERE TO HELP YOU.

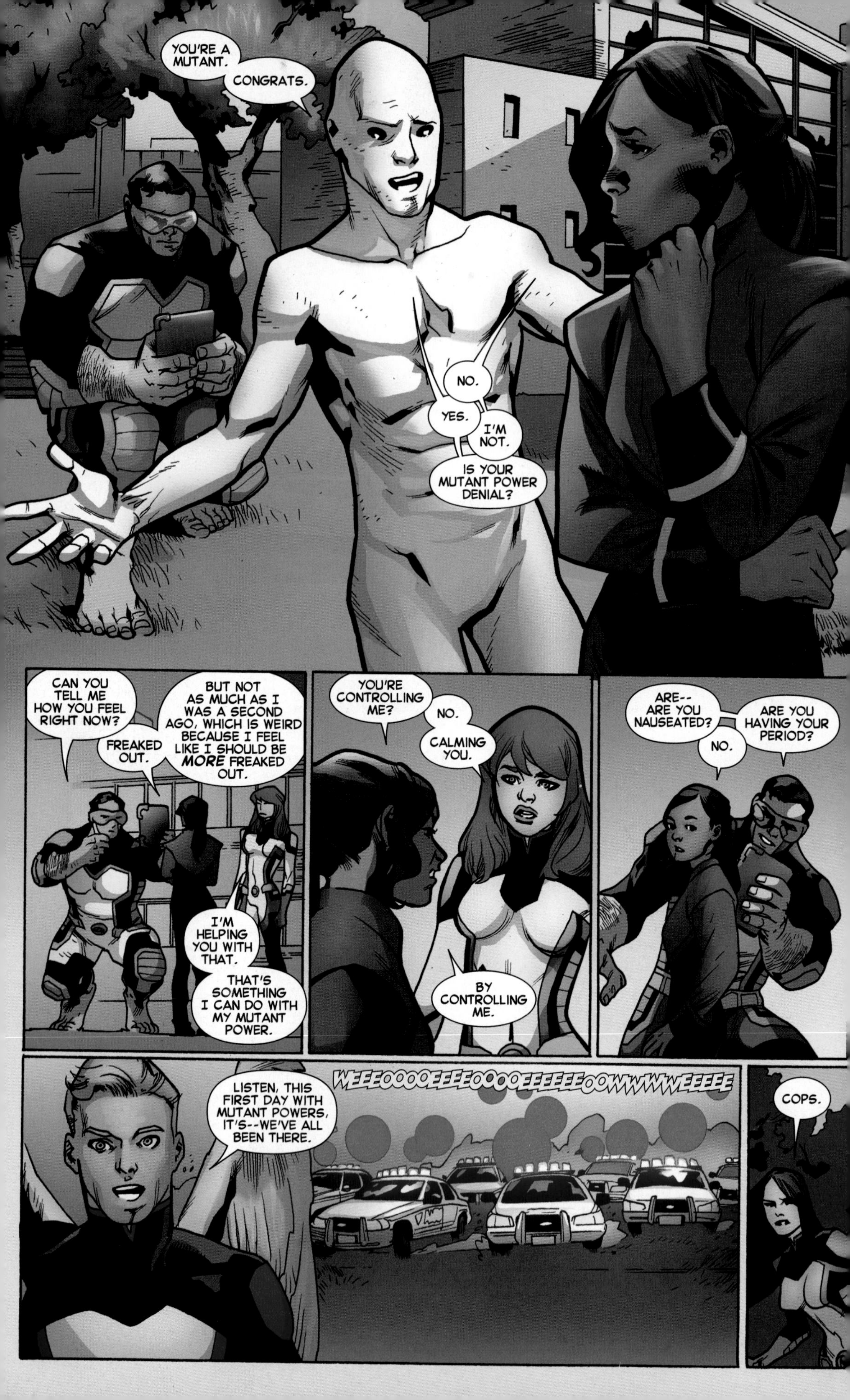
YOU'RE A MUTANT.
CONGRATS.
NO.
YES.
I'M NOT.
IS YOUR MUTANT POWER DENIAL?
CAN YOU TELL ME HOW YOU FEEL RIGHT NOW?
FREAKED OUT.
BUT NOT AS MUCH AS I WAS A SECOND AGO, WHICH IS WEIRD BECAUSE I FEEL LIKE I SHOULD BE MORE FREAKED OUT.
I'M HELPING YOU WITH THAT.
THAT'S SOMETHING I CAN DO WITH MY MUTANT POWER.
YOU'RE CONTROLLING ME?
NO.
CALMING YOU.
BY CONTROLLING ME.
ARE-- ARE YOU NAUSEATED?
NO.
ARE YOU HAVING YOUR PERIOD?
LISTEN, THIS FIRST DAY WITH MUTANT POWERS, IT'S--WE'VE ALL BEEN THERE.
WEEEOOOOEEEEOOOOEEEEEEOOWWWWEEEEE
COPS.

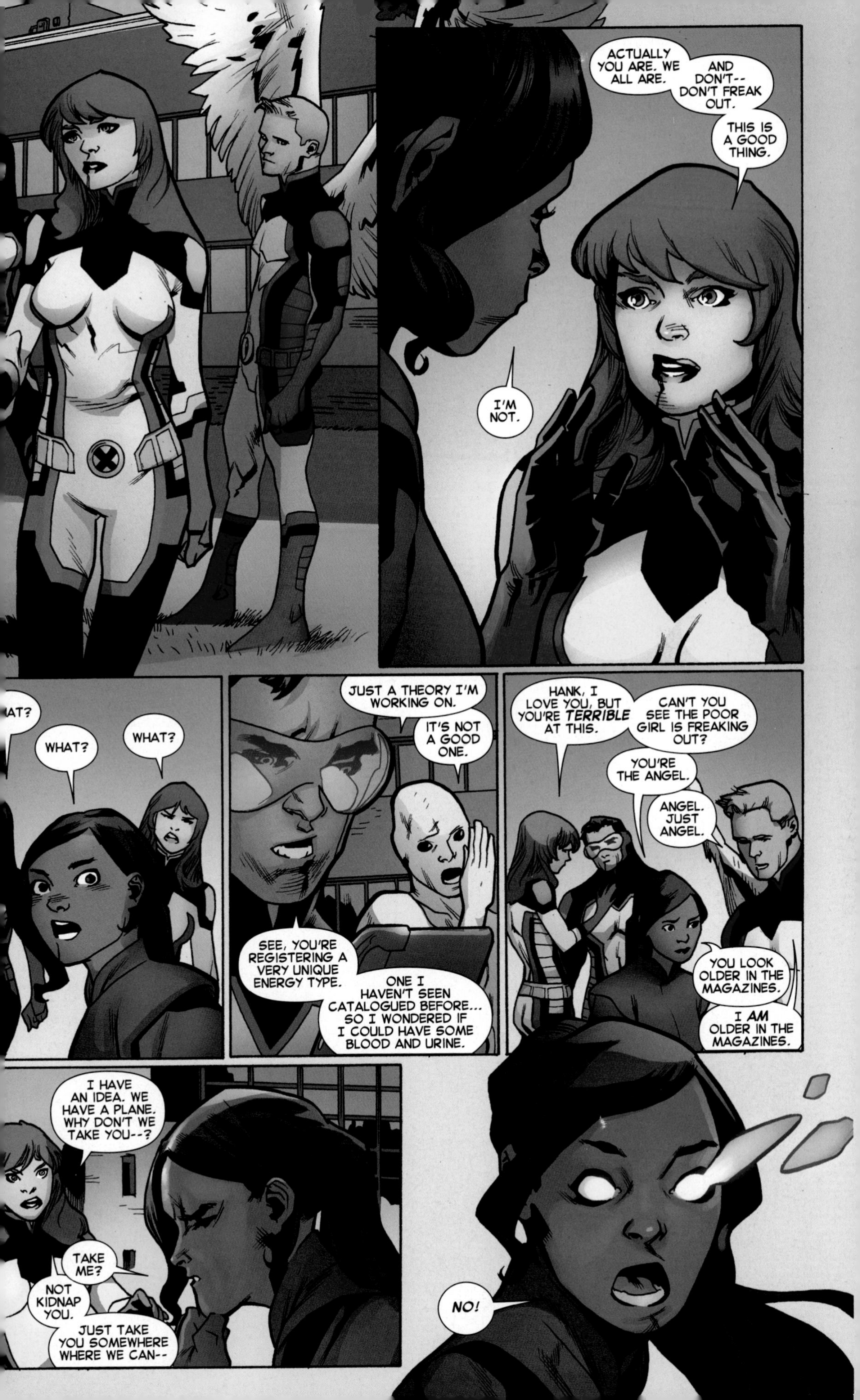
ACTUALLY YOU ARE. WE ALL ARE.
AND DON'T-- DON'T FREAK OUT.
THIS IS A GOOD THING.
I'M NOT.
AT?
WHAT?
WHAT?
JUST A THEORY I'M WORKING ON.
IT'S NOT A GOOD ONE.
SEE, YOU'RE REGISTERING A VERY UNIQUE ENERGY TYPE.
ONE I HAVEN'T SEEN CATALOGUED BEFORE... SO I WONDERED IF I COULD HAVE SOME BLOOD AND URINE.
HANK, I LOVE YOU, BUT YOU'RE *TERRIBLE* AT THIS.
CAN'T YOU SEE THE POOR GIRL IS FREAKING OUT?
YOU'RE THE ANGEL.
ANGEL. JUST ANGEL.
YOU LOOK OLDER IN THE MAGAZINES.
I *AM* OLDER IN THE MAGAZINES.
I HAVE AN IDEA. WE HAVE A PLANE. WHY DON'T WE TAKE YOU--?
TAKE ME?
NOT KIDNAP YOU.
JUST TAKE YOU SOMEWHERE WHERE WE CAN--
NO!

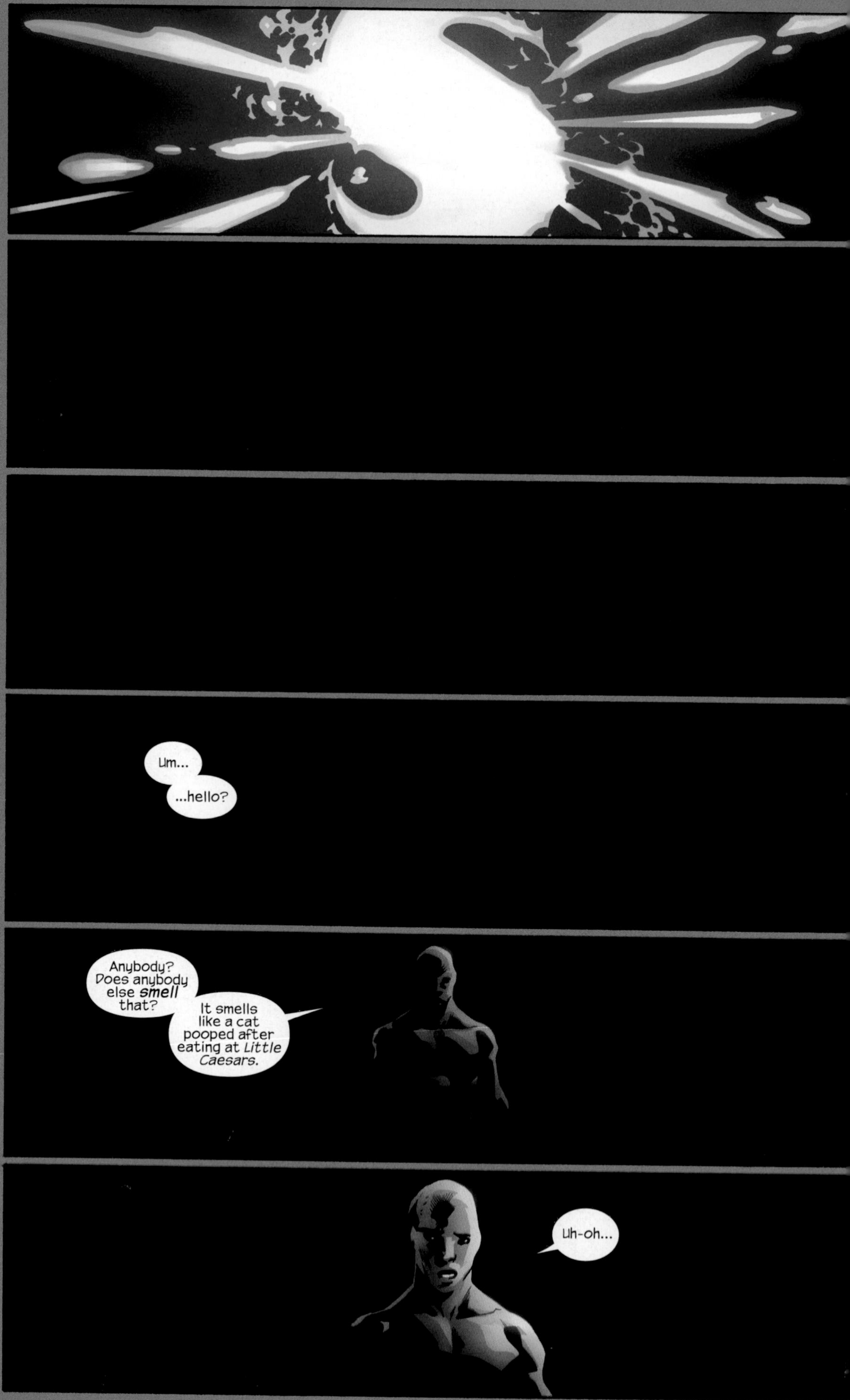
Um...
...hello?
Anybody? Does anybody else smell that?
It smells like a cat pooped after eating at Little Caesars.
Uh-oh...

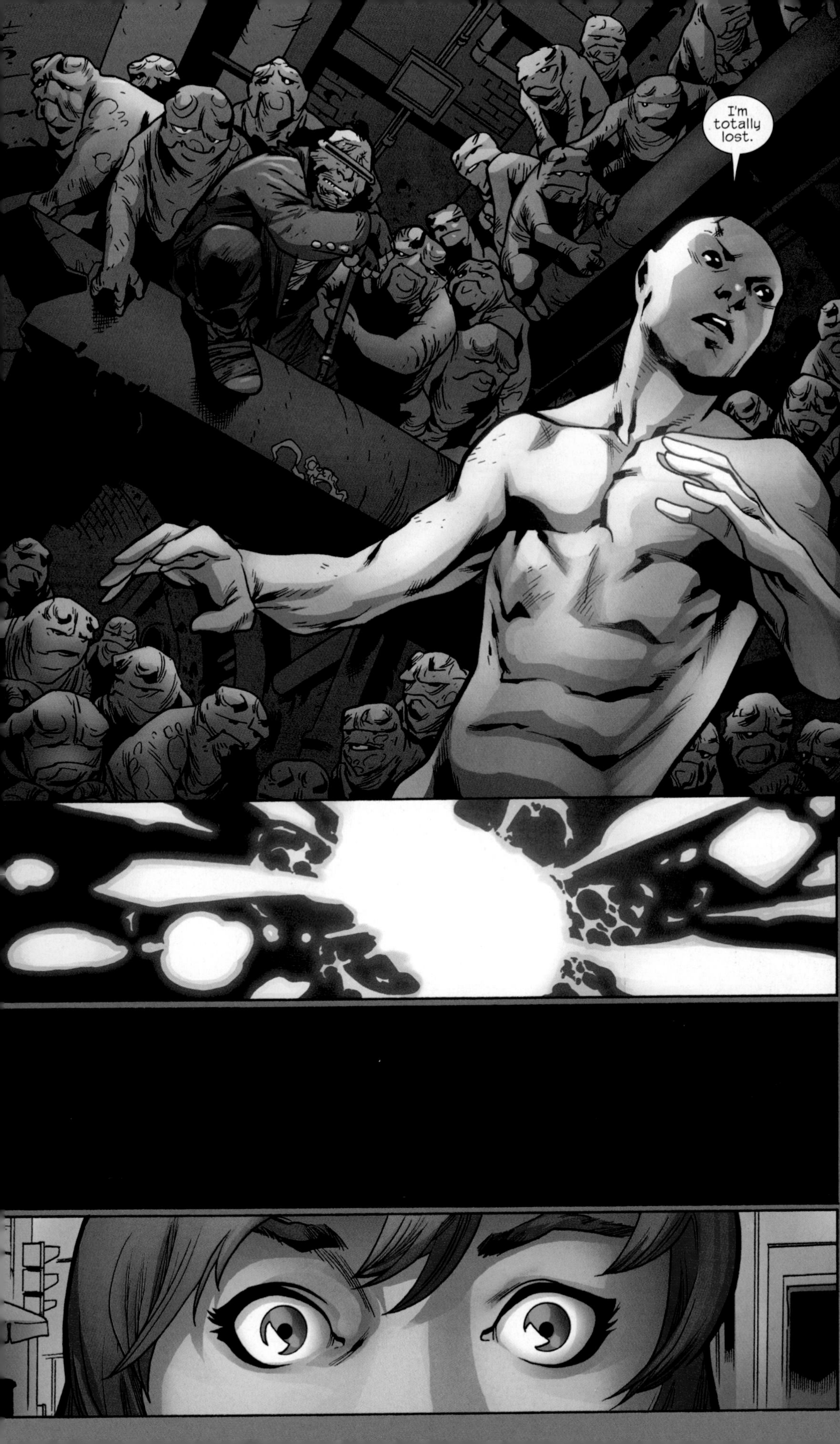
I'm totally lost.

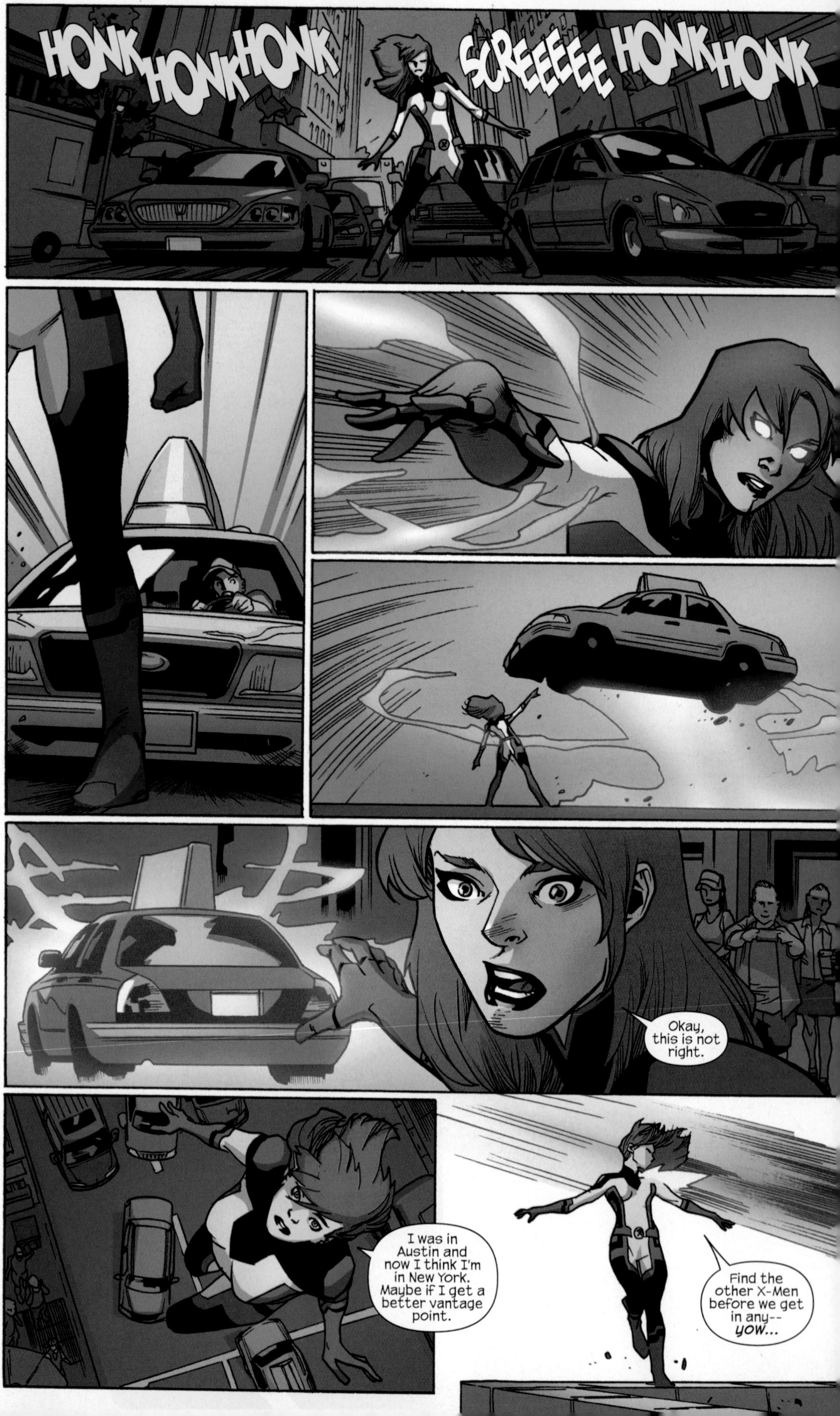
HONK HONK HONK
SCREEEEE HONK HONK
Okay, this is not right.
I was in Austin and now I think I'm in New York. Maybe if I get a better vantage point.
Find the other X-Men before we get in any-- YOW...

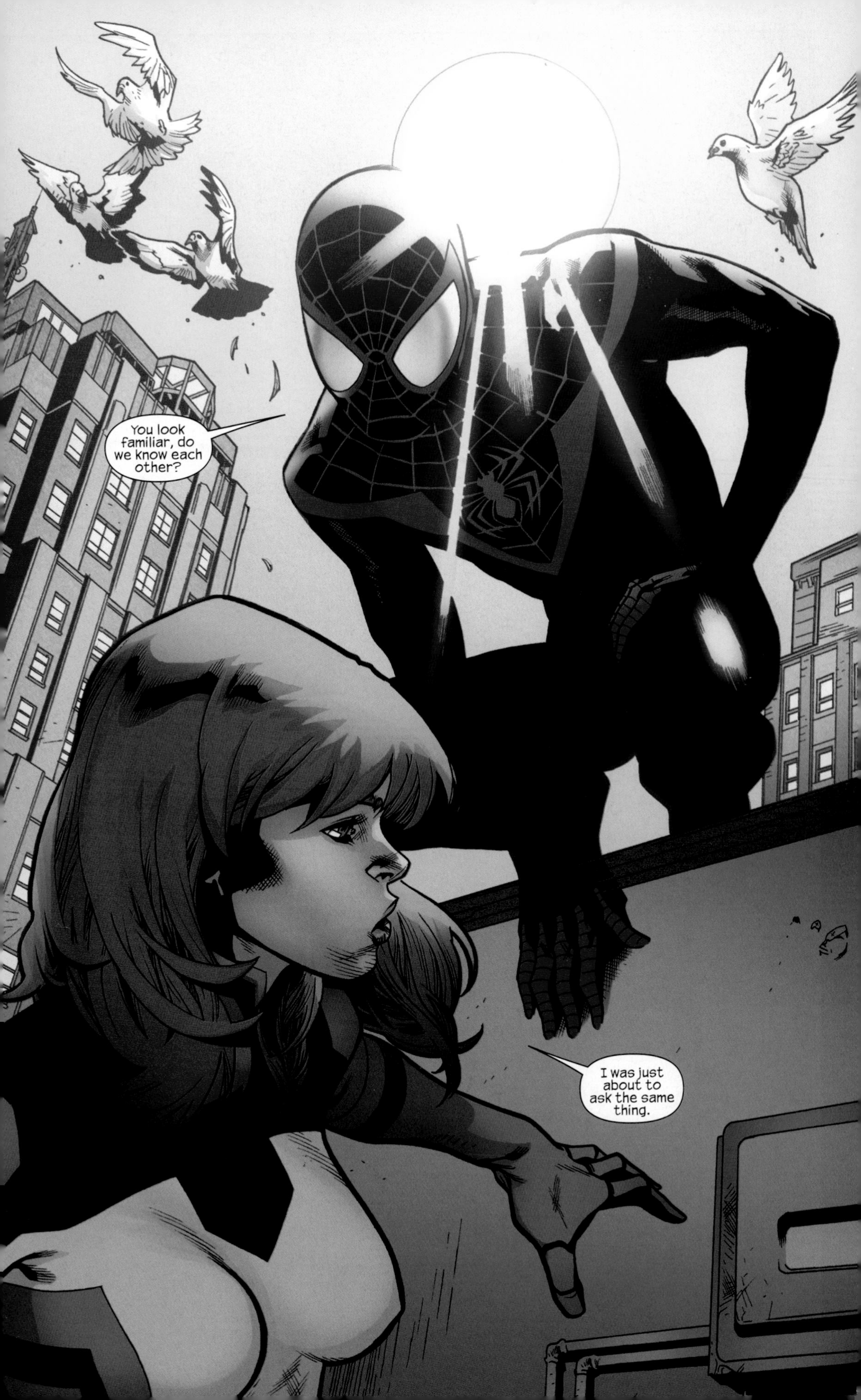
You look familiar, do we know each other?
I was just about to ask the same thing.

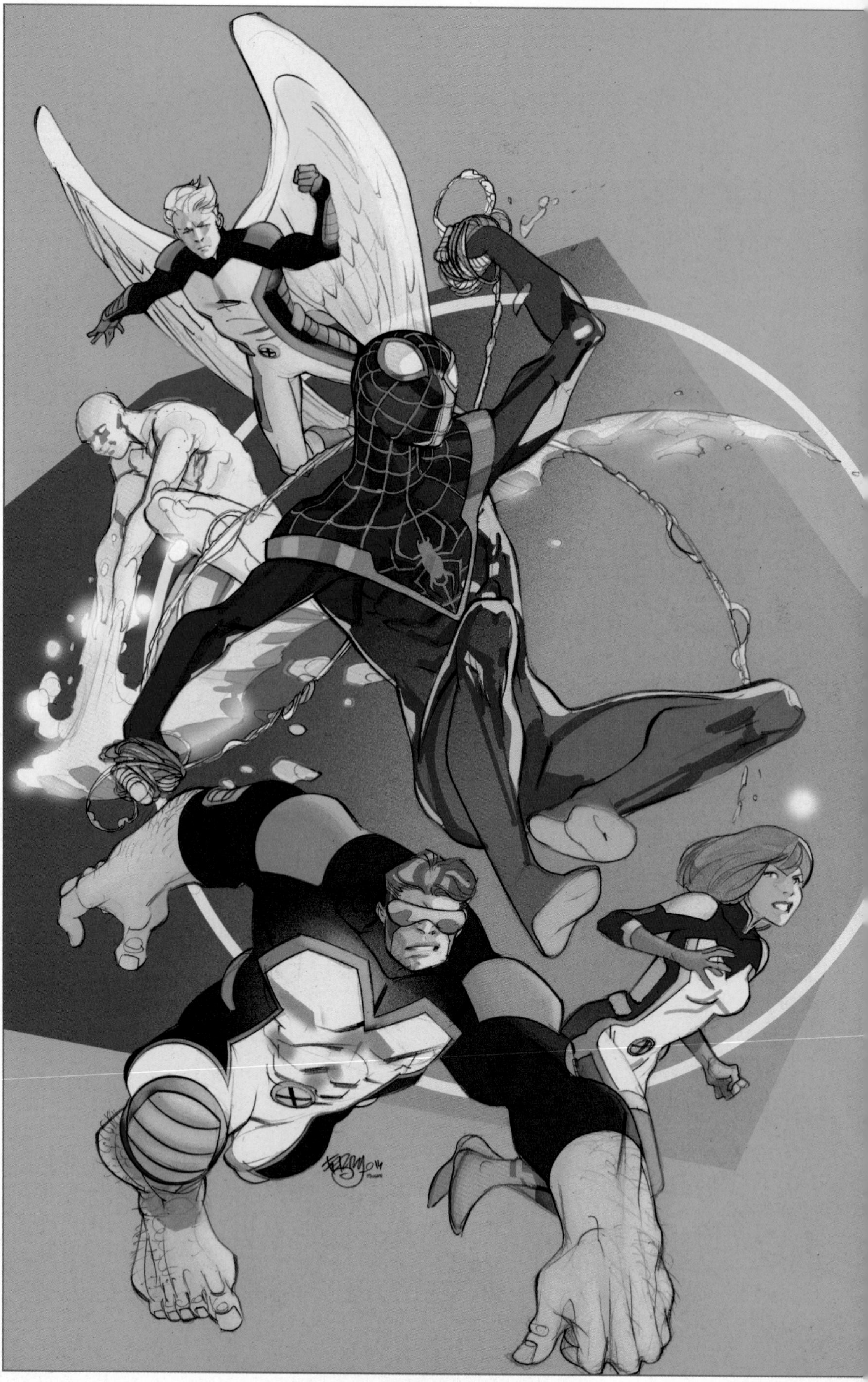

ALL-NEW X-MEN #33 VARIANT

BY PASQUAL FERRY & MATT HOLLINGSWORTH

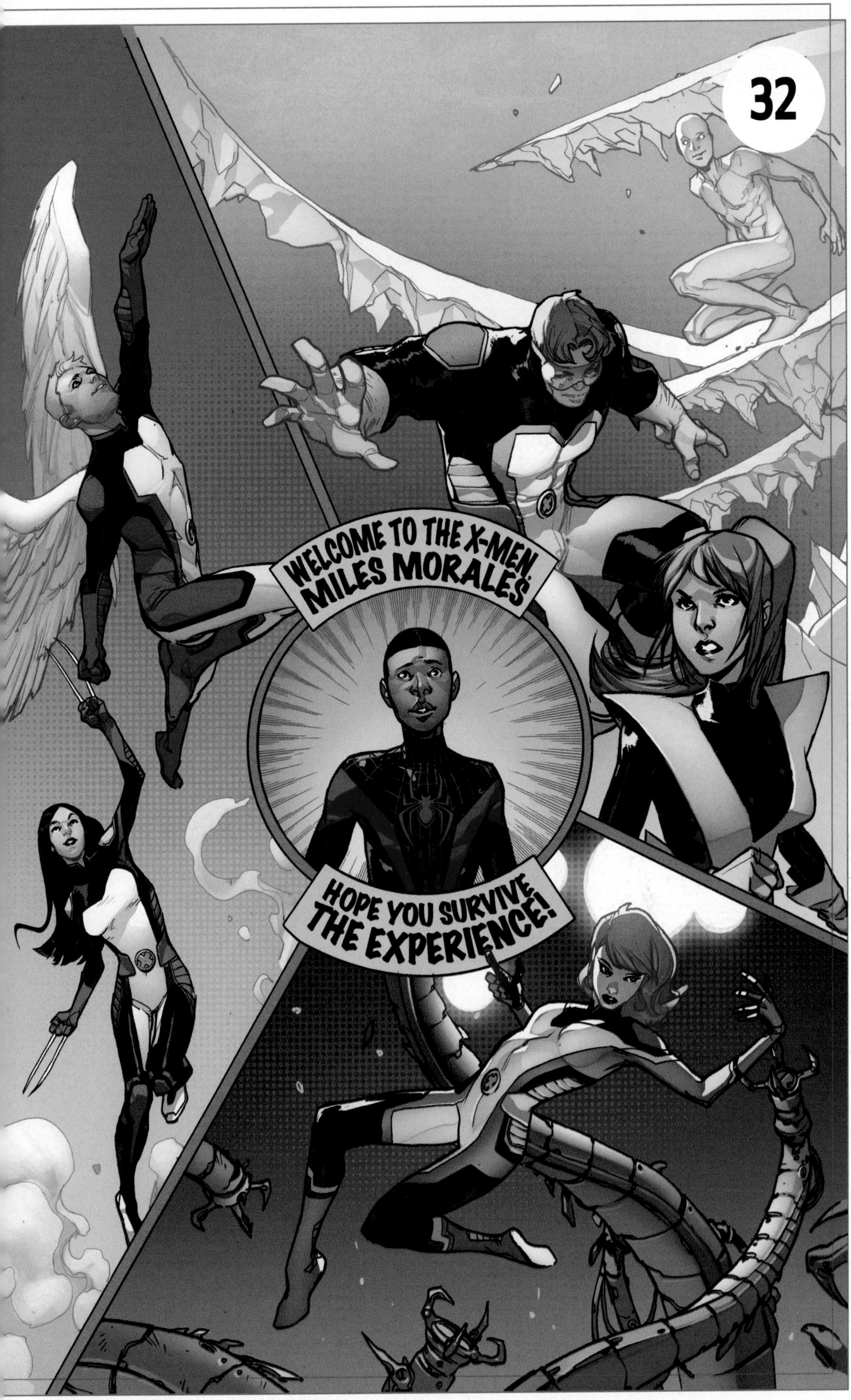
32
WELCOME TO THE X-MEN, MILES MORALES
HOPE YOU SURVIVE THE EXPERIENCE!

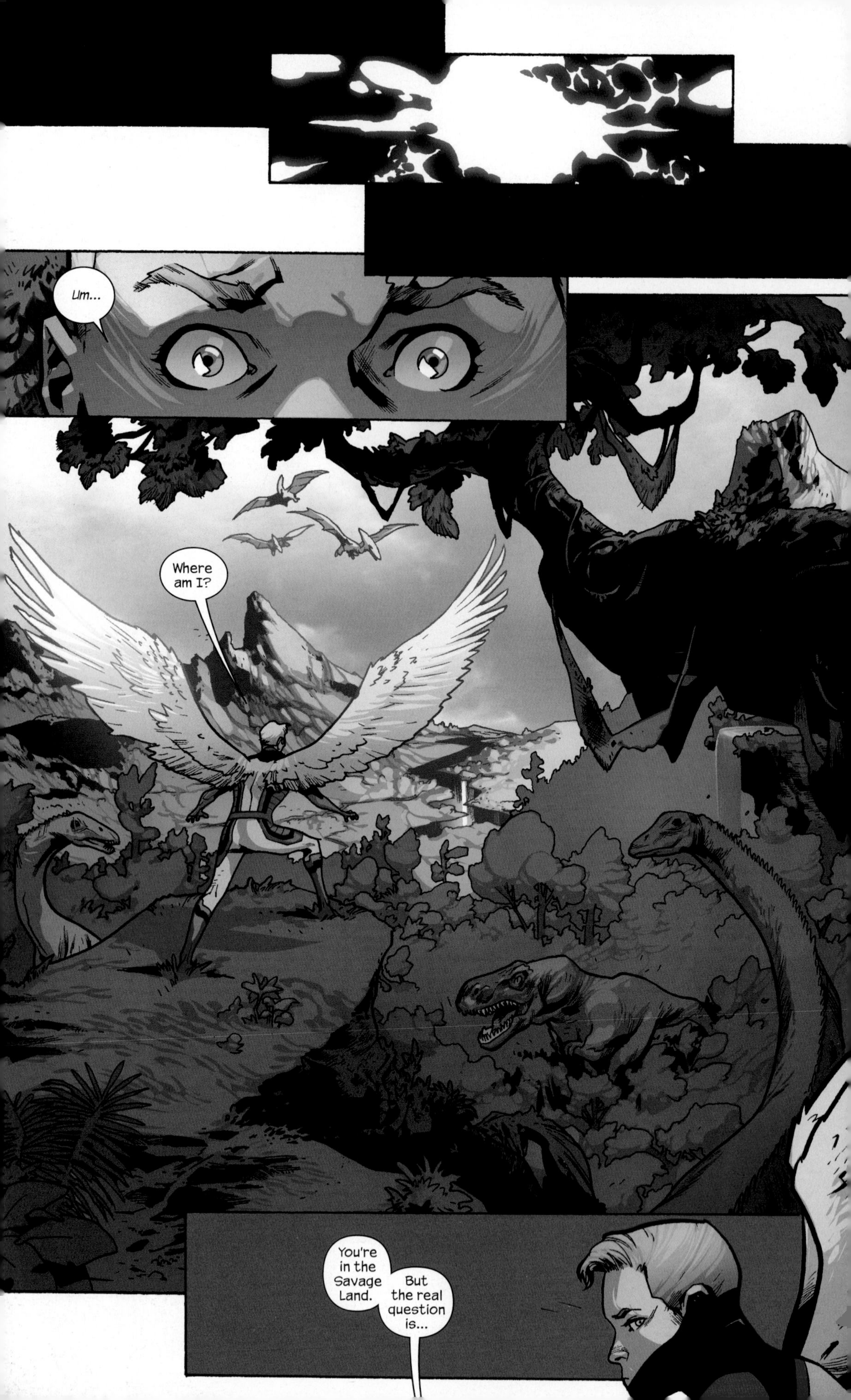
Um...
Where am I?
You're in the Savage Land.
But the real question is...

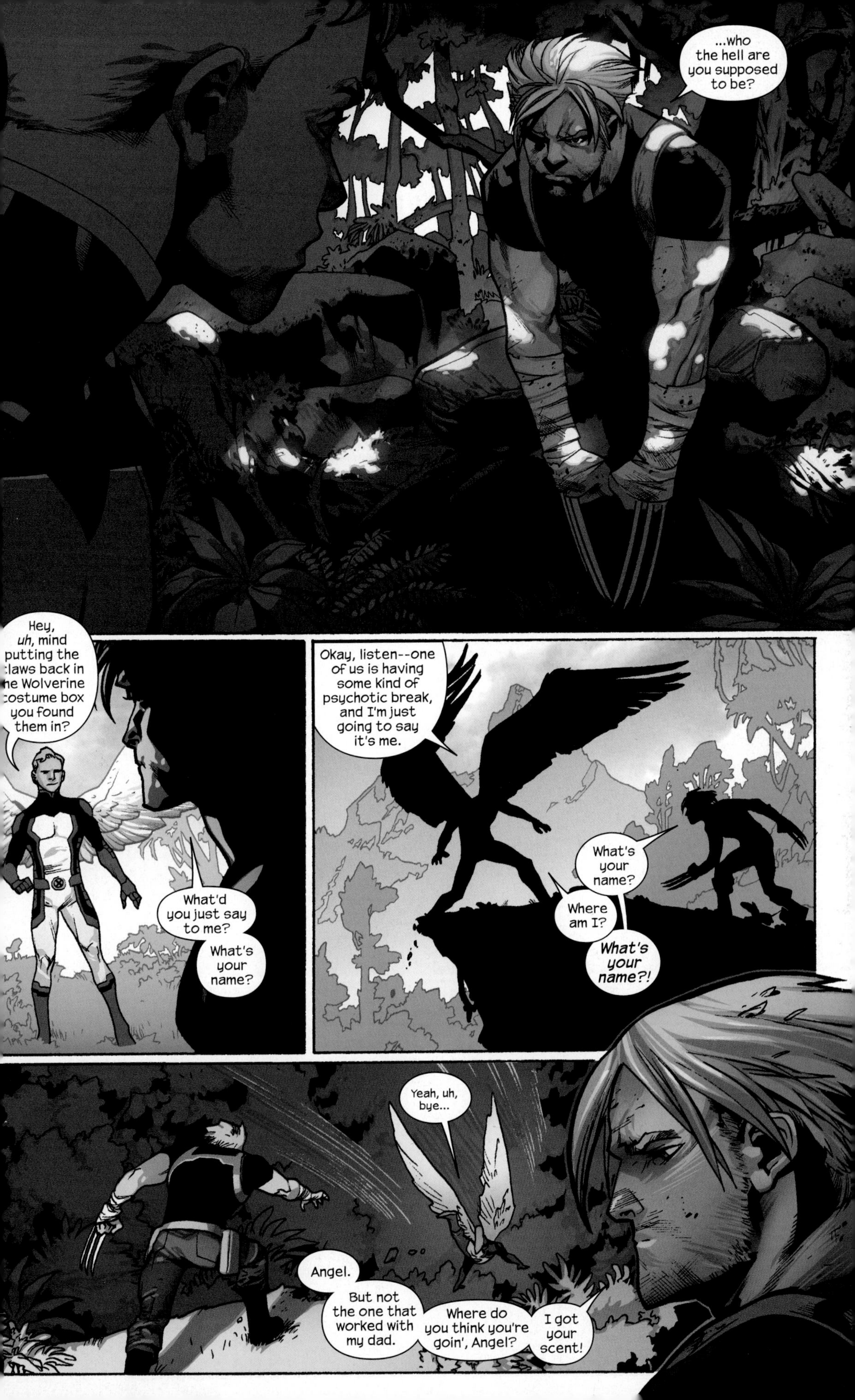
...who the hell are you supposed to be?
Hey, uh, mind putting the claws back in the Wolverine costume box you found them in?
What'd you just say to me?
What's your name?
Okay, listen--one of us is having some kind of psychotic break, and I'm just going to say it's me.
What's your name?
Where am I?
What's your name?!
Yeah, uh, bye...
Angel.
But not the one that worked with my dad.
Where do you think you're goin', Angel?
I got your scent!

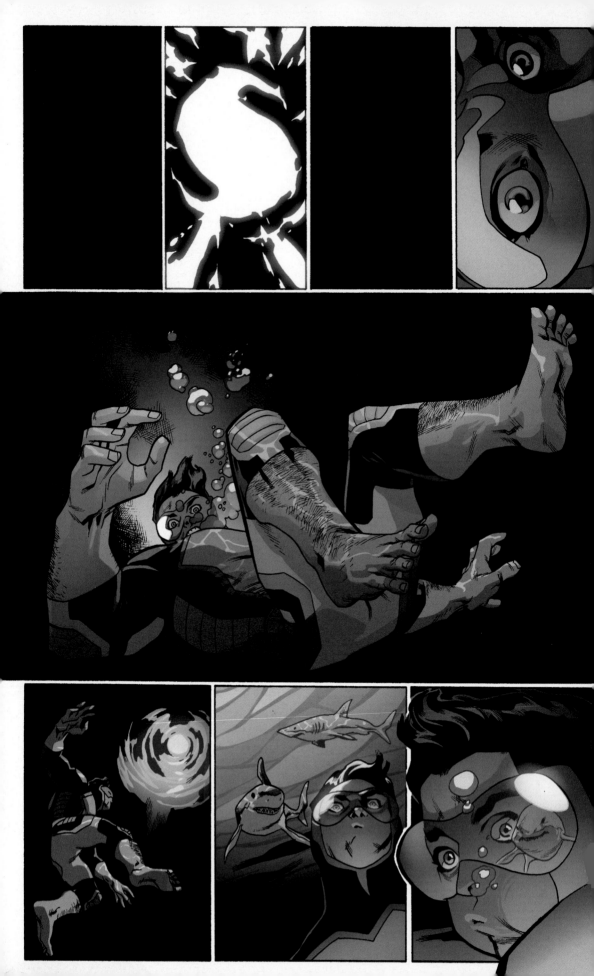

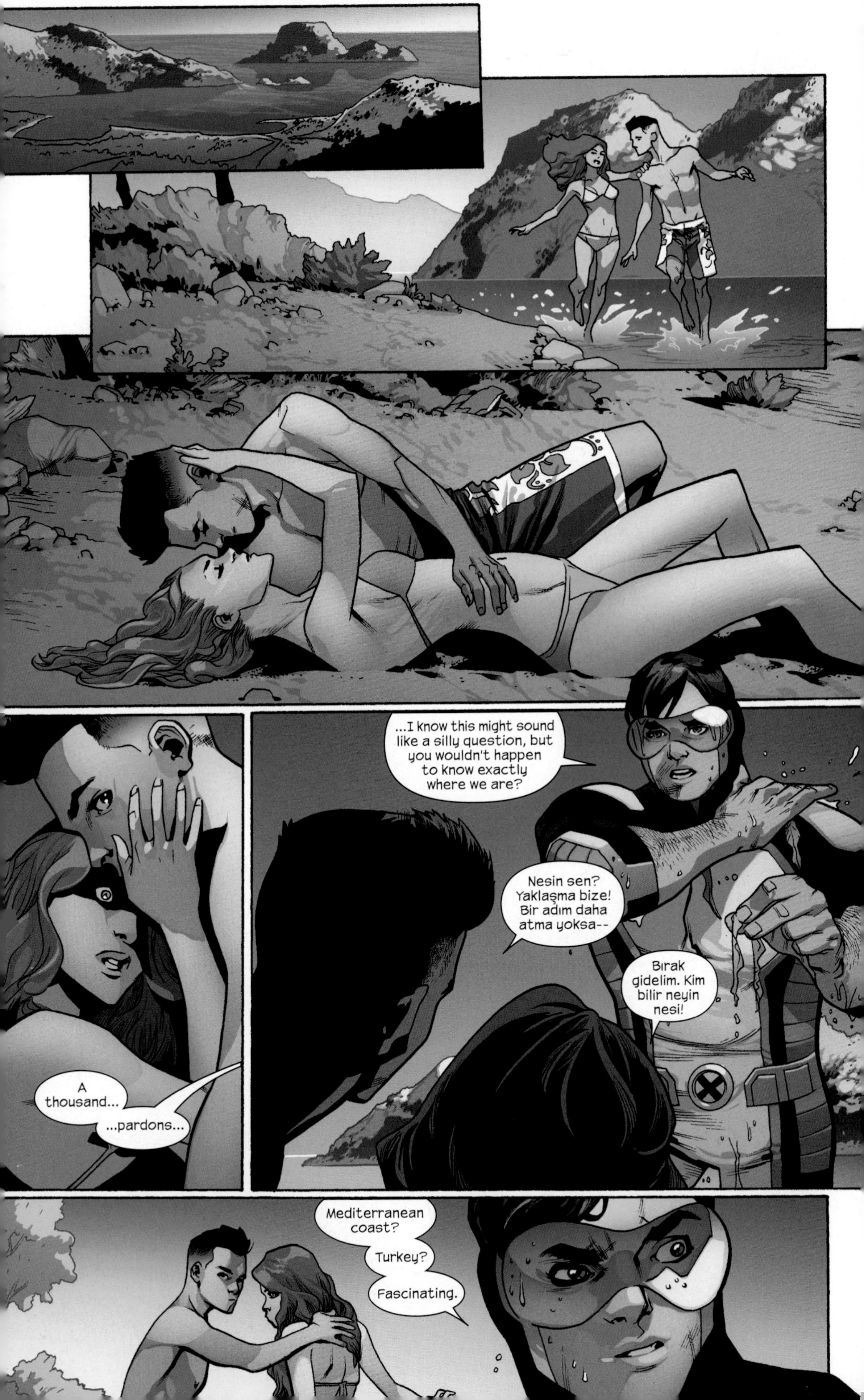
A thousand...
...pardons...
...I know this might sound like a silly question, but you wouldn't happen to know exactly where we are?
Nesin sen? Yaklaşma bize! Bir adım daha atma yoksa--
Bırak gidelim. Kim bilir neyin nesi!
Mediterranean coast?
Turkey?
Fascinating.

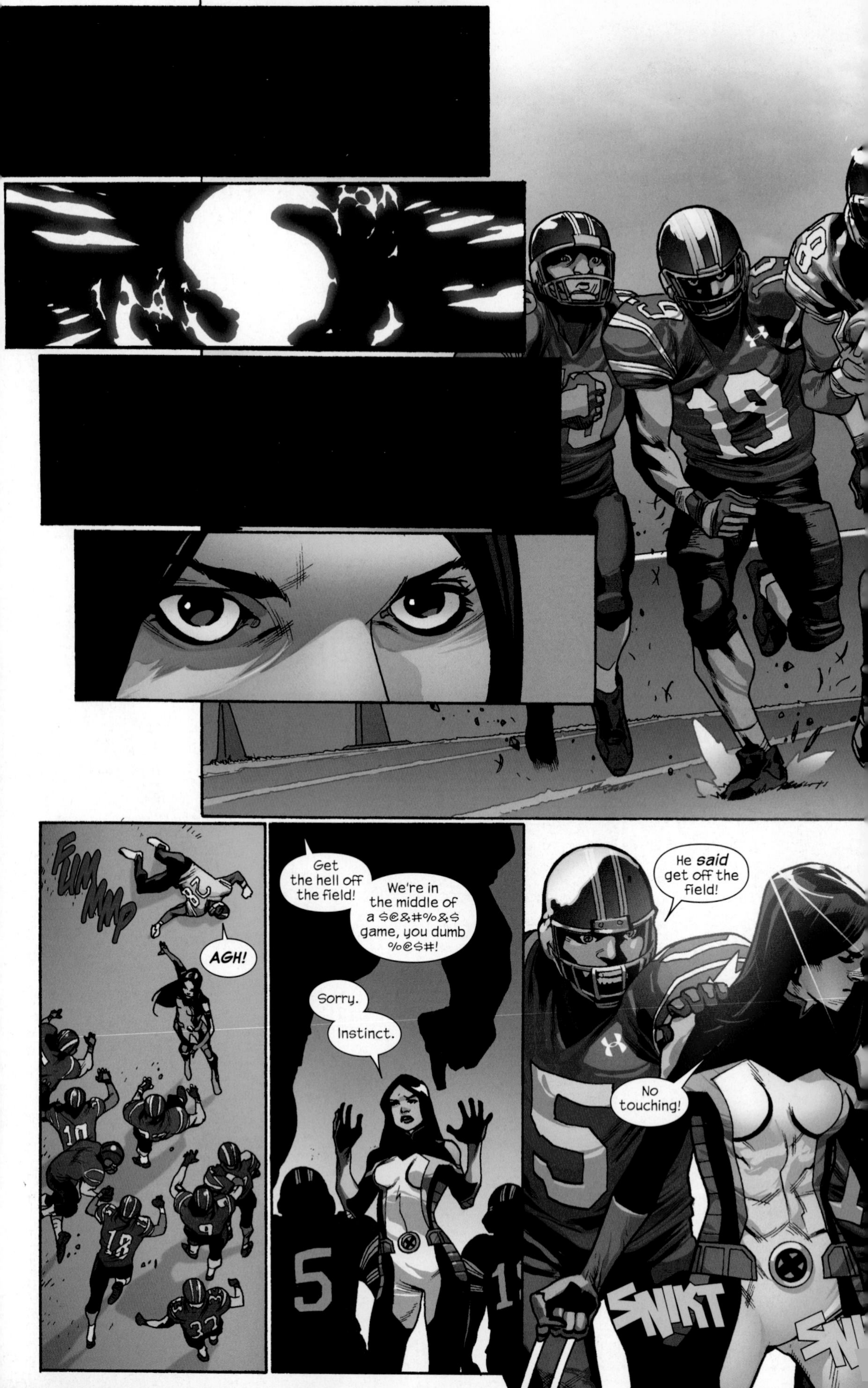
FUMMMP
AGH!
Get the hell off the field!
We're in the middle of a $@&#%&$ game, you dumb %@$#!
Sorry.
Instinct.
He *said* get off the field!
No touching!
SNIKT

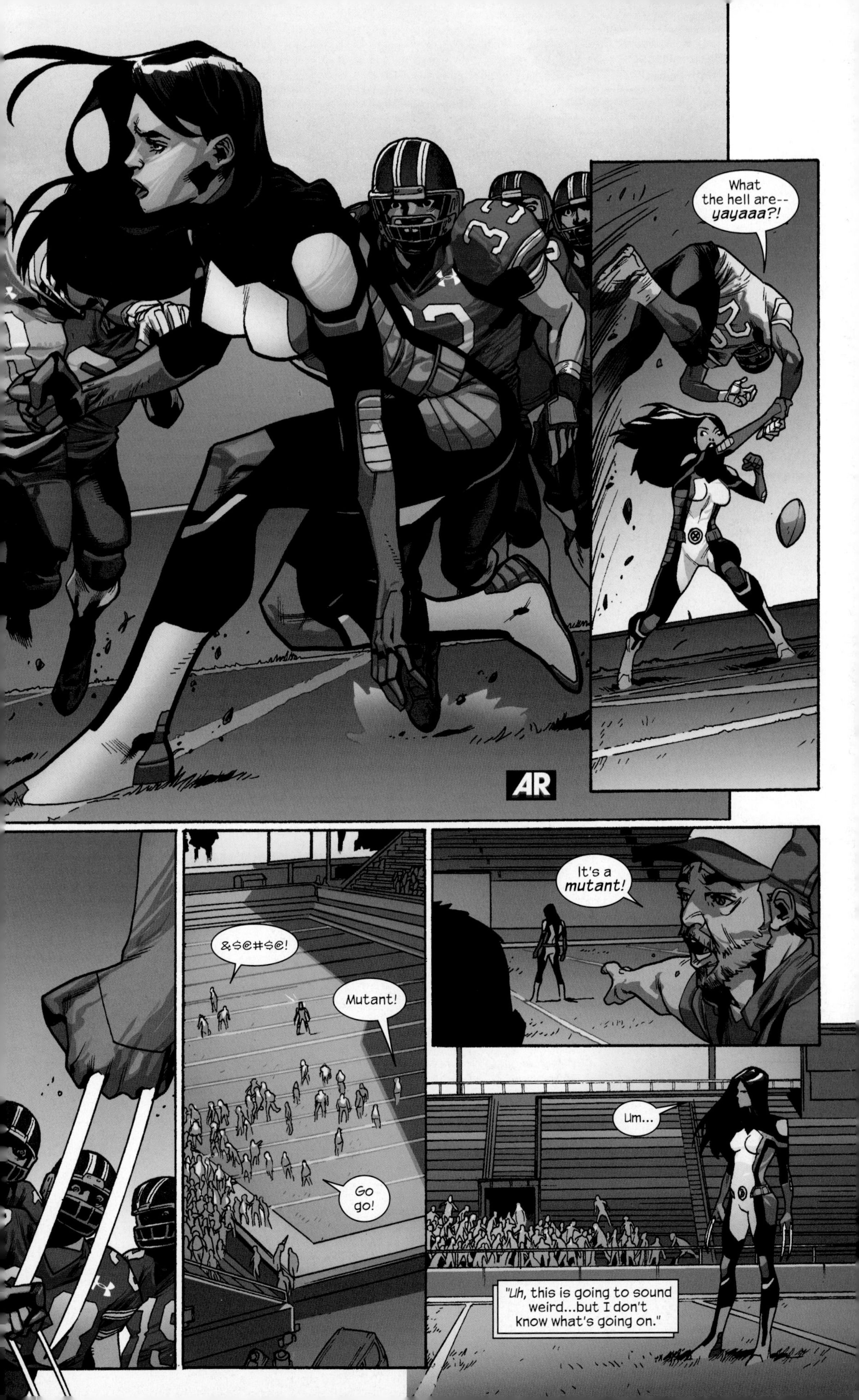
AR
What the hell are-- yayaaa?!
&$@#$@!
Mutant!
Go go!
It's a mutant!
Um...
"Uh, this is going to sound weird...but I don't know what's going on."

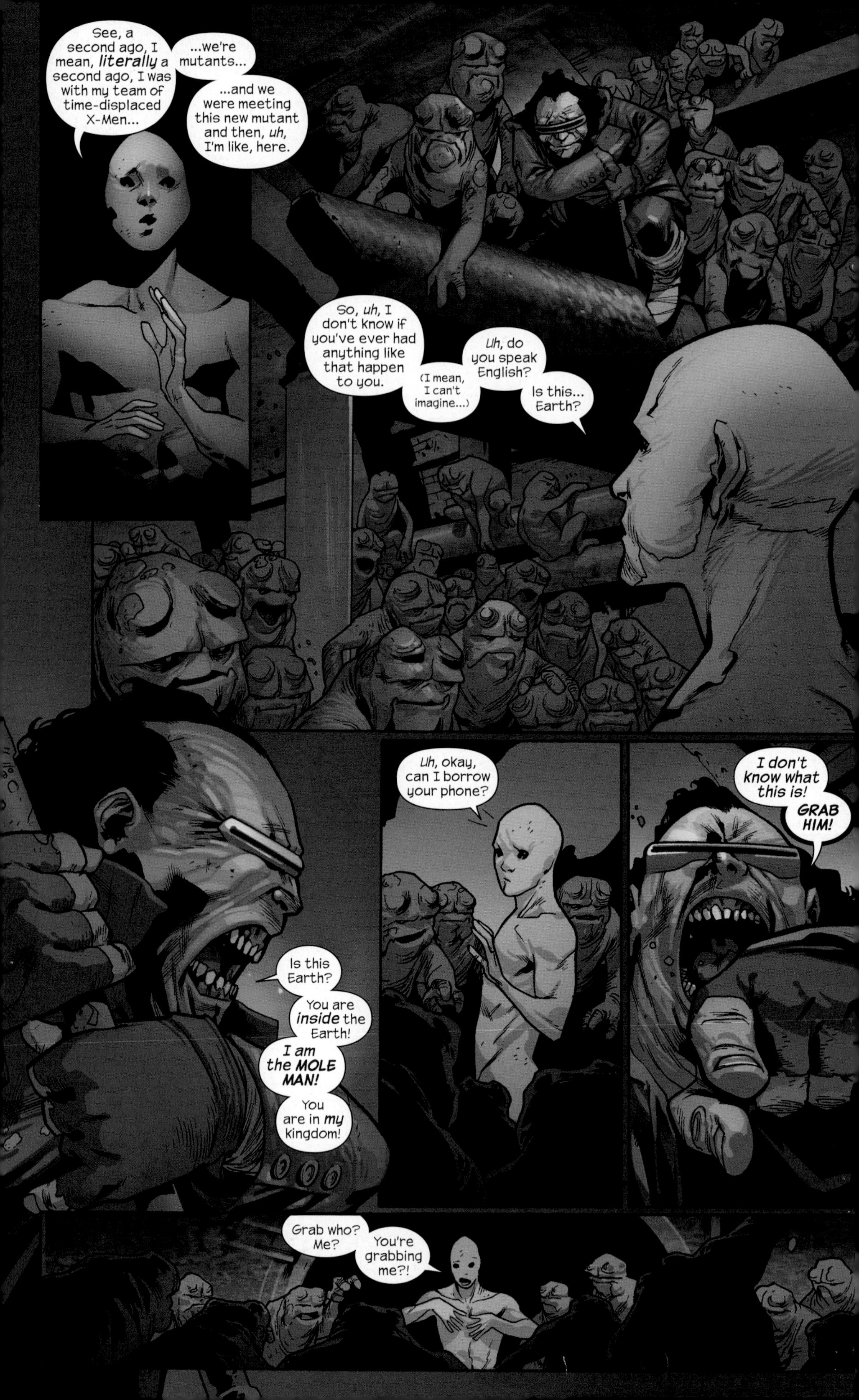
See, a second ago, I mean, *literally* a second ago, I was with my team of time-displaced X-Men...
...we're mutants...
...and we were meeting this new mutant and then, *uh*, I'm like, here.
So, *uh*, I don't know if you've ever had anything like that happen to you.
(I mean, I can't imagine...)
Uh, do you speak English?
Is this... Earth?
Is this Earth?
You are *inside* the Earth!
I am the MOLE MAN!
You are in *my* kingdom!
Uh, okay, can I borrow your phone?
I don't know what this is!
GRAB HIM!
Grab who? Me?
You're grabbing me?!

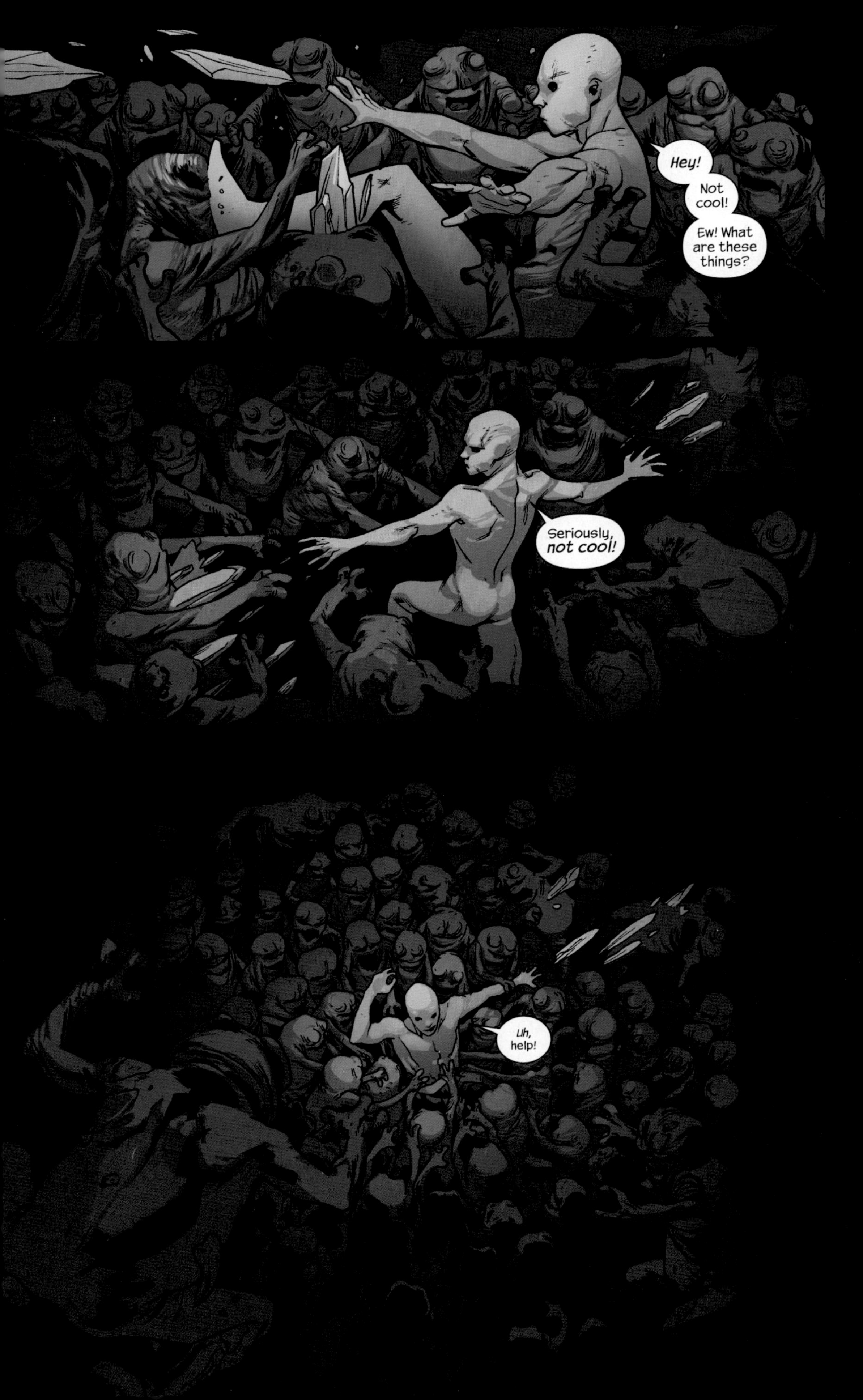
Hey!
Not cool!
Ew! What are these things?
Seriously, not cool!
Uh, help!

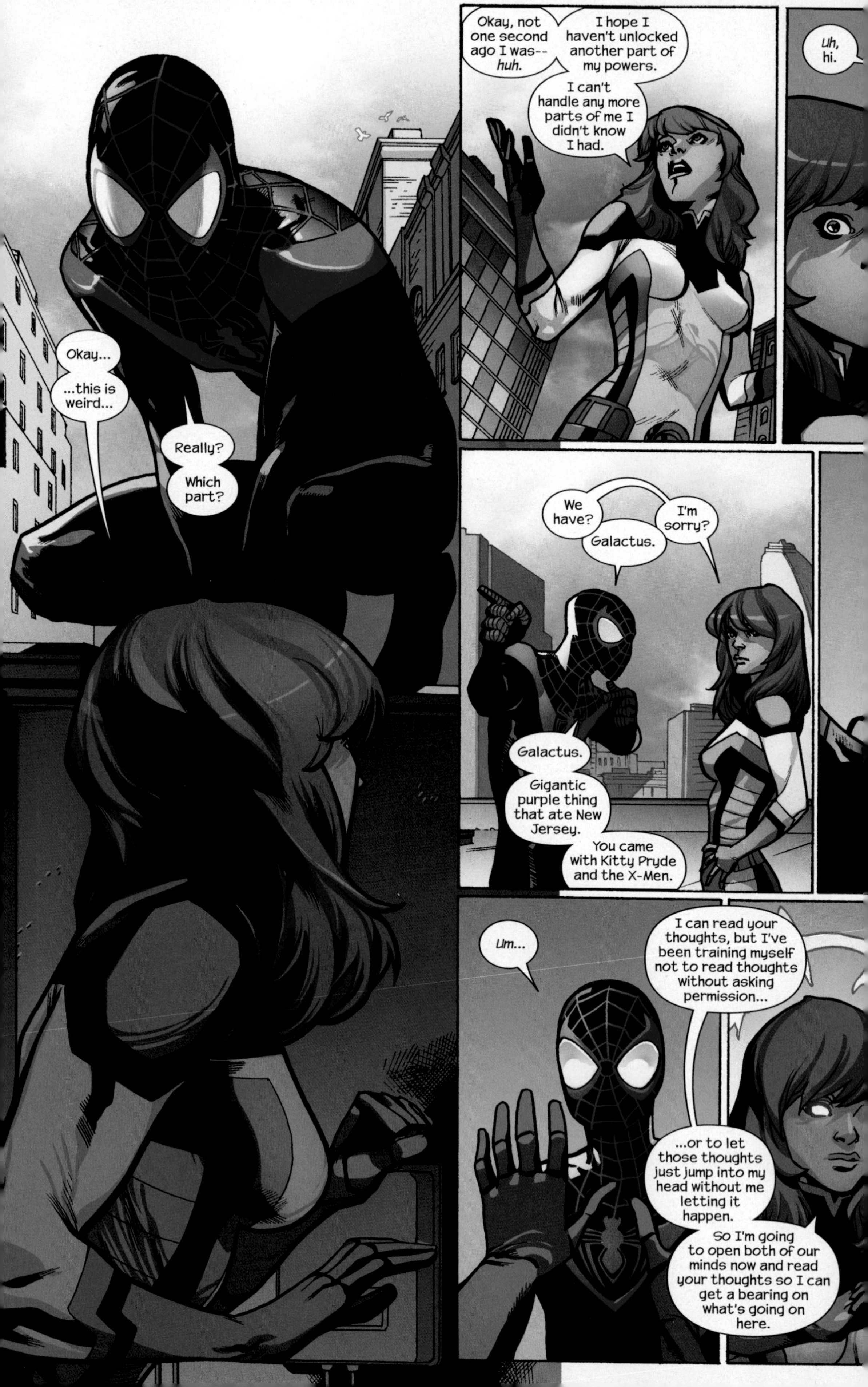
Okay...
...this is weird...
Really?
Which part?
Okay, not one second ago I was-- huh.
I hope I haven't unlocked another part of my powers.
I can't handle any more parts of me I didn't know I had.
Uh, hi.
We have?
Galactus.
I'm sorry?
Galactus.
Gigantic purple thing that ate New Jersey.
You came with Kitty Pryde and the X-Men.
Um...
I can read your thoughts, but I've been training myself not to read thoughts without asking permission...
...or to let those thoughts just jump into my head without me letting it happen.
So I'm going to open both of our minds now and read your thoughts so I can get a bearing on what's going on here.

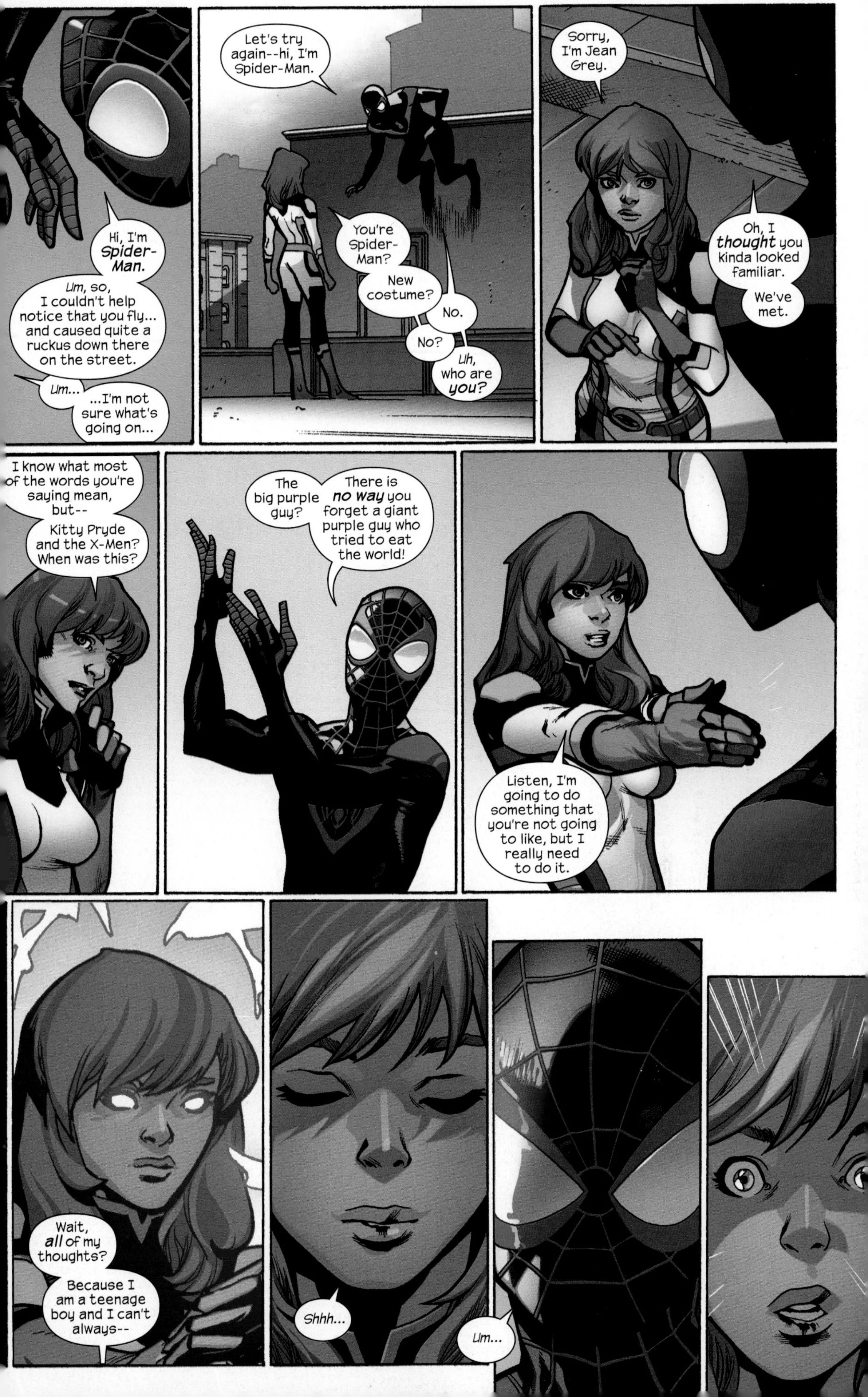
Hi, I'm Spider-Man.
Um, so, I couldn't help notice that you fly... and caused quite a ruckus down there on the street.
Um...
...I'm not sure what's going on...
Let's try again--hi, I'm Spider-Man.
You're Spider-Man?
New costume?
No.
No?
Uh, who are you?
Sorry, I'm Jean Grey.
Oh, I thought you kinda looked familiar.
We've met.
I know what most of the words you're saying mean, but--
Kitty Pryde and the X-Men? When was this?
The big purple guy?
There is no way you forget a giant purple guy who tried to eat the world!
Listen, I'm going to do something that you're not going to like, but I really need to do it.
Wait, all of my thoughts?
Because I am a teenage boy and I can't always--
Shhh...
Um...

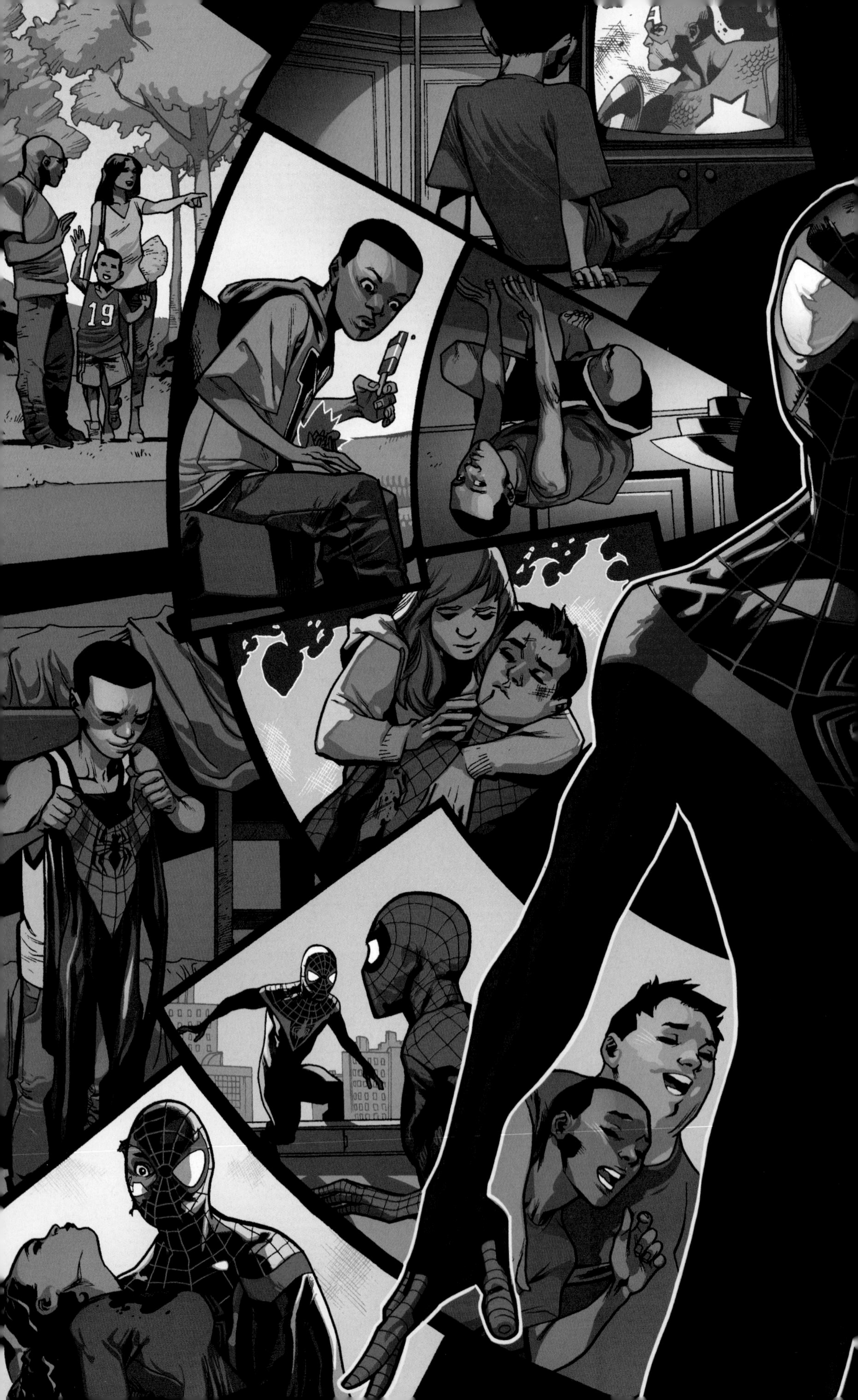
19

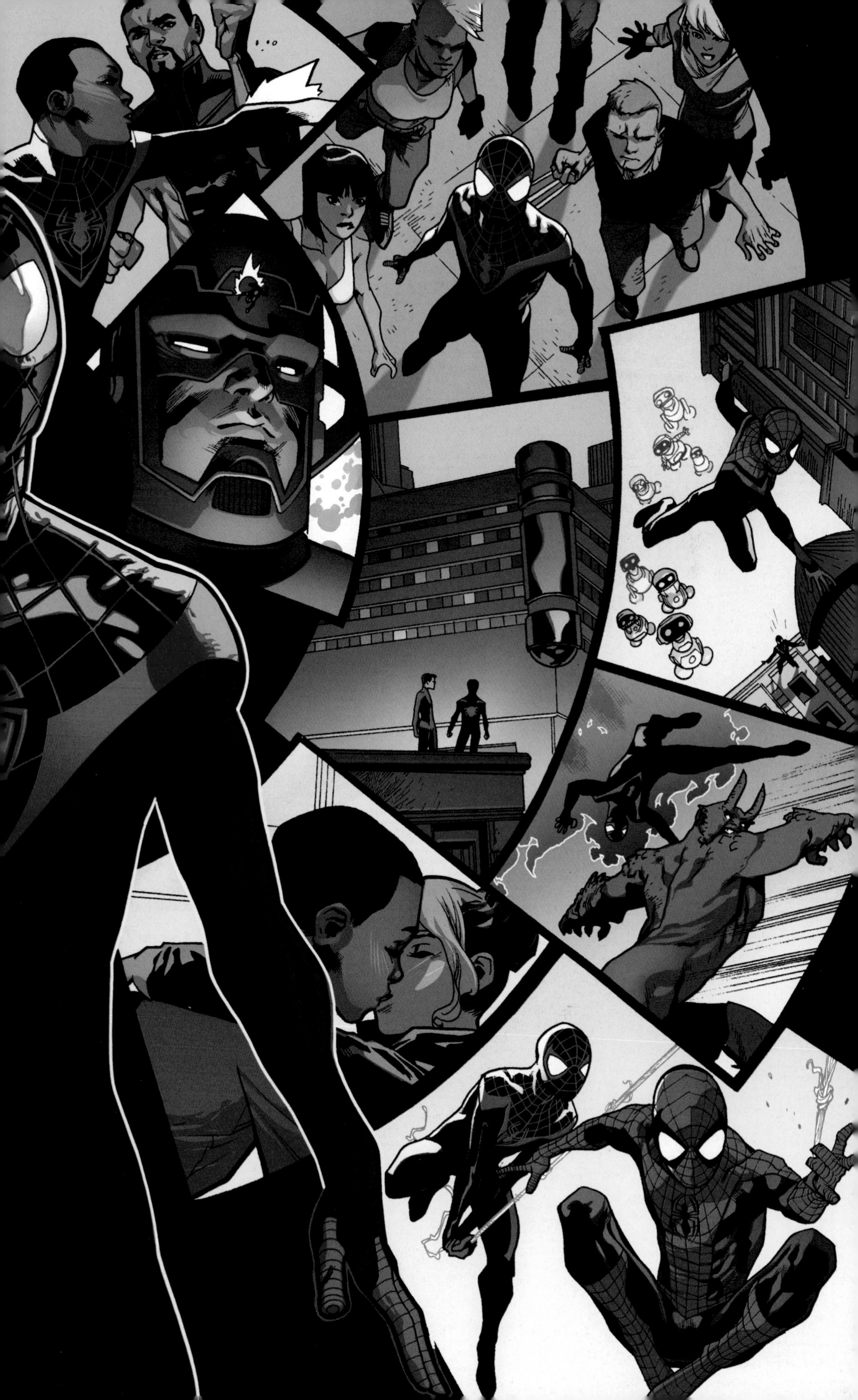

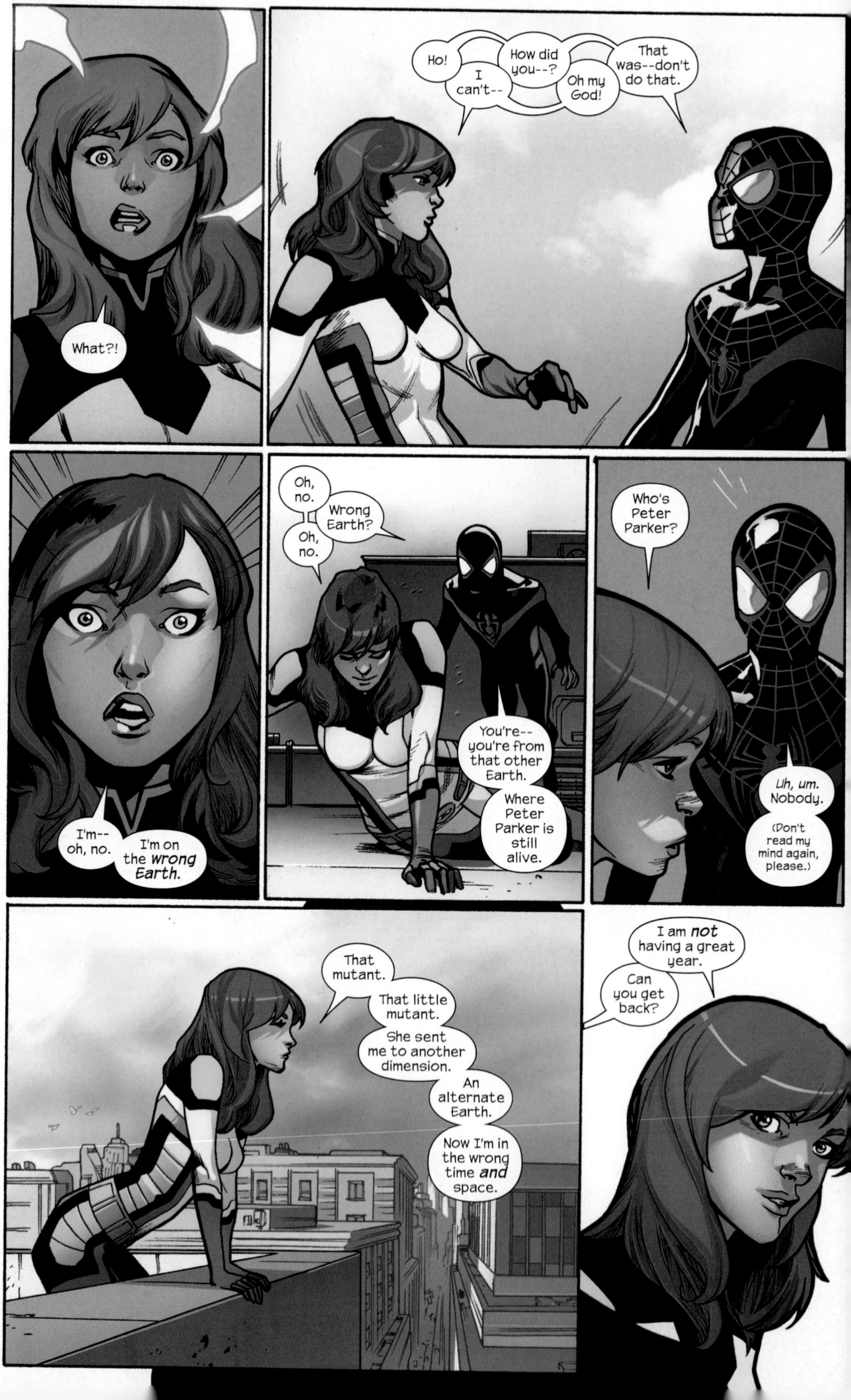
What?!
Ho!
I can't--
How did you--?
Oh my God!
That was--don't do that.
I'm-- oh, no.
I'm on the *wrong Earth.*
Oh, no.
Wrong Earth?
Oh, no.
You're-- you're from that other Earth.
Where Peter Parker is still alive.
Who's Peter Parker?
Uh, um. Nobody.
(Don't read my mind again, please.)
That mutant.
That little mutant.
She sent me to another dimension.
An alternate Earth.
Now I'm in the wrong time *and* space.
I am *not* having a great year.
Can you get back?

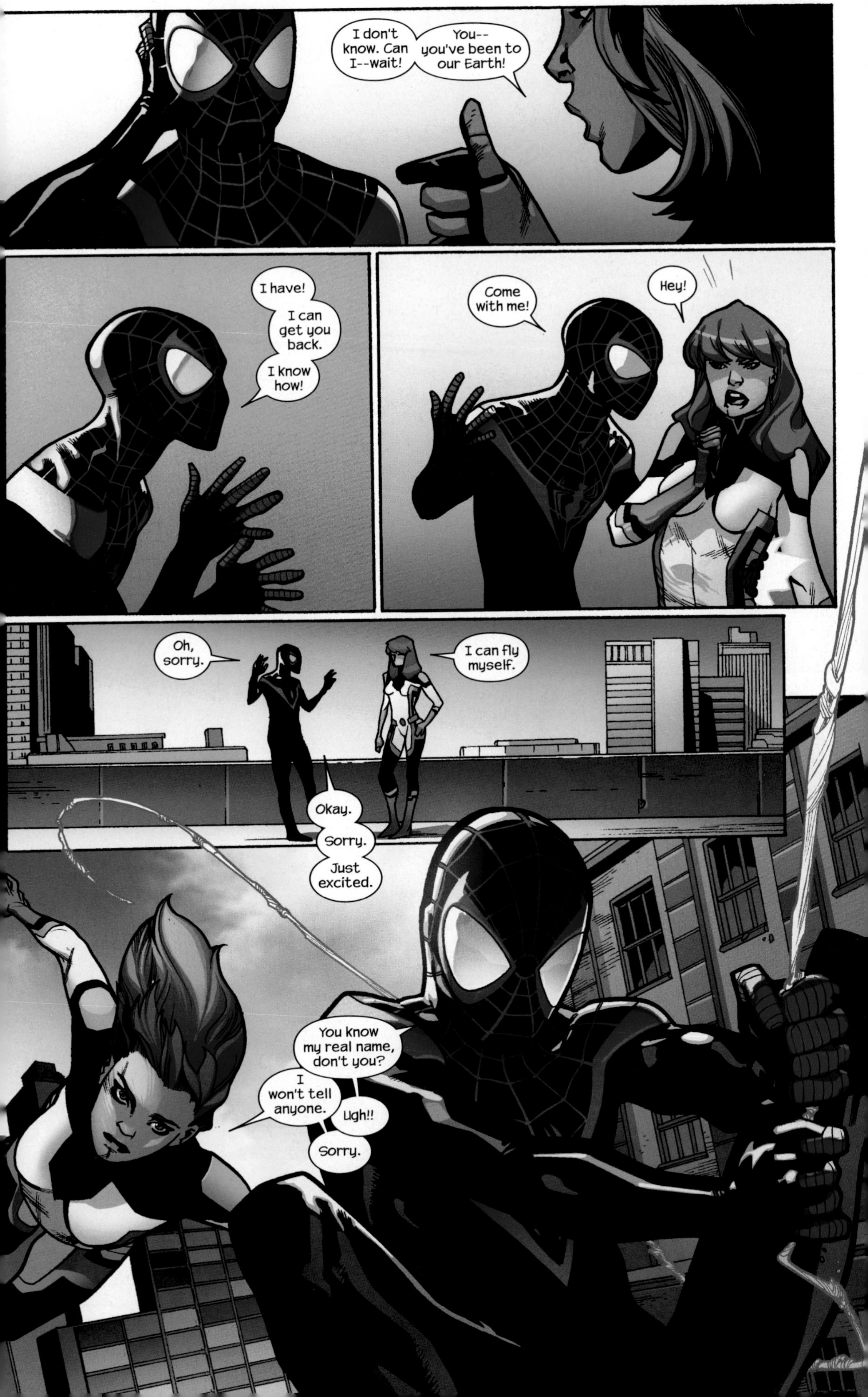
I don't know. Can I--wait!
You-- you've been to our Earth!
I have!
I can get you back.
I know how!
Come with me!
Hey!
Oh, sorry.
I can fly myself.
Okay.
Sorry.
Just excited.
You know my real name, don't you?
I won't tell anyone.
Ugh!!
Sorry.

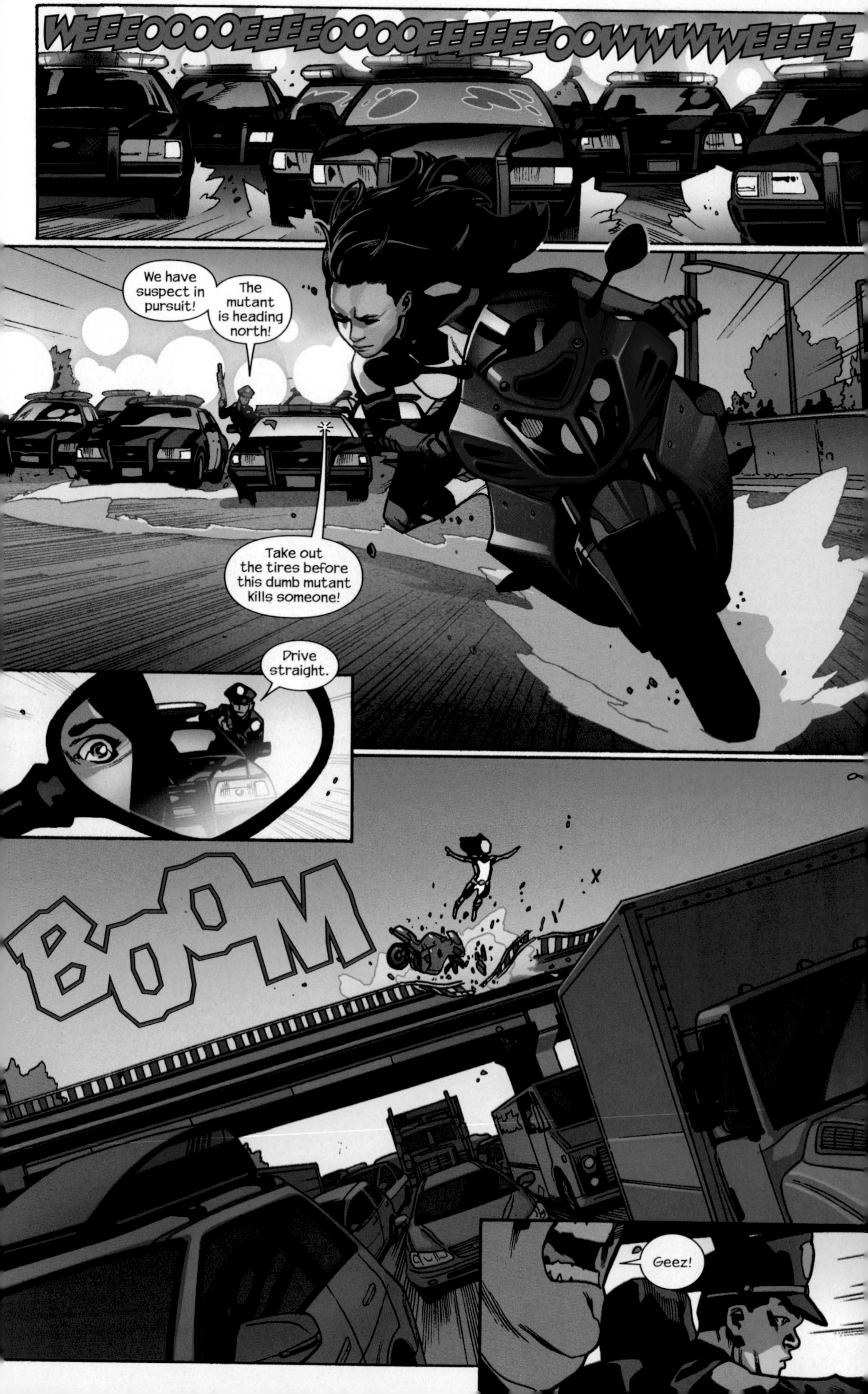
WEEEOOOOEEEEOOOOEEEEEEOOWWWWEEEEE
We have suspect in pursuit!
The mutant is heading north!
Take out the tires before this dumb mutant kills someone!
Drive straight.
BOOM
Geez!

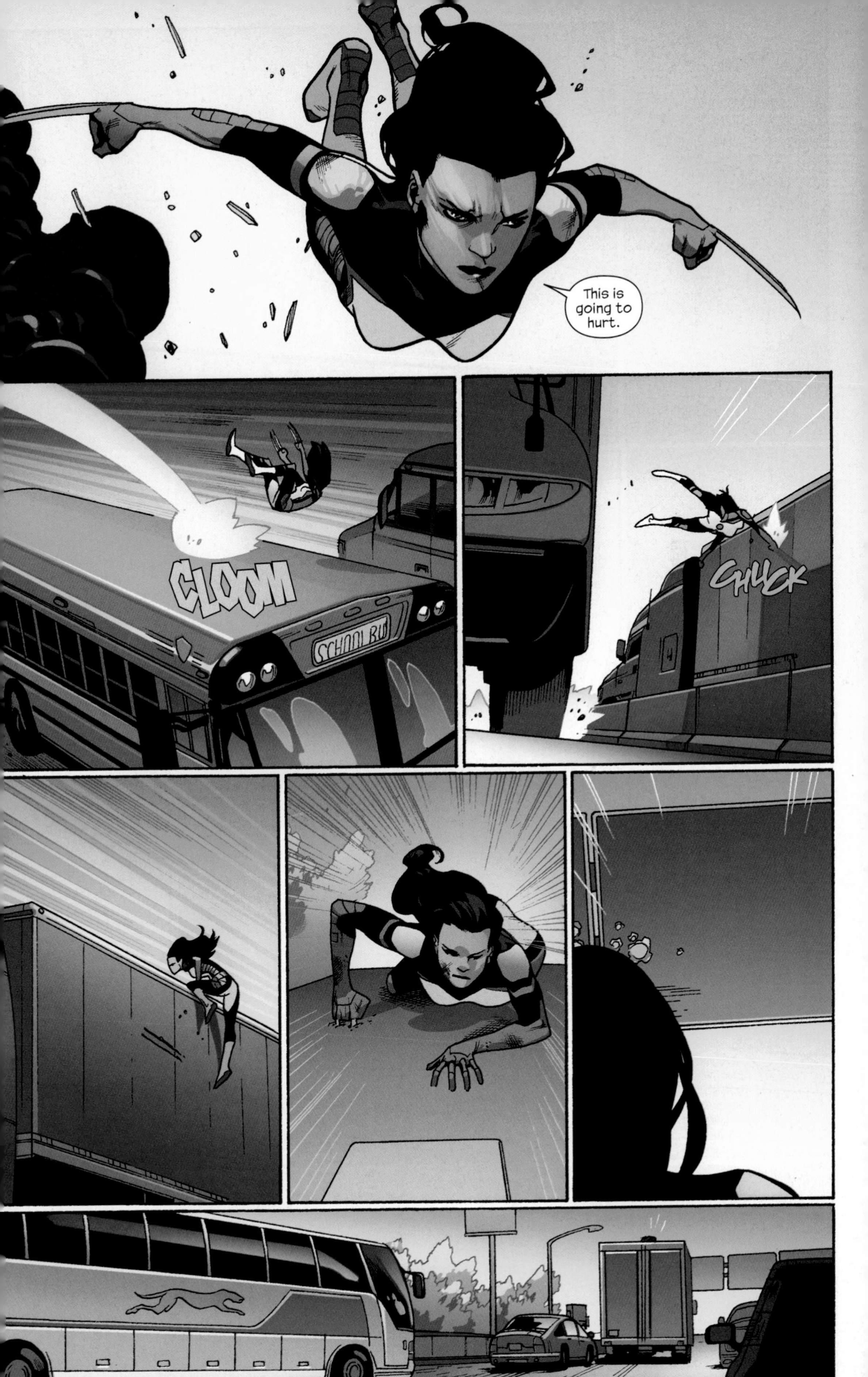
This is going to hurt.
CLOOM
CHUCK

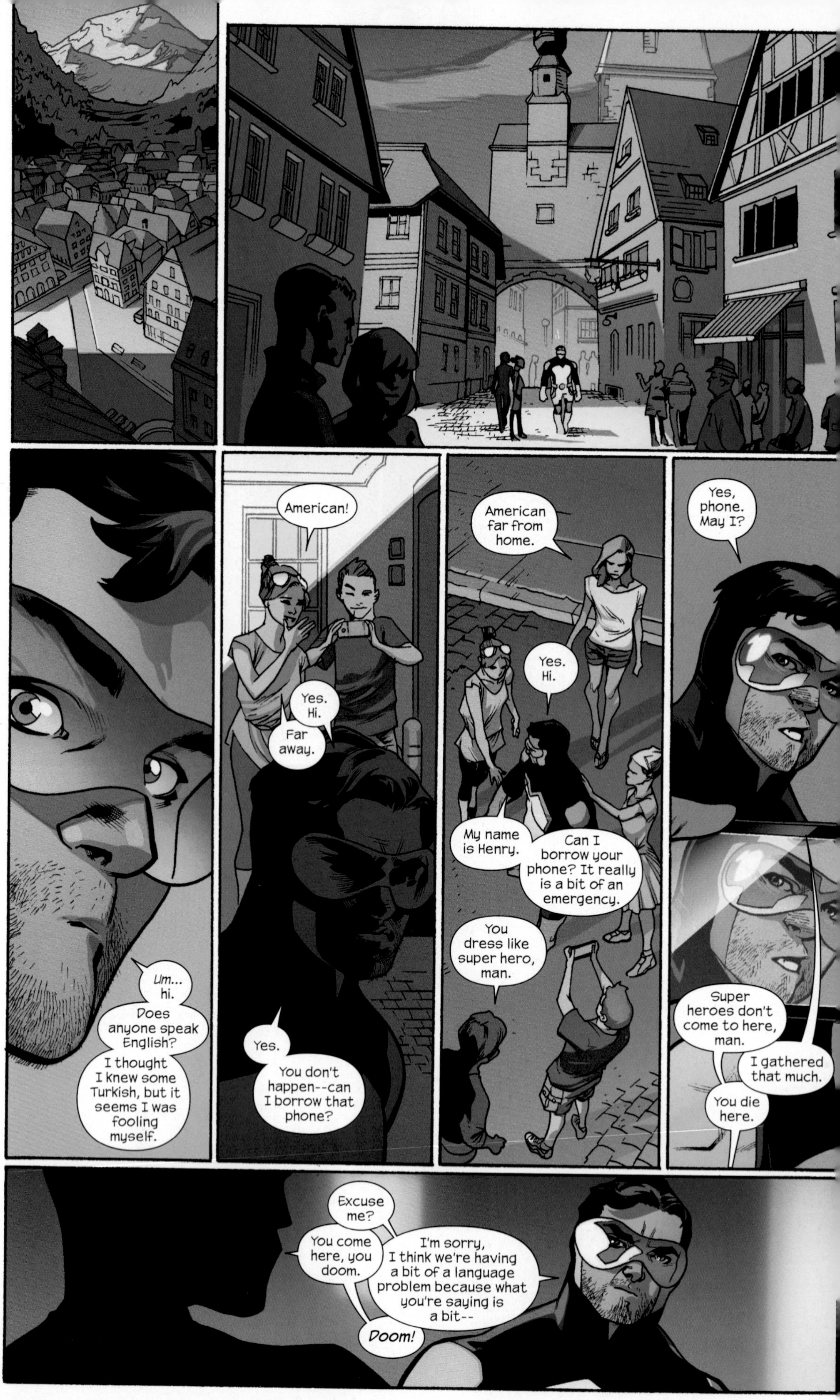
Um... hi.
Does anyone speak English?
I thought I knew some Turkish, but it seems I was fooling myself.
American!
Yes. Hi.
Far away.
Yes.
You don't happen--can I borrow that phone?
American far from home.
Yes. Hi.
My name is Henry.
Can I borrow your phone? It really is a bit of an emergency.
You dress like super hero, man.
Yes, phone. May I?
Super heroes don't come to here, man.
I gathered that much.
You die here.
Excuse me?
You come here, you doom.
I'm sorry, I think we're having a bit of a language problem because what you're saying is a bit--
Doom!

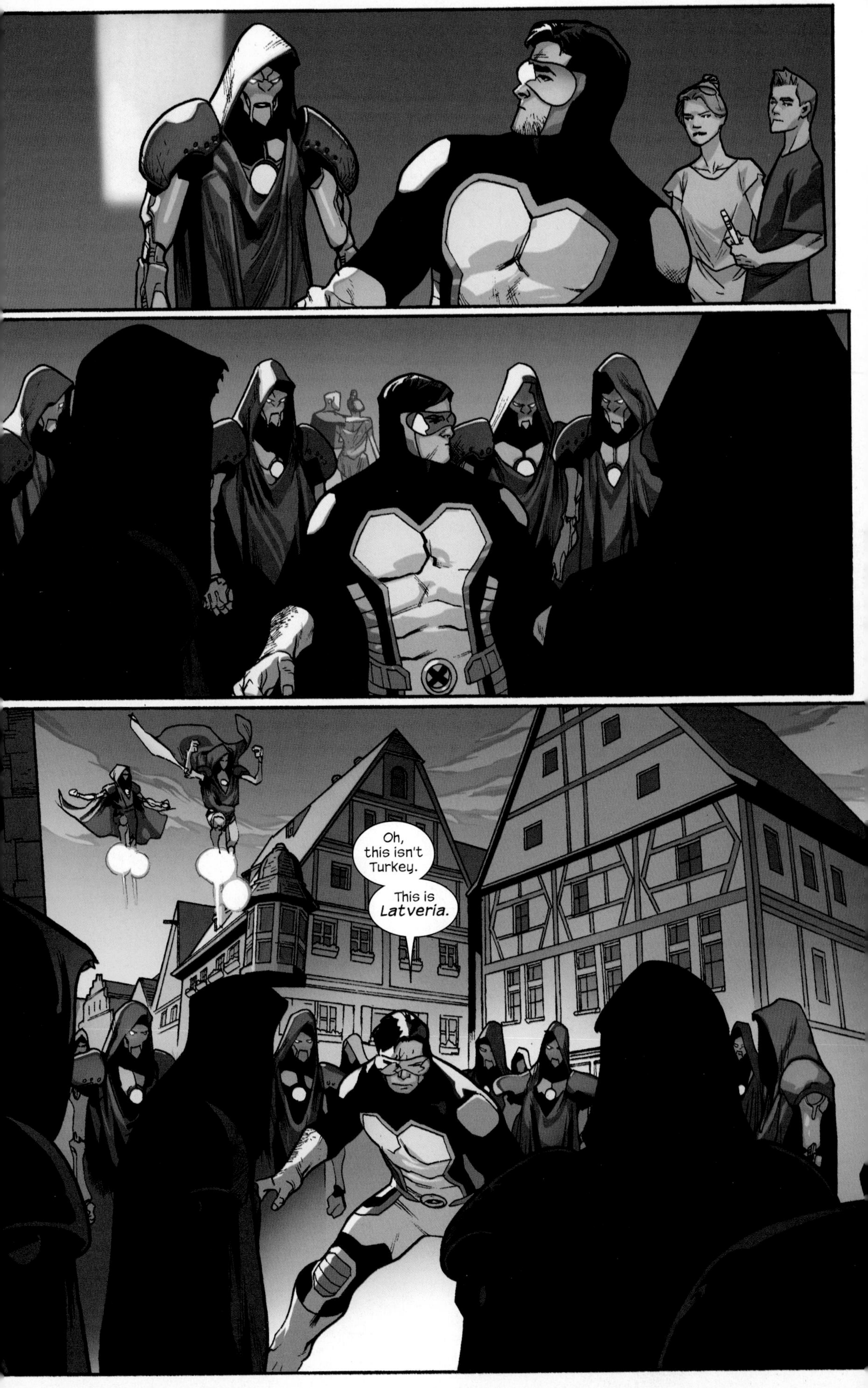
Oh, this isn't Turkey.
This is Latveria.

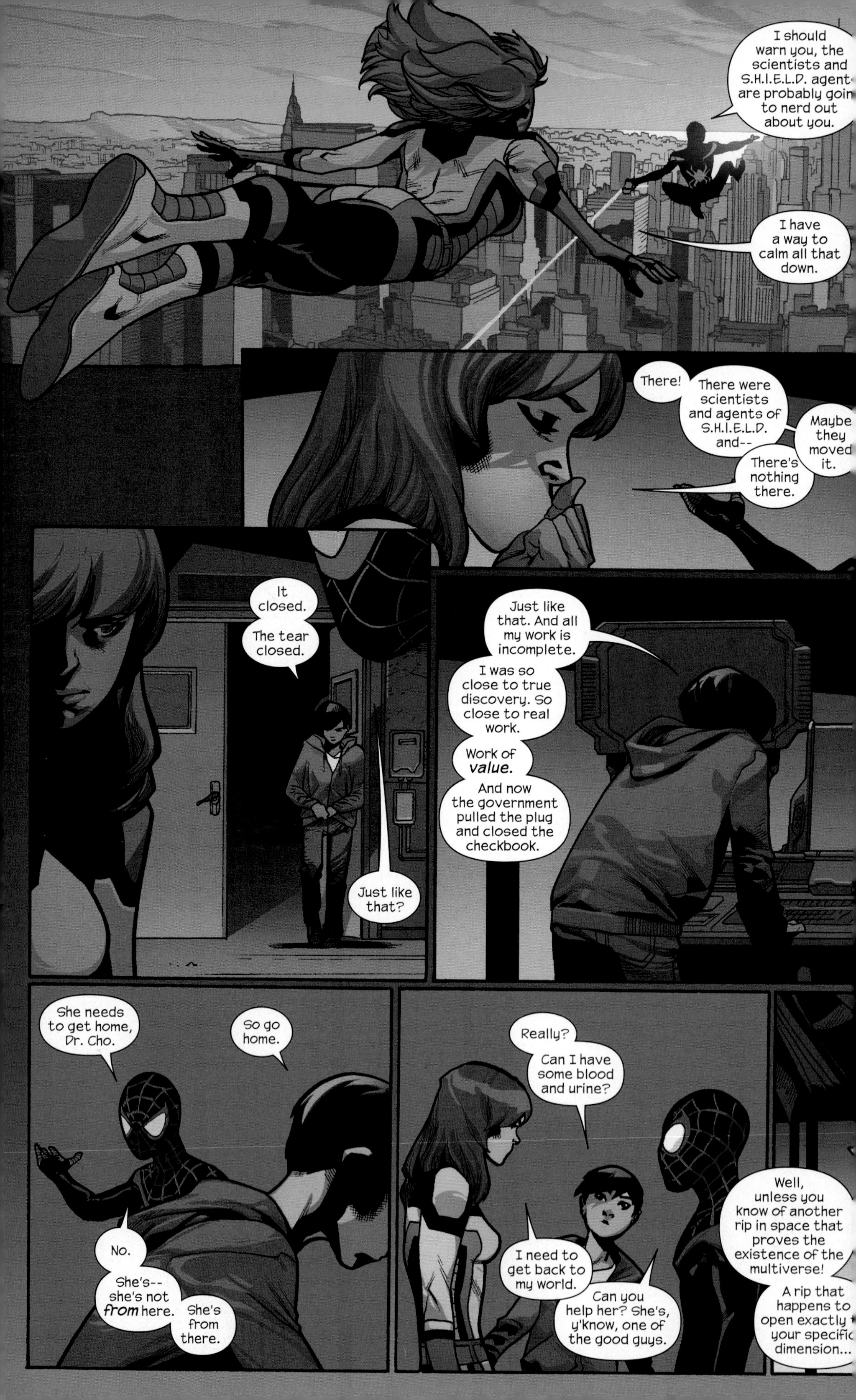

I should warn you, the scientists and S.H.I.E.L.D. agent are probably goin to nerd out about you.
I have a way to calm all that down.
There!
There were scientists and agents of S.H.I.E.L.D. and--
Maybe they moved it.
There's nothing there.
It closed.
The tear closed.
Just like that?
Just like that. And all my work is incomplete.
I was so close to true discovery. So close to real work.
Work of *value.*
And now the government pulled the plug and closed the checkbook.
She needs to get home, Dr. Cho.
So go home.
No.
She's-- she's not *from* here.
She's from there.
Really?
Can I have some blood and urine?
I need to get back to my world.
Can you help her? She's, y'know, one of the good guys.
Well, unless you know of another rip in space that proves the existence of the multiverse!
A rip that happens to open exactly your specific dimension...

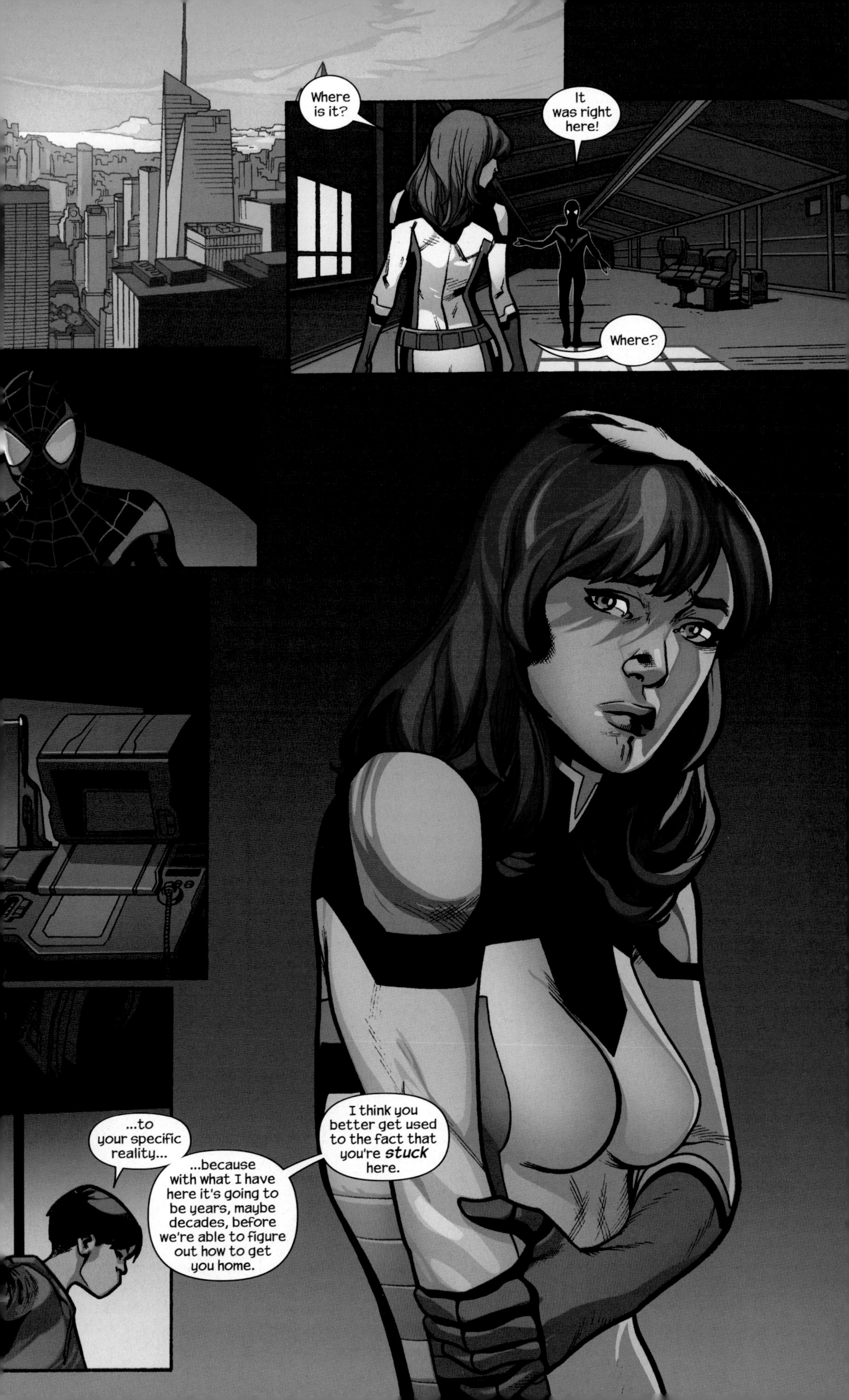
Where is it?
It was right here!
Where?
...to your specific reality...
...because with what I have here it's going to be years, maybe decades, before we're able to figure out how to get you home.
I think you better get used to the fact that you're *stuck* here.

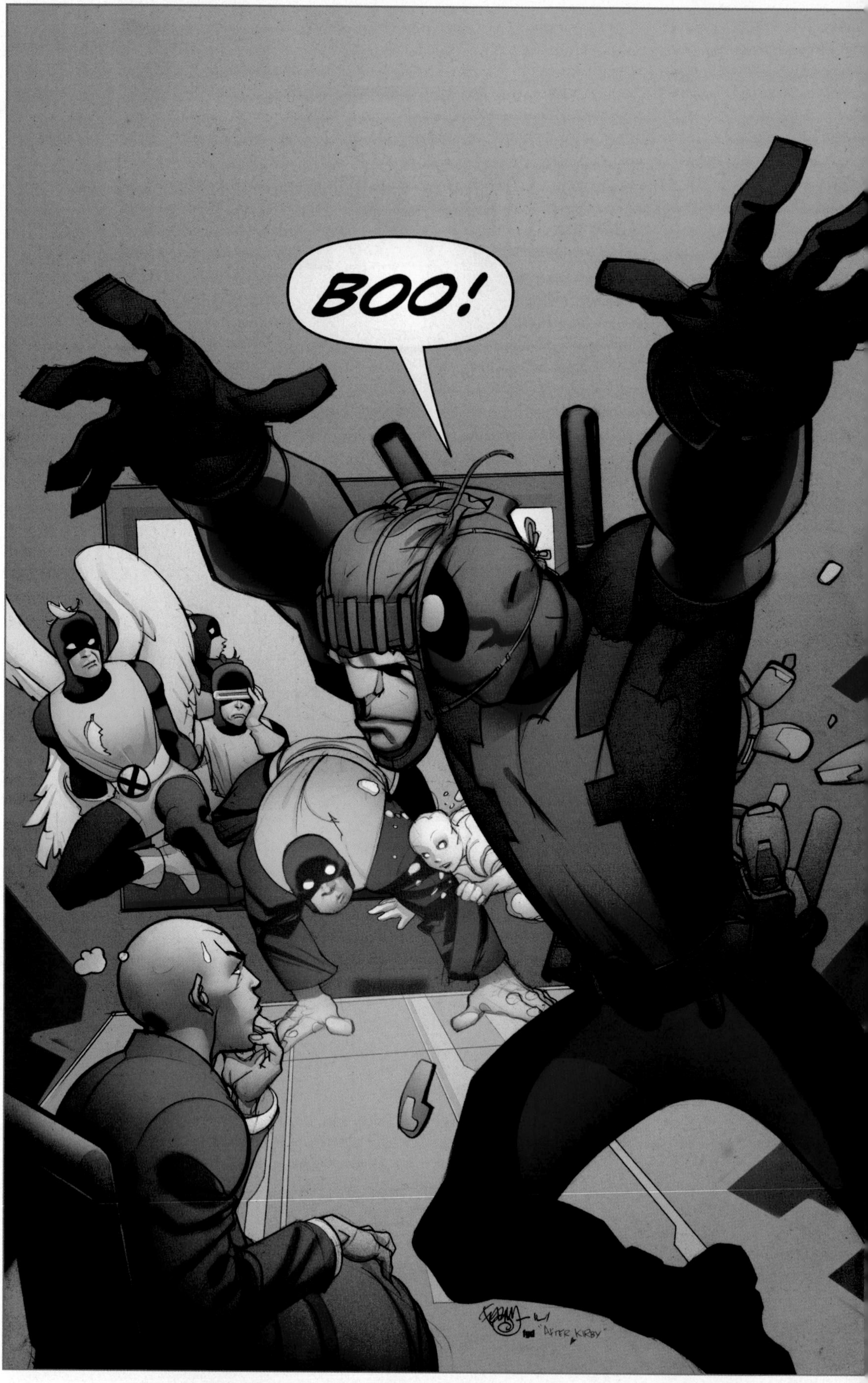
BOO!

ALL-NEW X-MEN #33 DEADPOOL 75TH ANNIVERSARY VARIANT
BY PASQUAL FERRY & FRANK D'ARMATA

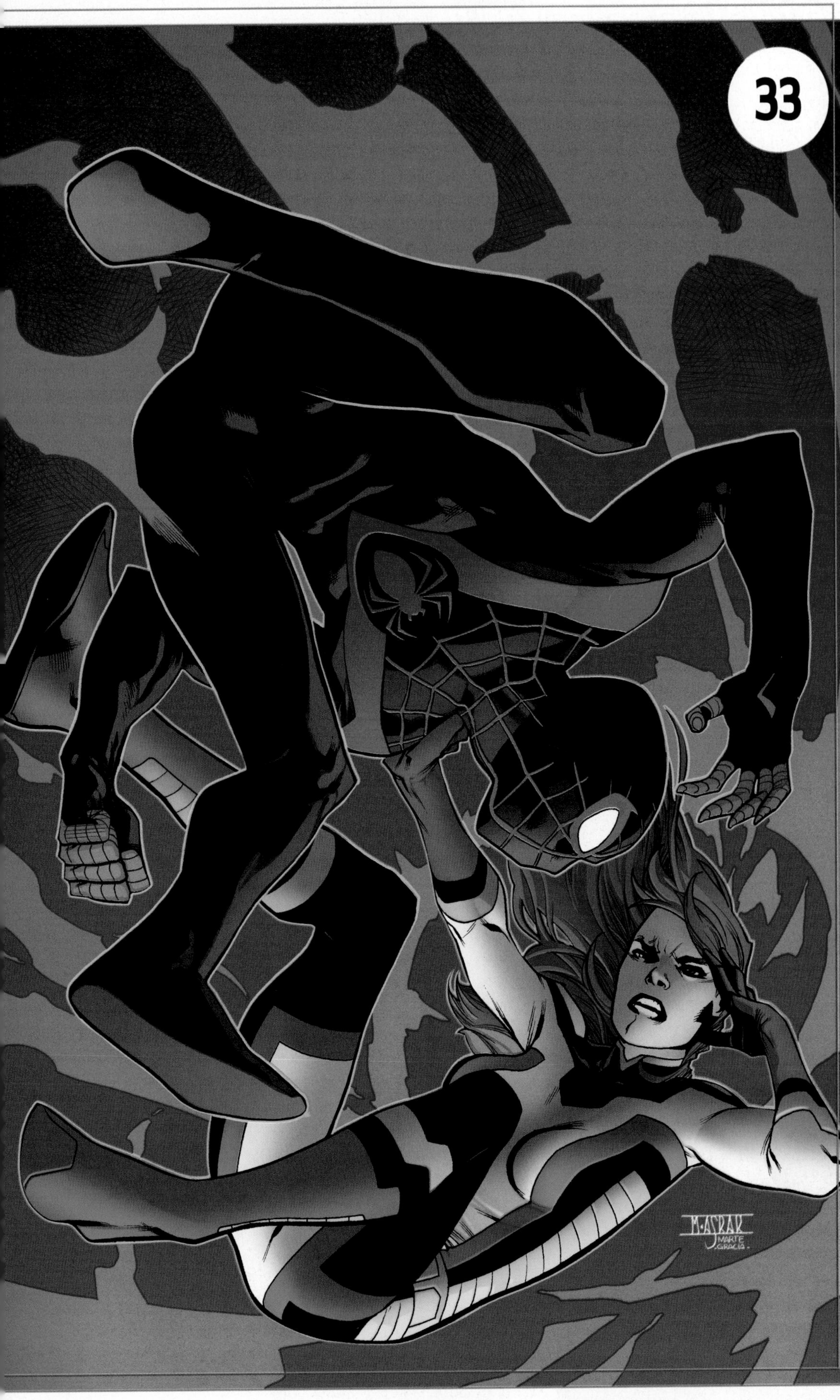
33
M.ASRAR
MARTE GRACIA

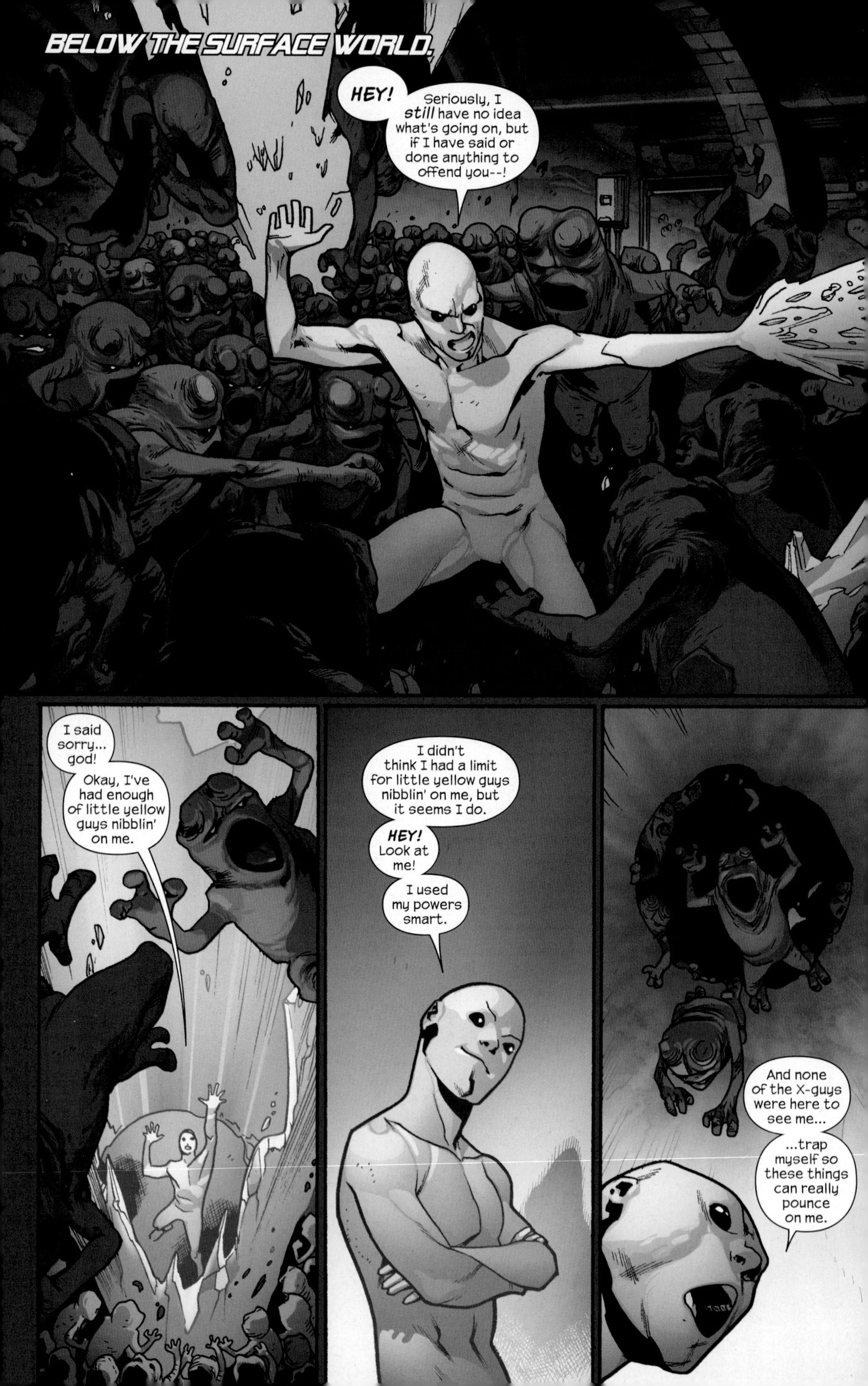
BELOW THE SURFACE WORLD.
HEY!
Seriously, I still have no idea what's going on, but if I have said or done anything to offend you--!
I said sorry... god!
Okay, I've had enough of little yellow guys nibblin' on me.
I didn't think I had a limit for little yellow guys nibblin' on me, but it seems I do.
HEY! Look at me!
I used my powers smart.
And none of the X-guys were here to see me...
...trap myself so these things can really pounce on me.

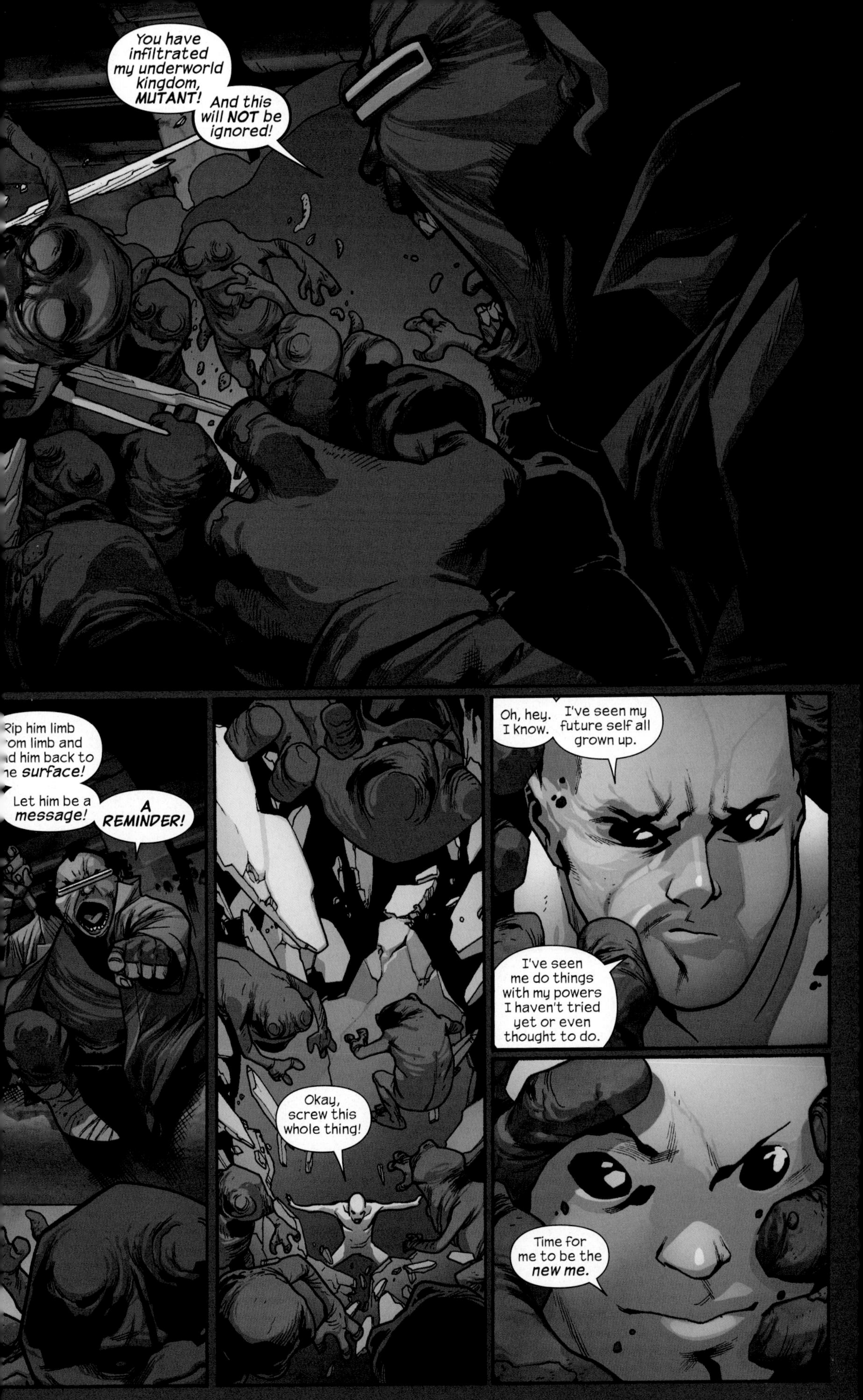
You have infiltrated my underworld kingdom, MUTANT!
And this will NOT be ignored!
Rip him limb rom limb and d him back to e surface!
Let him be a message!
A REMINDER!
Okay, screw this whole thing!
Oh, hey. I know.
I've seen my future self all grown up.
I've seen me do things with my powers I haven't tried yet or even thought to do.
Time for me to be the new me.

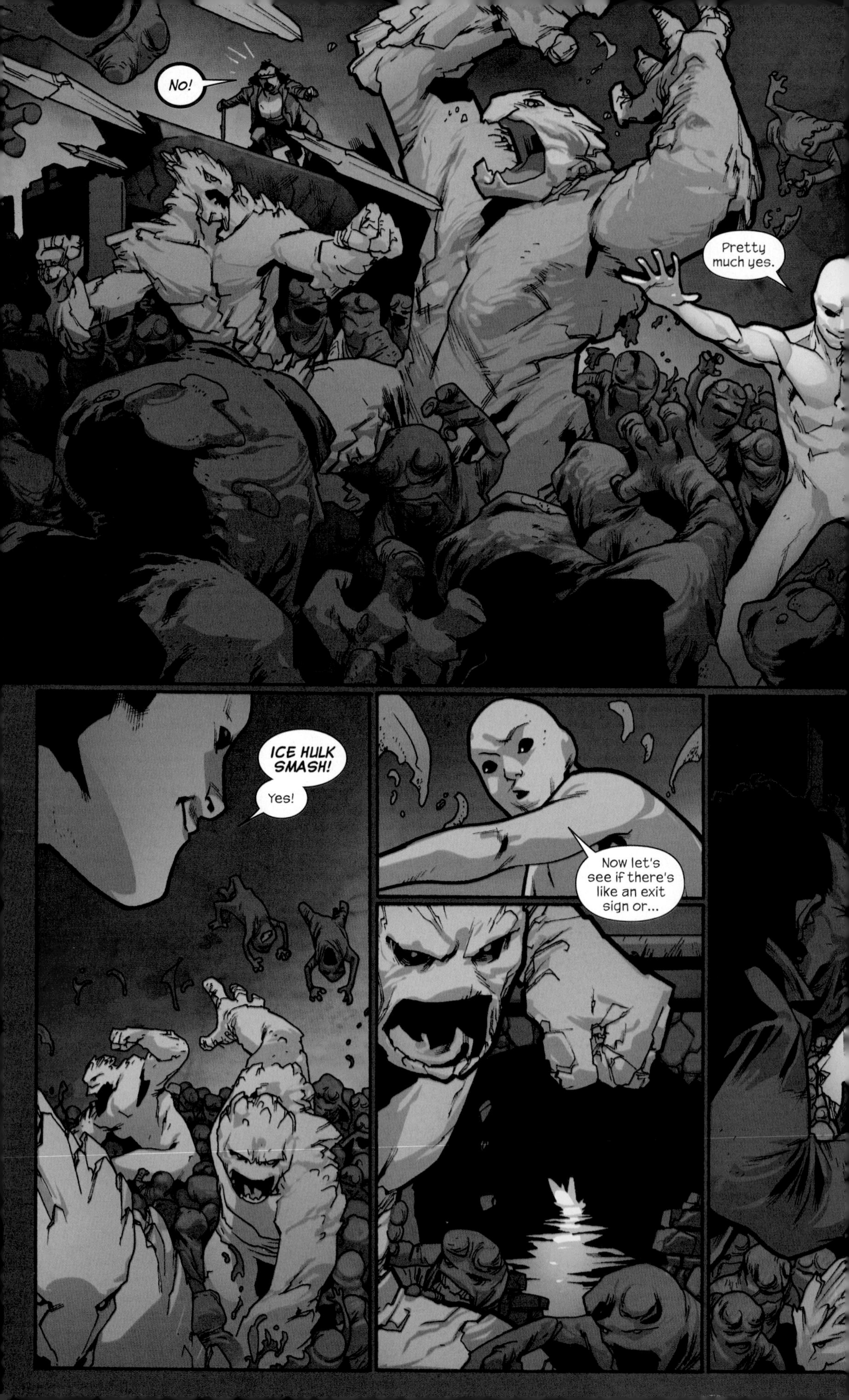
No!
Pretty much yes.
ICE HULK SMASH!
Yes!
Now let's see if there's like an exit sign or...

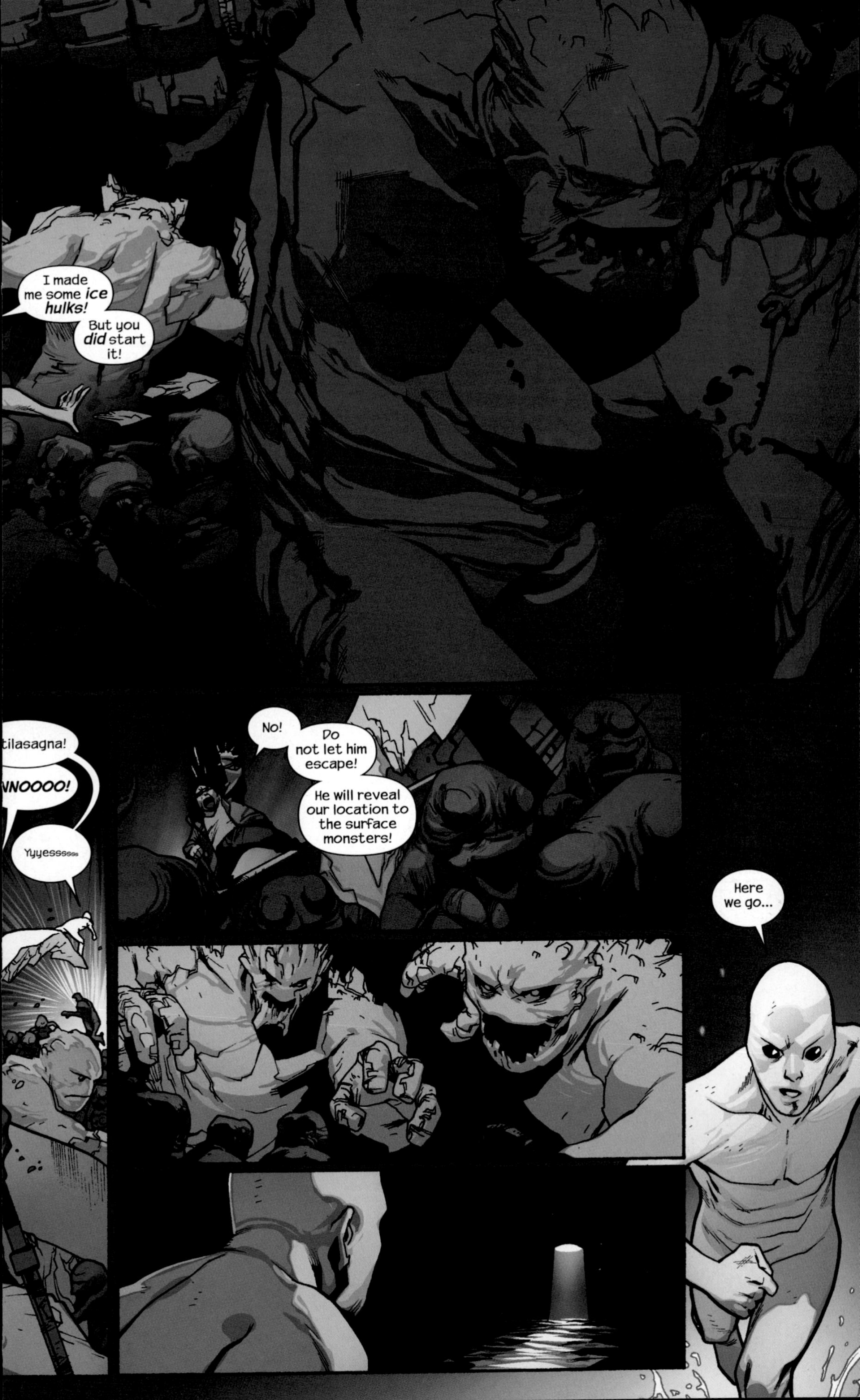
I made me some *ice hulks!*
But you *did* start it!
tilasagna!
NNOOOO!
Yyyesssss
No!
Do not let him escape!
He will reveal our location to the surface monsters!
Here we go...

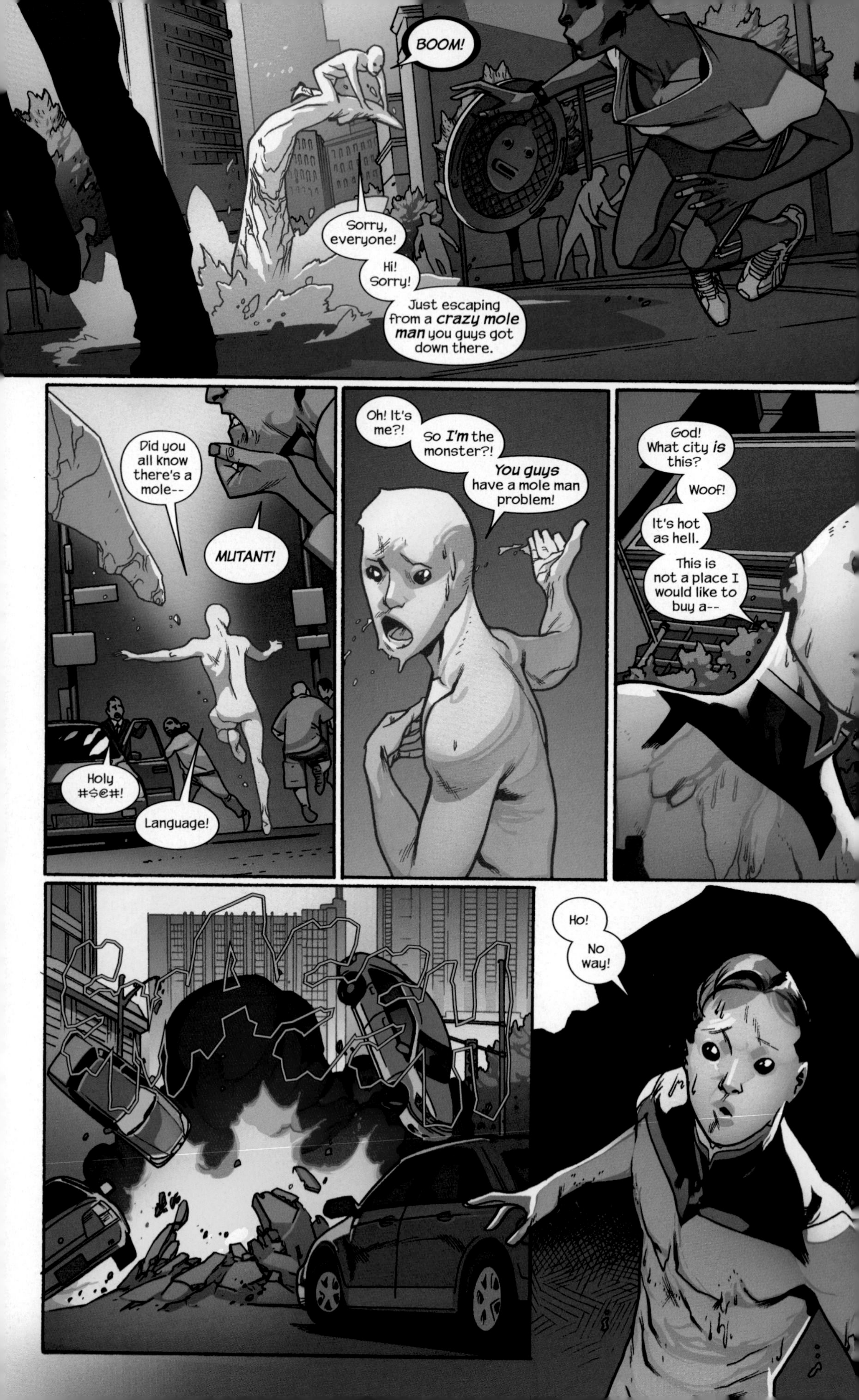
BOOM!
Sorry, everyone!
Hi! Sorry!
Just escaping from a crazy mole man you guys got down there.
Did you all know there's a mole--
MUTANT!
Holy #$@#!
Language!
Oh! It's me?!
So I'm the monster?!
You guys have a mole man problem!
God! What city is this?
Woof!
It's hot as hell.
This is not a place I would like to buy a--
Ho!
No way!

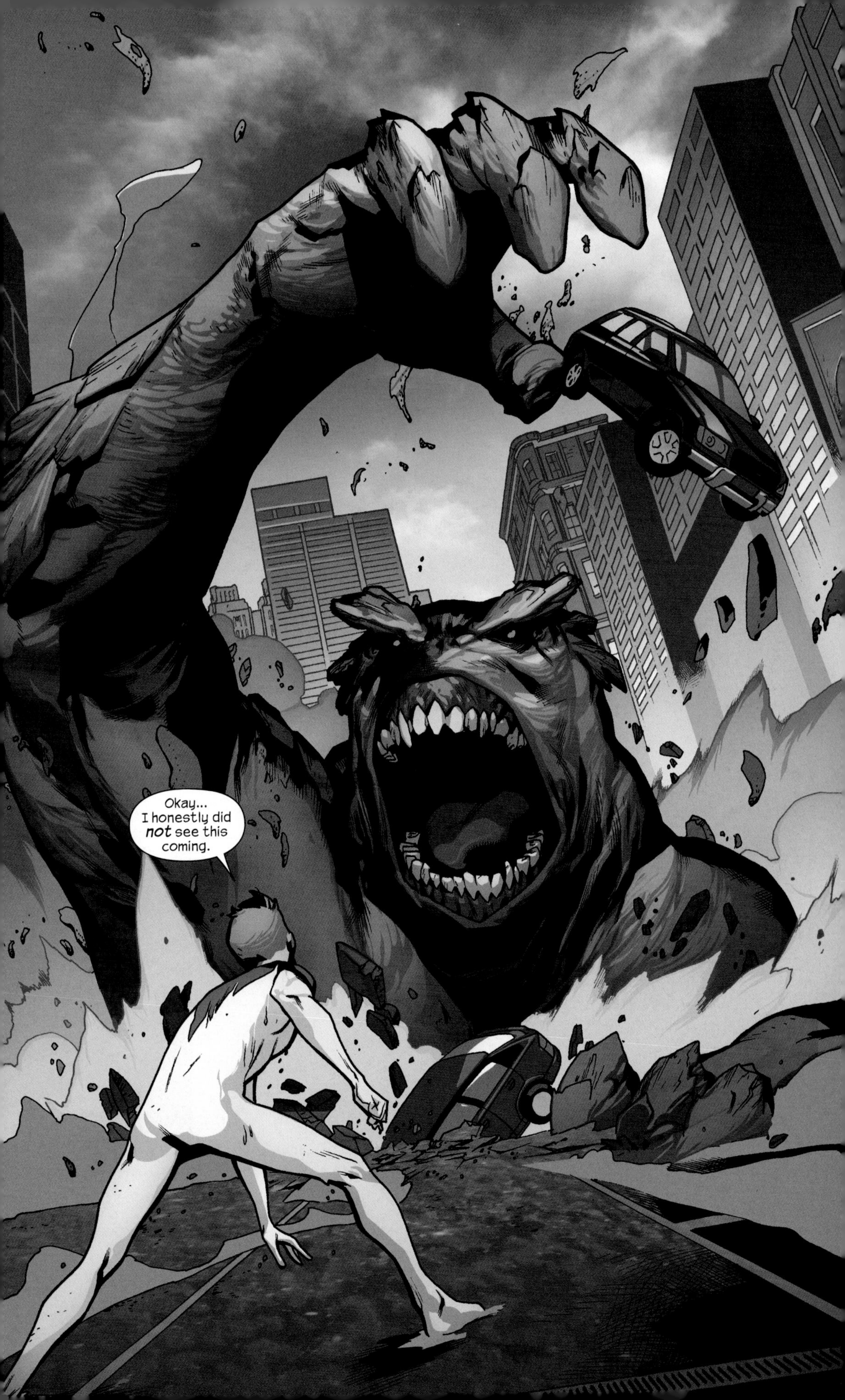
Okay... I honestly did *not* see this coming.

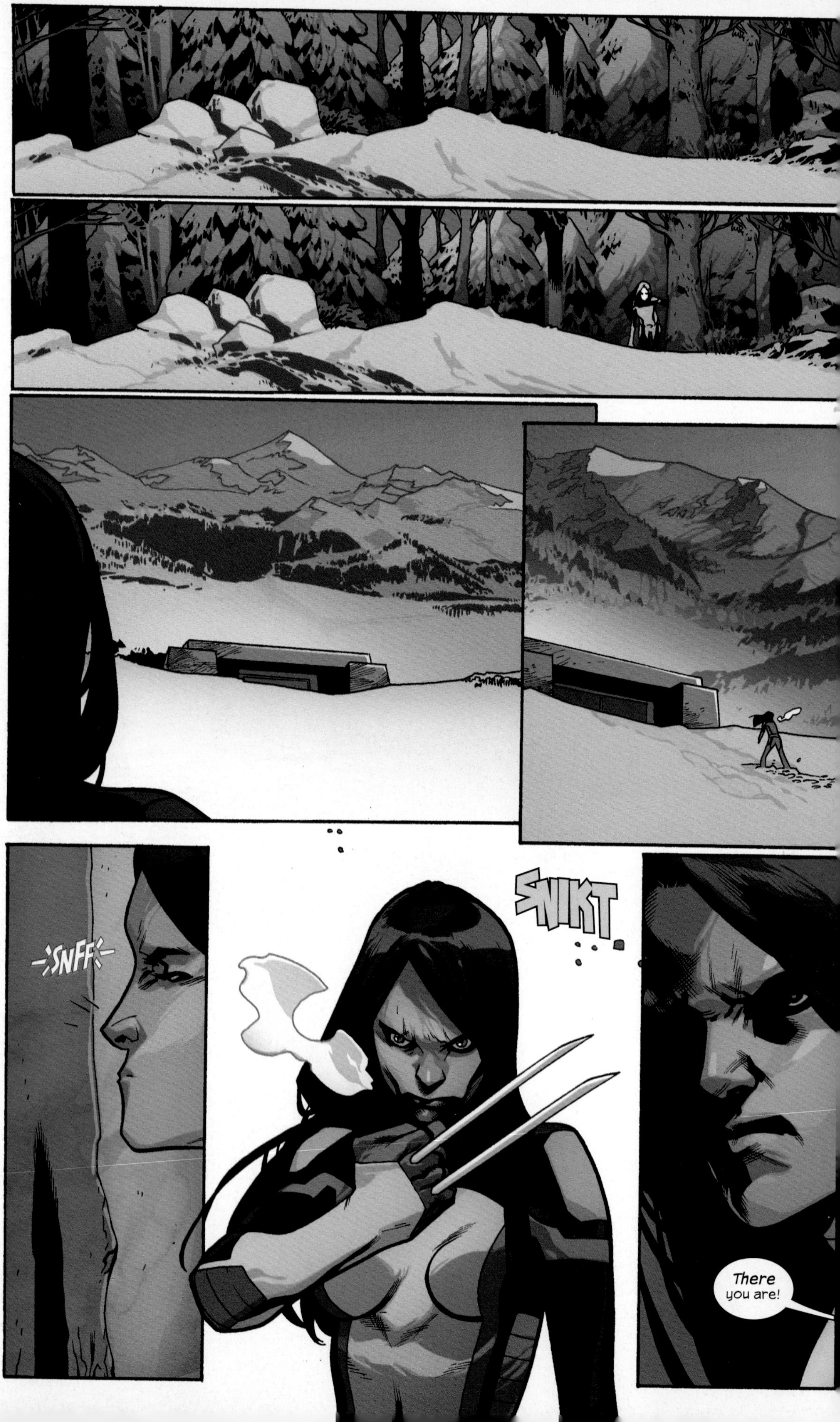
SNFF
SNIKT
There you are!

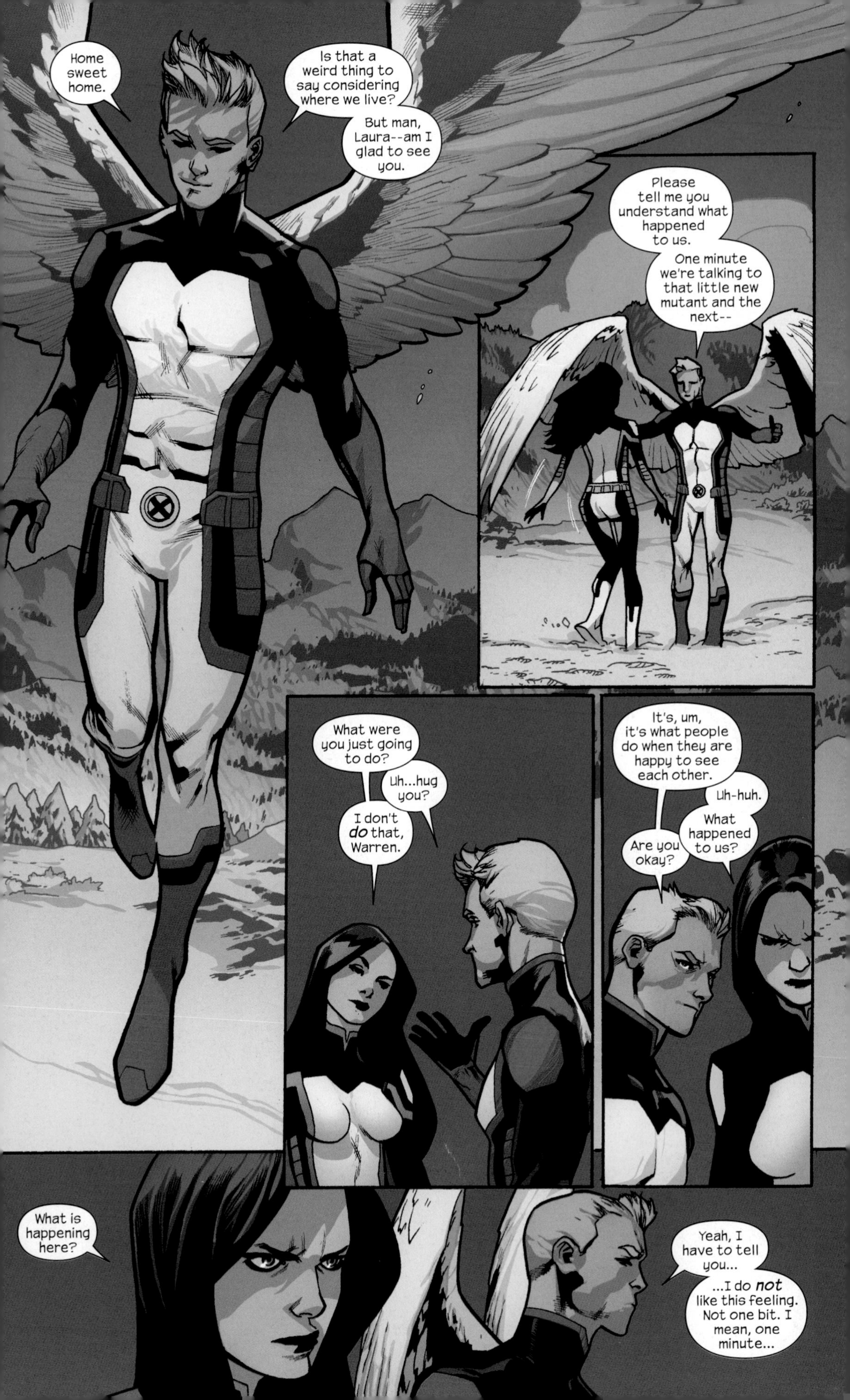
Home sweet home.
Is that a weird thing to say considering where we live?
But man, Laura--am I glad to see you.
Please tell me you understand what happened to us.
One minute we're talking to that little new mutant and the next--
What were you just going to do?
Uh...hug you?
I don't *do* that, Warren.
It's, um, it's what people do when they are happy to see each other.
Uh-huh.
What happened to us?
Are you okay?
What is happening here?
Yeah, I have to tell you...
...I do ***not*** like this feeling. Not one bit. I mean, one minute...

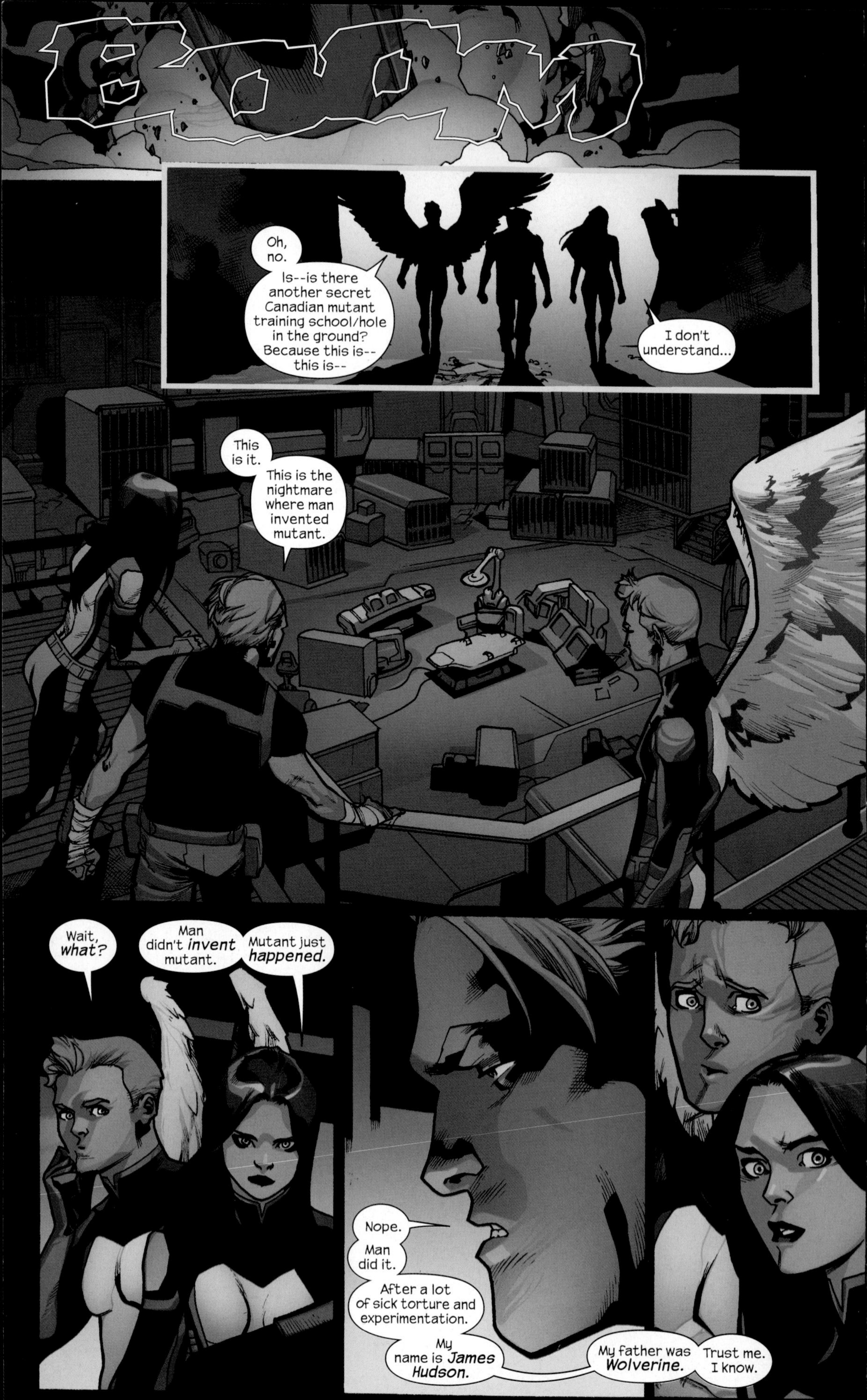
Oh, no.
Is--is there another secret Canadian mutant training school/hole in the ground? Because this is-- this is--
I don't understand...
This is it.
This is the nightmare where man invented mutant.
Wait, *what?*
Man didn't *invent* mutant.
Mutant just *happened.*
Nope.
Man did it.
After a lot of sick torture and experimentation.
My name is *James Hudson.*
My father was *Wolverine.*
Trust me. I know.

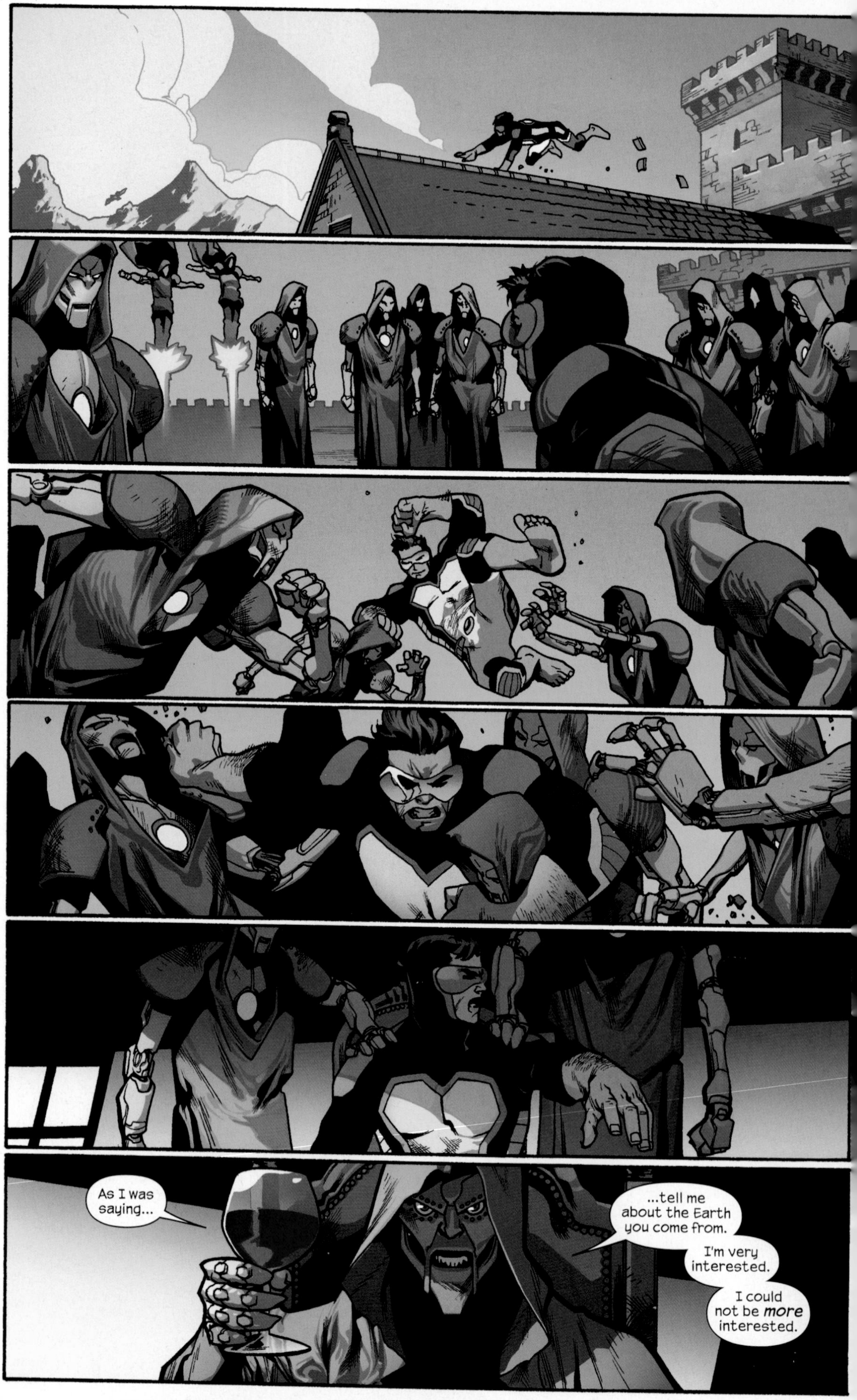
As I was saying...
...tell me about the Earth you come from.
I'm very interested.
I could not be *more* interested.

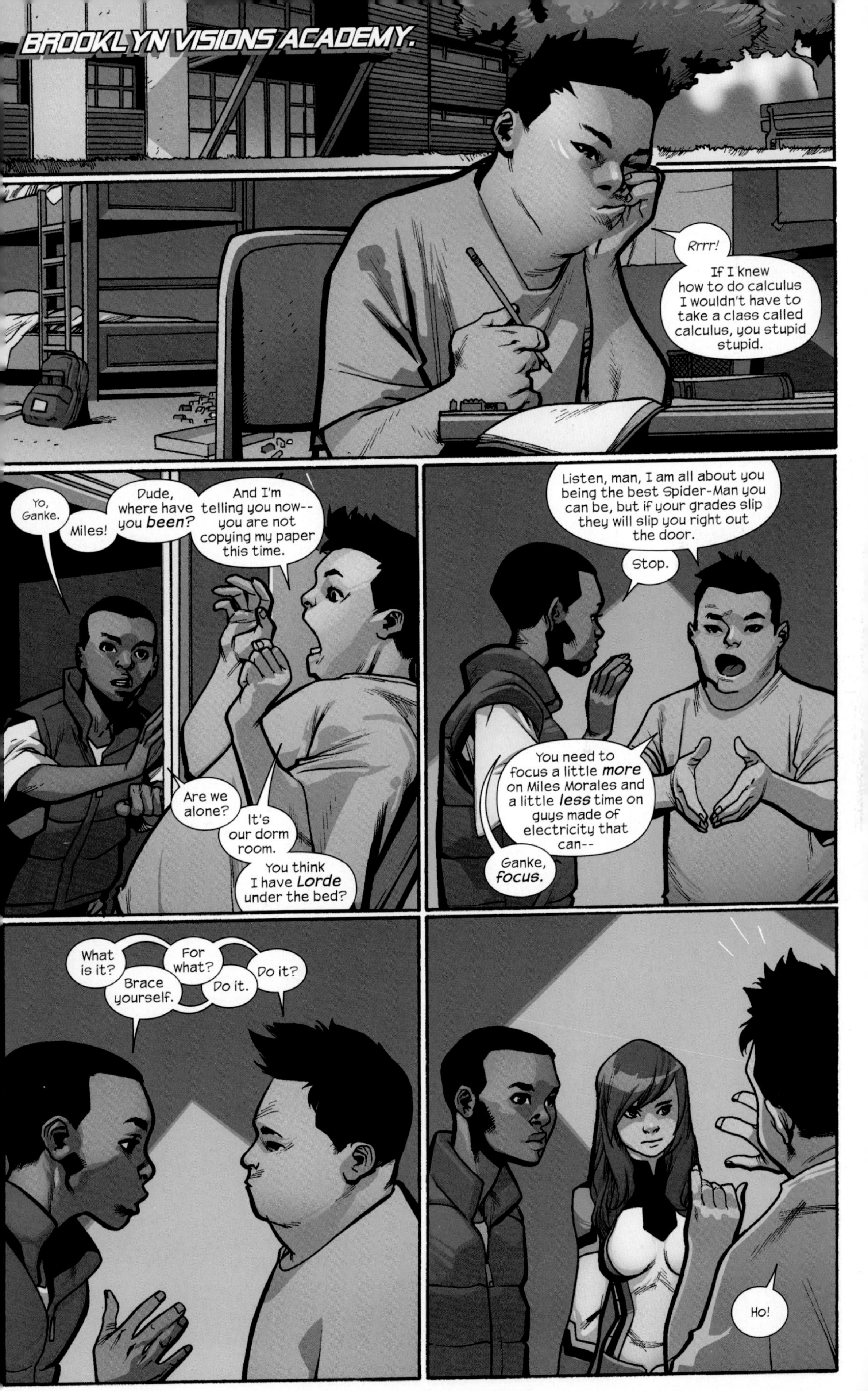
BROOKLYN VISIONS ACADEMY.
Rrrr!
If I knew how to do calculus I wouldn't have to take a class called calculus, you stupid stupid.
Yo, Ganke.
Miles!
Dude, where have you been?
And I'm telling you now--you are not copying my paper this time.
Are we alone?
It's our dorm room.
You think I have Lorde under the bed?
Listen, man, I am all about you being the best Spider-Man you can be, but if your grades slip they will slip you right out the door.
Stop.
You need to focus a little more on Miles Morales and a little less time on guys made of electricity that can--
Ganke, focus.
What is it?
Brace yourself.
For what?
Do it.
Do it?
Ho!

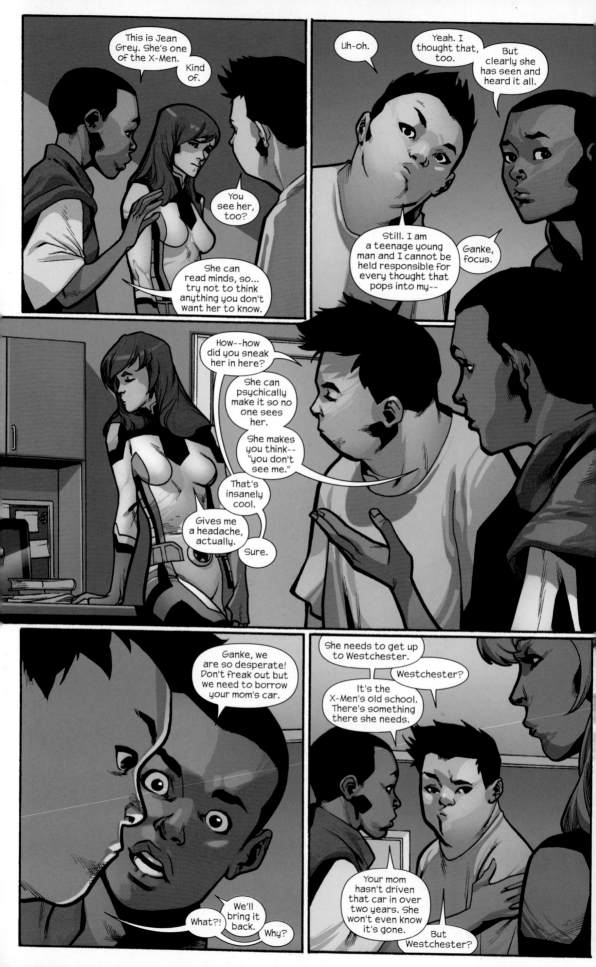

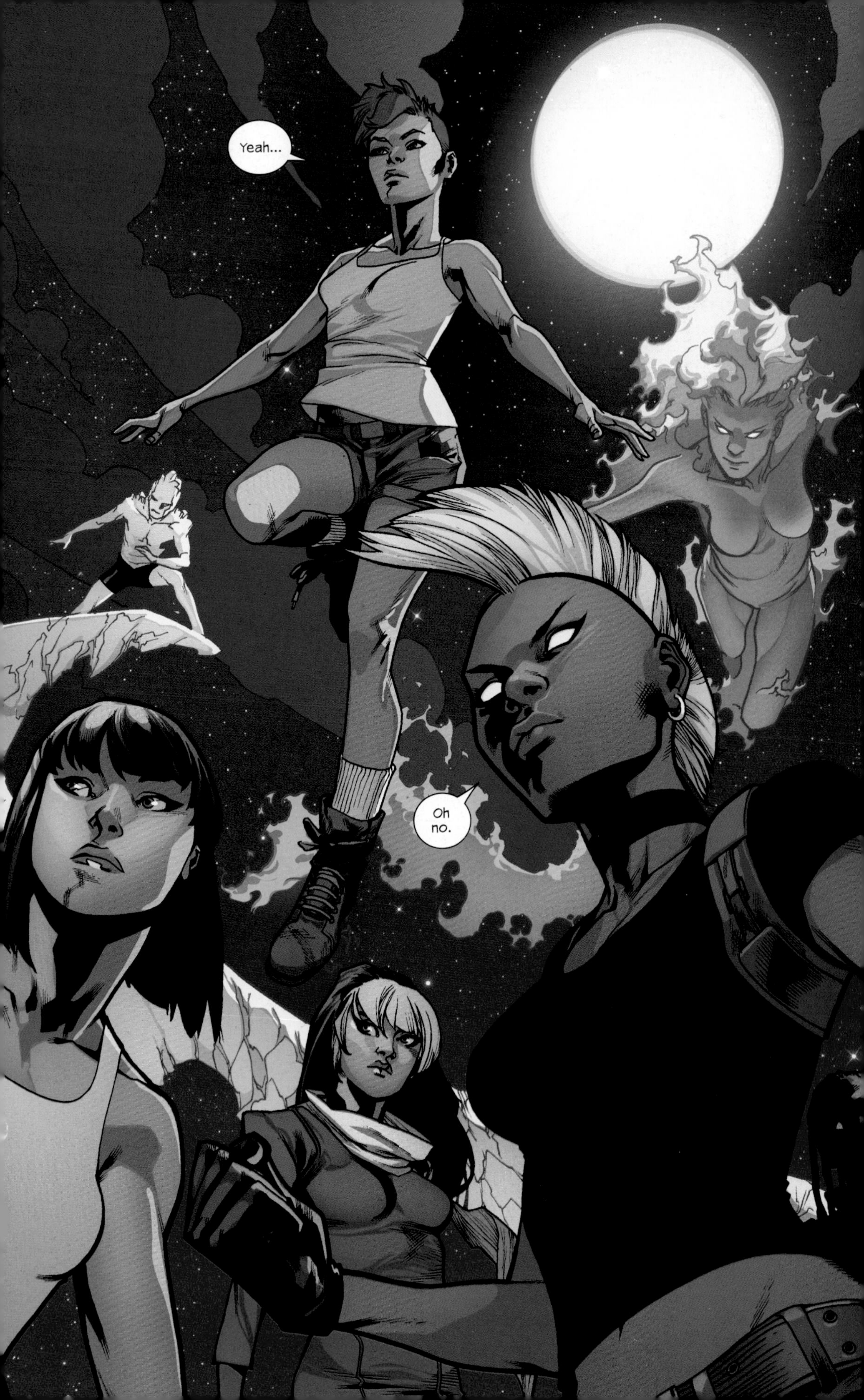
Yeah...
Oh no.

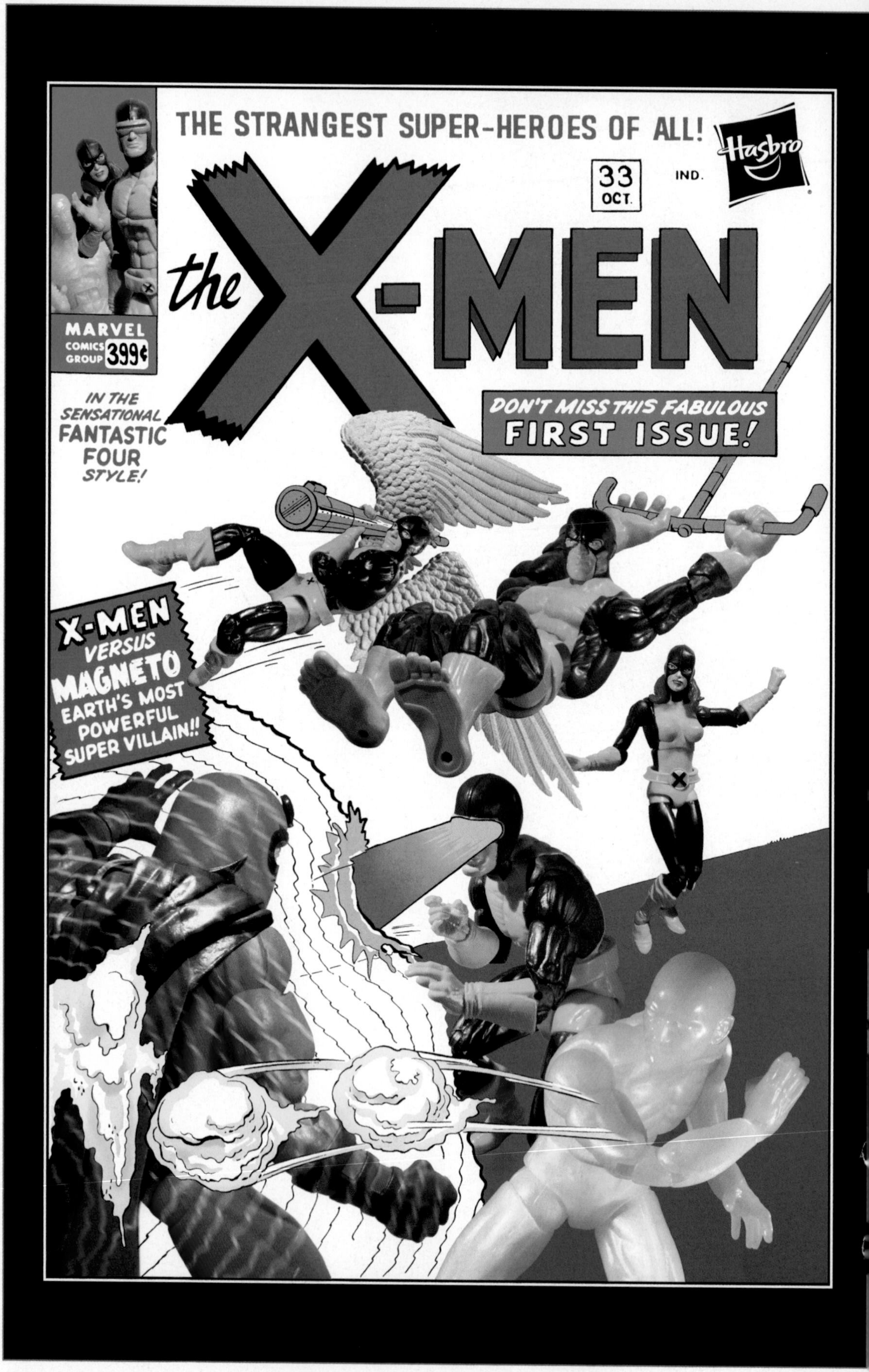
THE STRANGEST SUPER-HEROES OF ALL!
Hasbro
33
OCT.
IND.
the X-MEN
MARVEL
COMICS GROUP 399¢
IN THE SENSATIONAL FANTASTIC FOUR STYLE!
DON'T MISS THIS FABULOUS FIRST ISSUE!
X-MEN VERSUS MAGNETO EARTH'S MOST POWERFUL SUPER VILLAIN!!

ALL-NEW X-MEN #33 HASBRO VARIANT

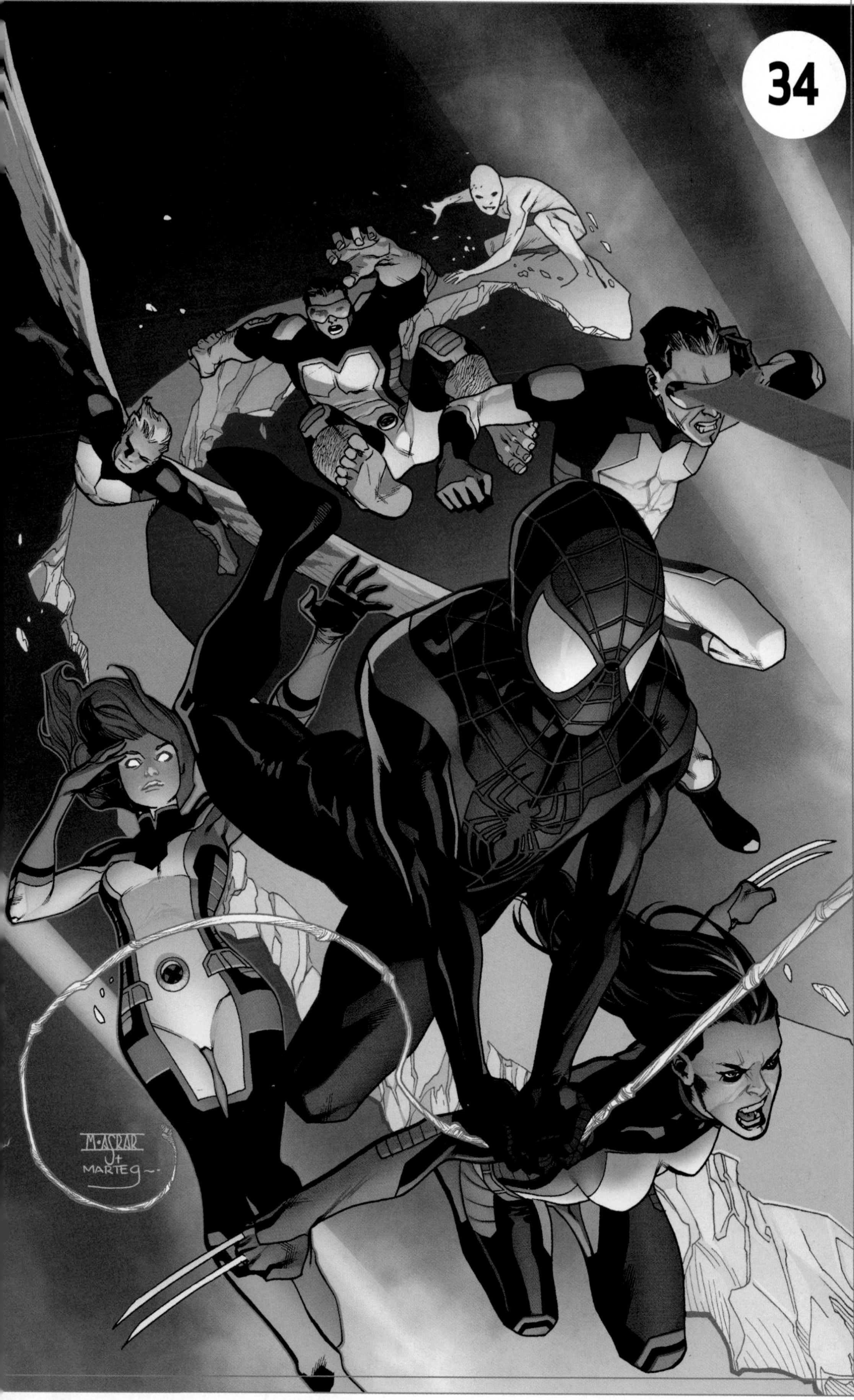
34
M·ASRAR
J+
MARTEG

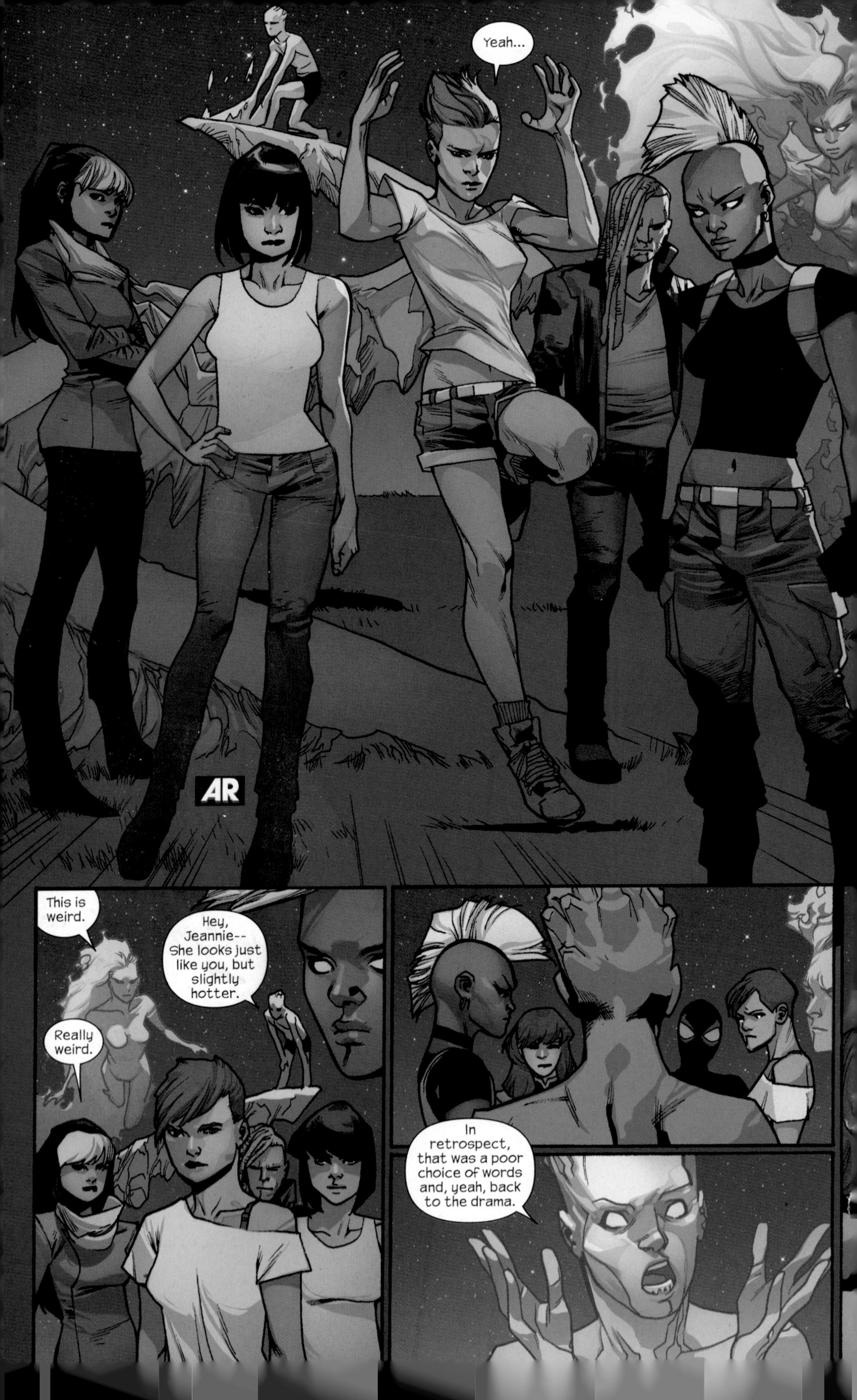
Yeah...
AR
This is weird.
Hey, Jeannie-- She looks just like you, but slightly hotter.
Really weird.
In retrospect, that was a poor choice of words and, yeah, back to the drama.

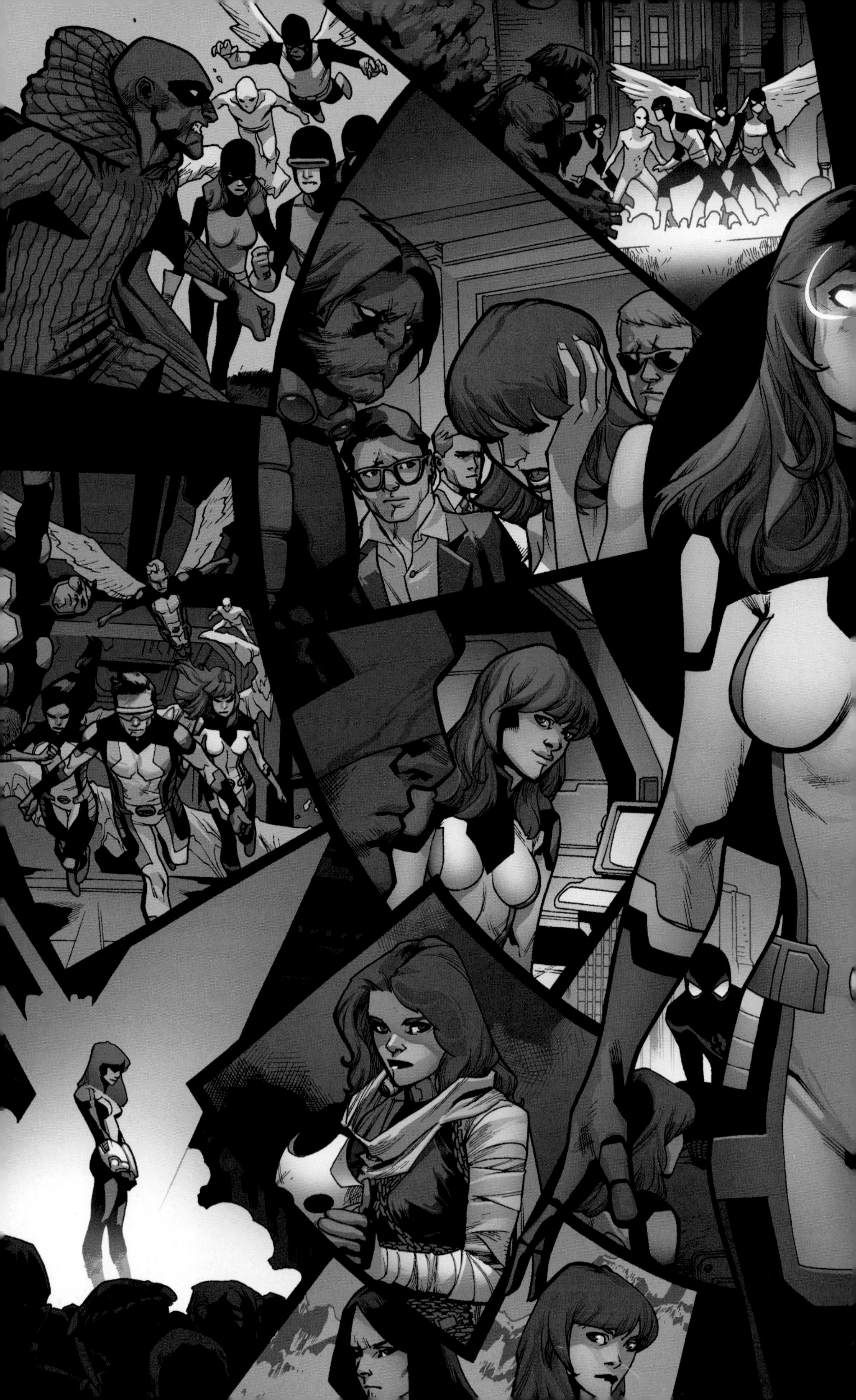

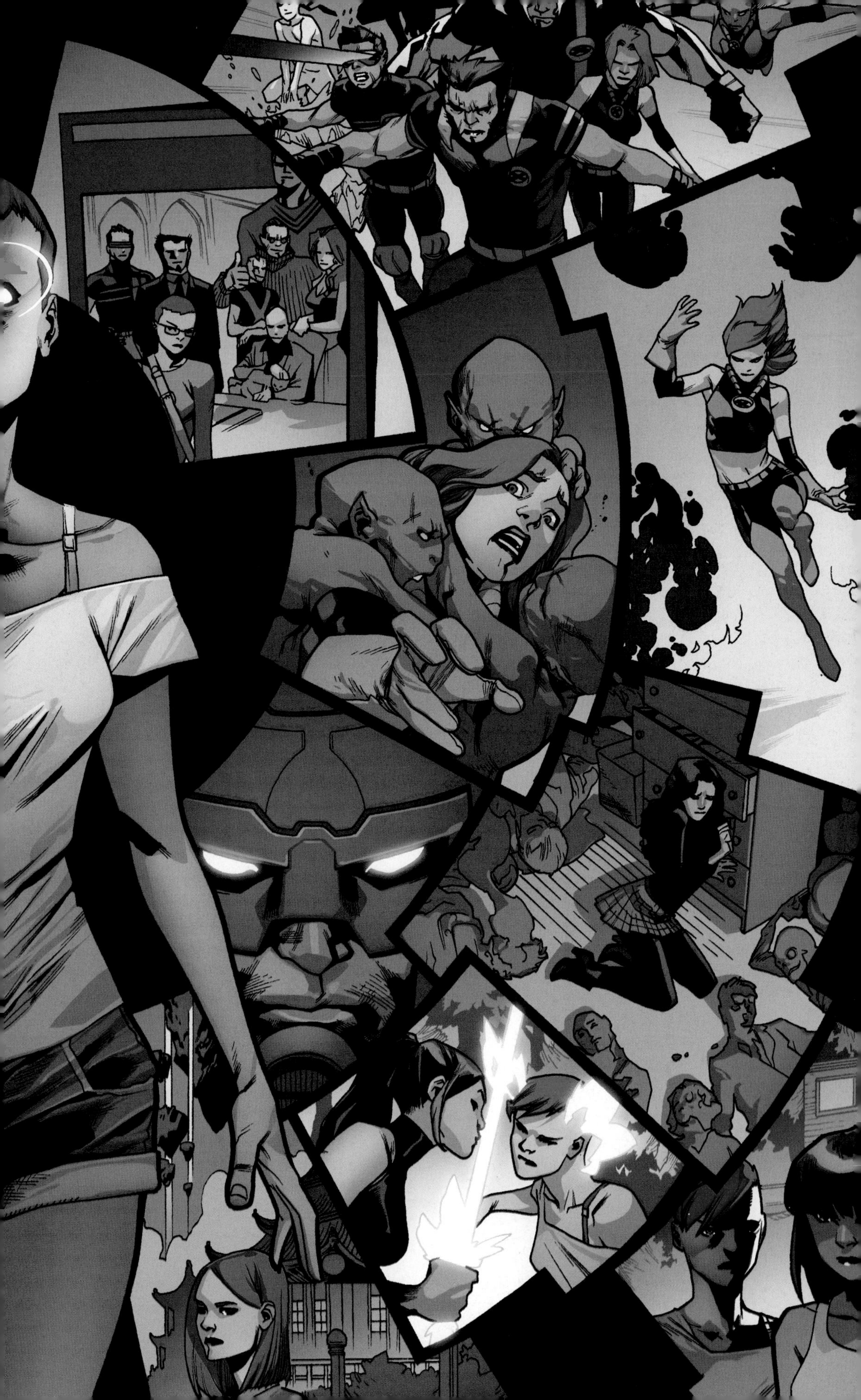

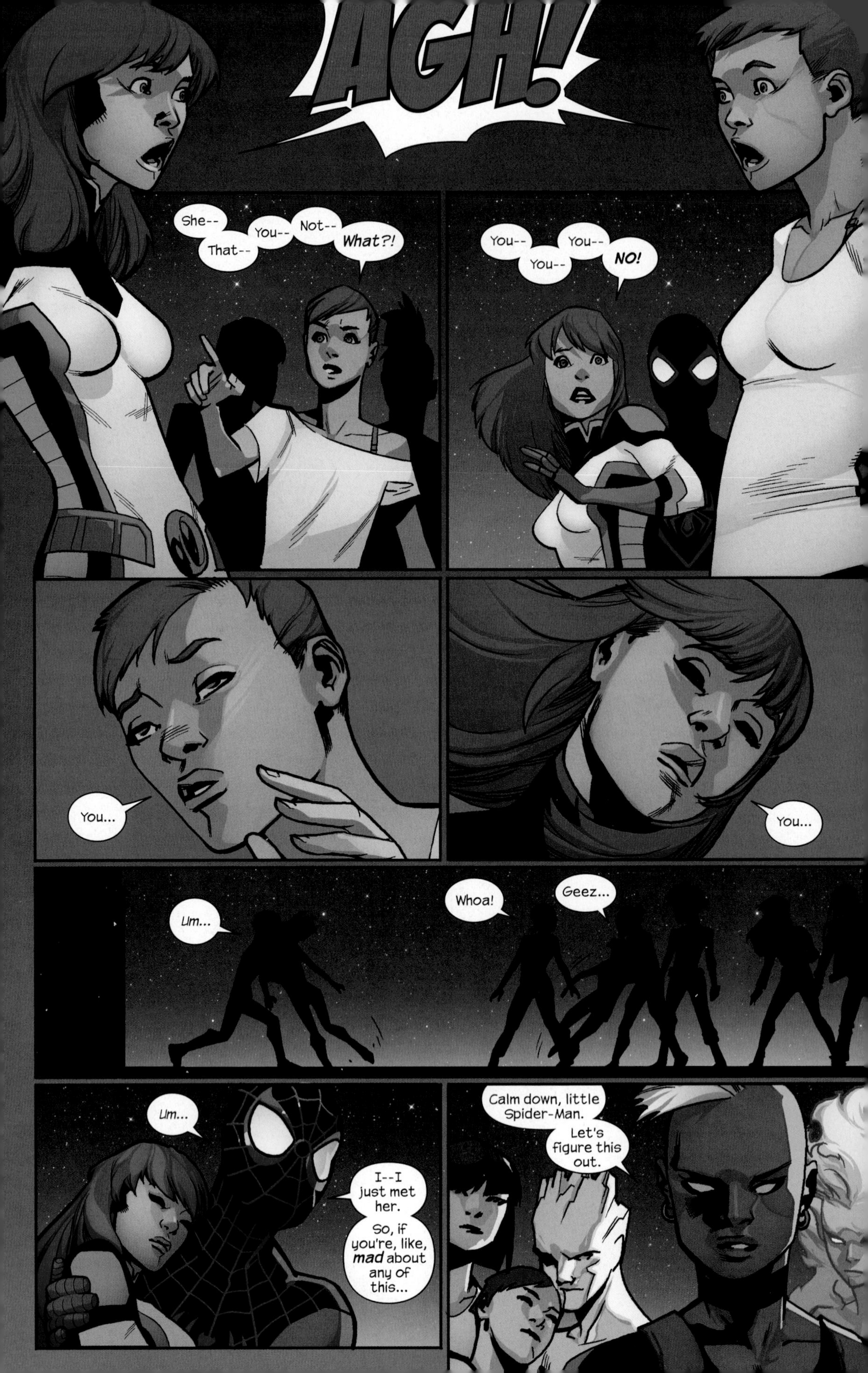
AGH!
She--
That--
You--
Not--
What?!
You--
You--
You--
NO!
You...
You...
Um...
Whoa!
Geez...
Um...
I--I just met her.
So, if you're, like, mad about any of this...
Calm down, little Spider-Man.
Let's figure this out.

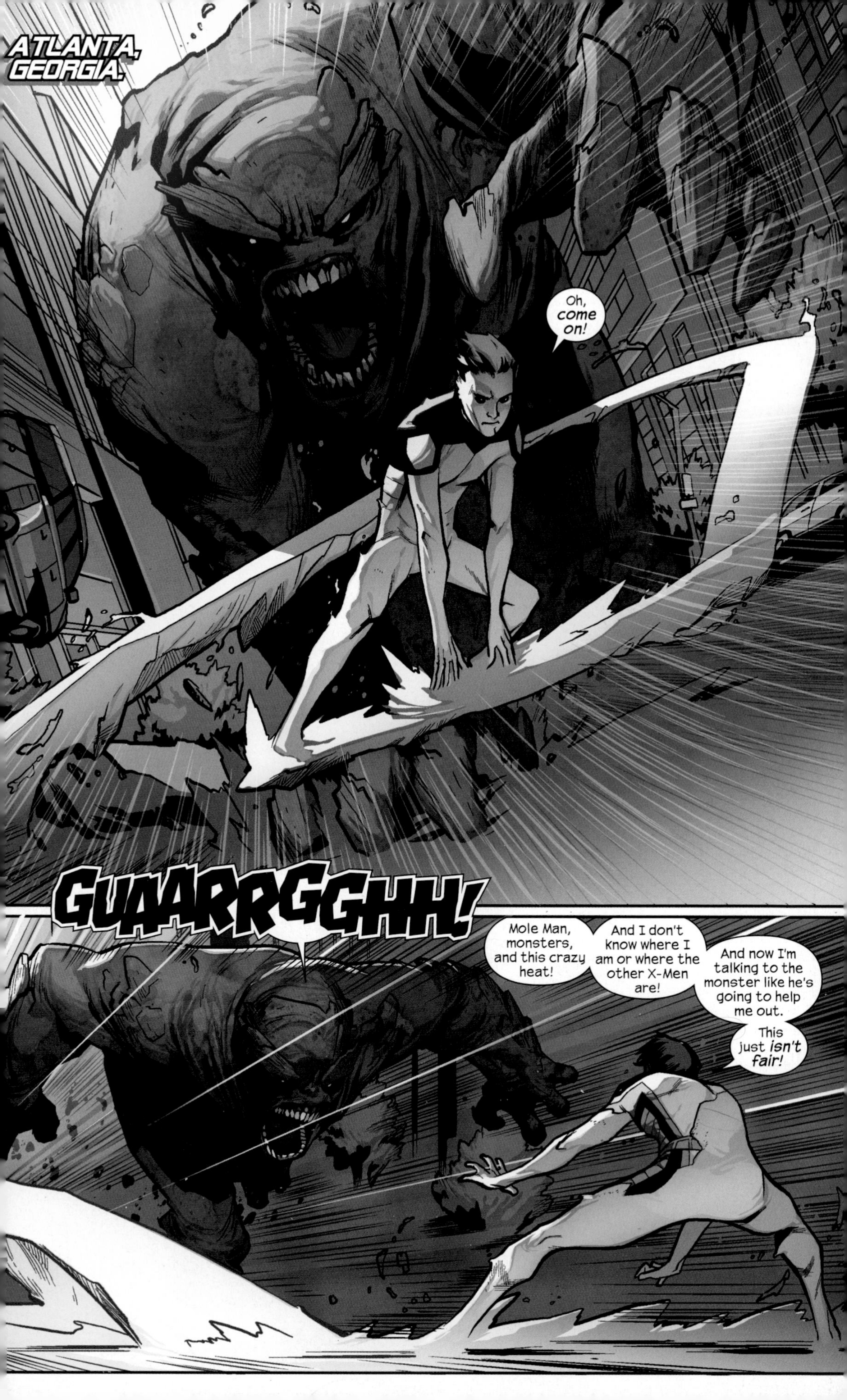
ATLANTA, GEORGIA.
Oh, come on!
GUAARRGGHHH!
Mole Man, monsters, and this crazy heat!
And I don't know where I am or where the other X-Men are!
And now I'm talking to the monster like he's going to help me out.
This just isn't fair!

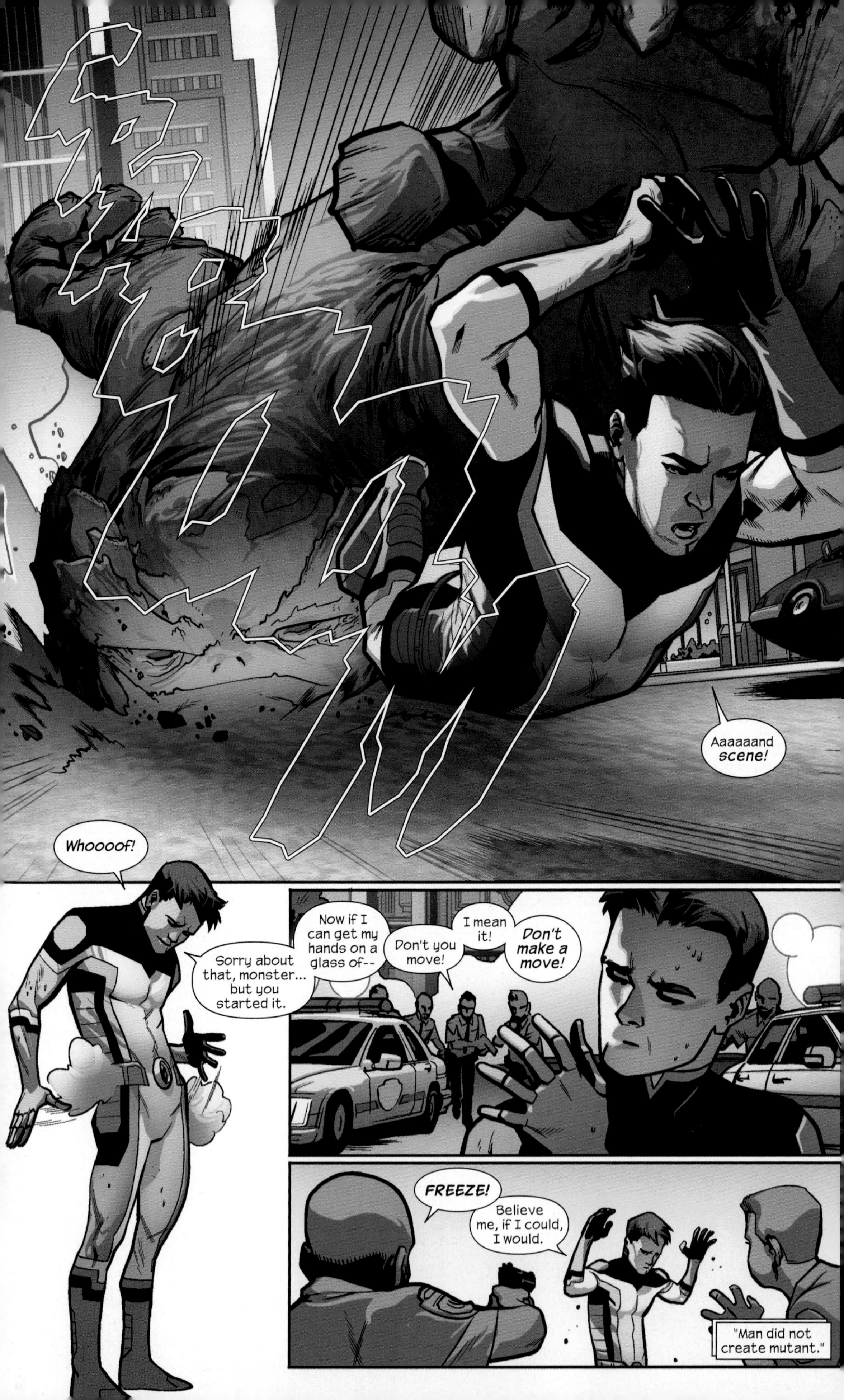
Aaaaaand scene!
Whoooof!
Sorry about that, monster... but you started it.
Now if I can get my hands on a glass of--
Don't you move!
I mean it!
Don't make a move!
FREEZE!
Believe me, if I could, I would.
"Man did not create mutant."

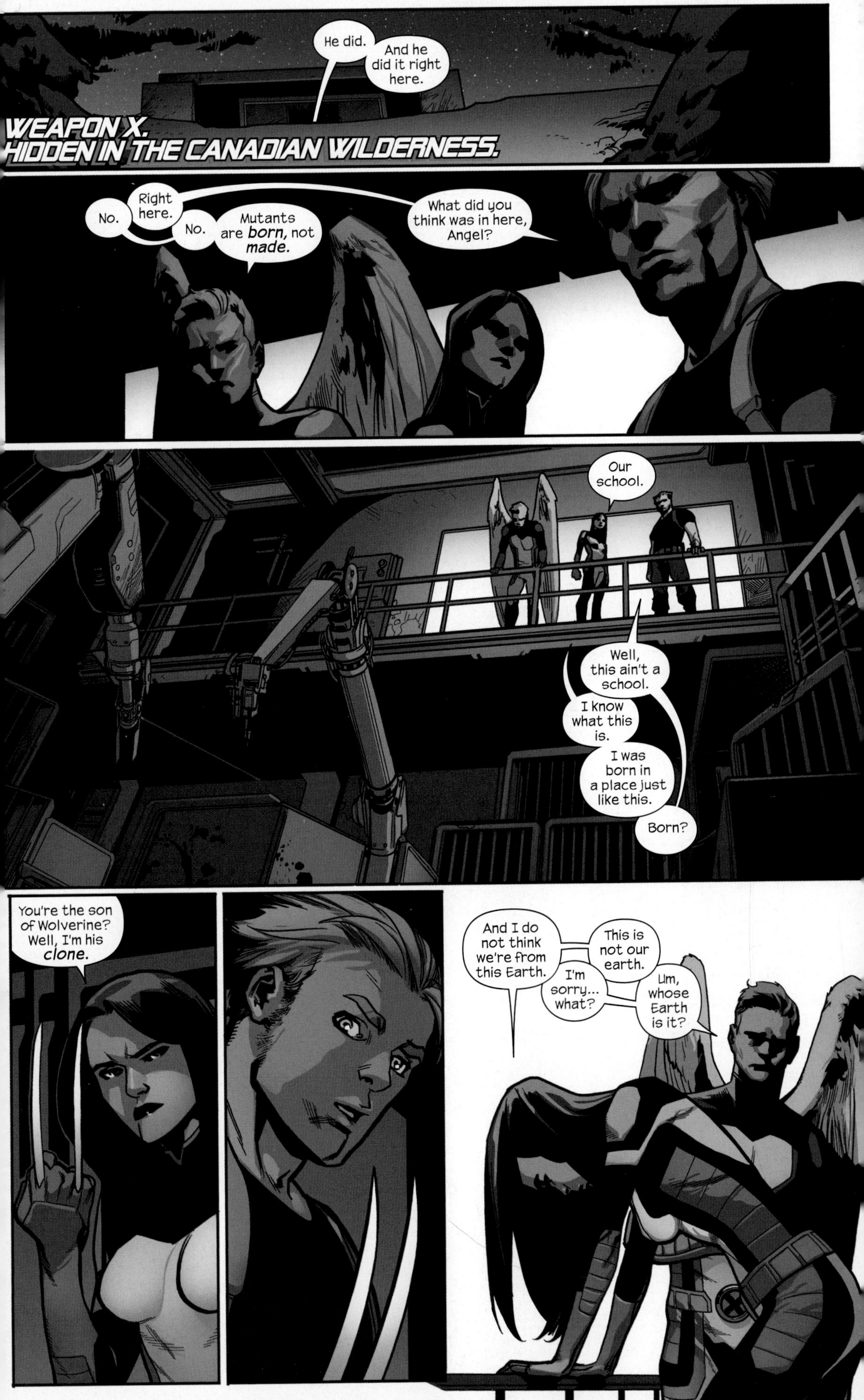
He did.
And he did it right here.
WEAPON X.
HIDDEN IN THE CANADIAN WILDERNESS.
No.
Right here.
No.
Mutants are born, not made.
What did you think was in here, Angel?
Our school.
Well, this ain't a school.
I know what this is.
I was born in a place just like this.
Born?
You're the son of Wolverine? Well, I'm his clone.
And I do not think we're from this Earth.
This is not our earth.
I'm sorry... what?
Um, whose Earth is it?

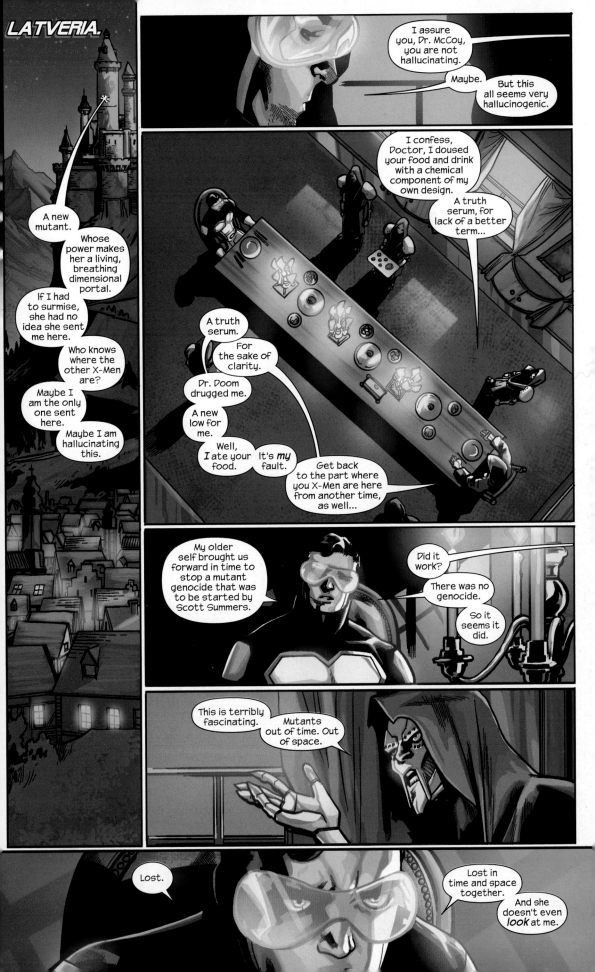

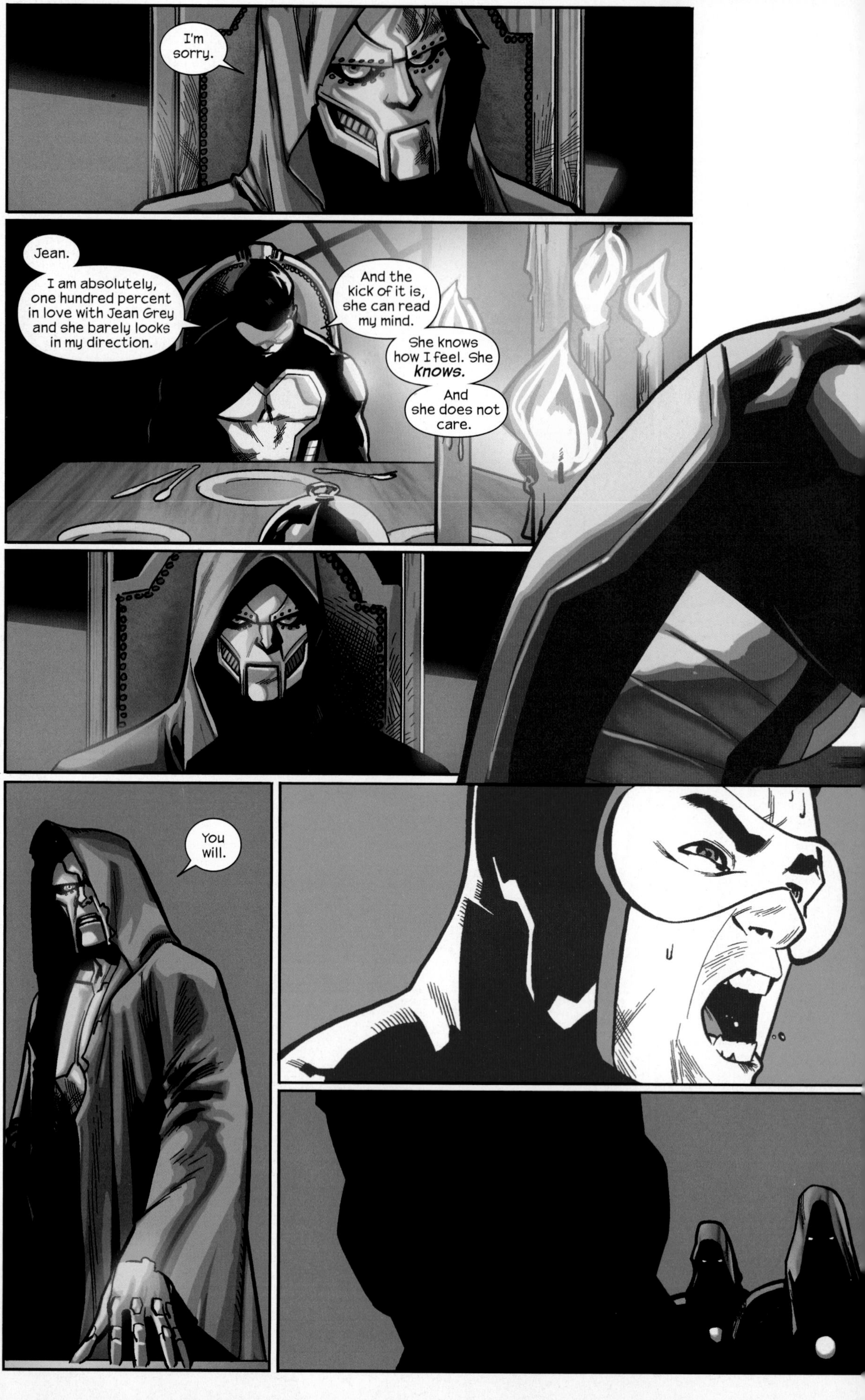
I'm sorry.
Jean.
I am absolutely, one hundred percent in love with Jean Grey and she barely looks in my direction.
And the kick of it is, she can read my mind.
She knows how I feel. She *knows.*
And she does not care.
You will.

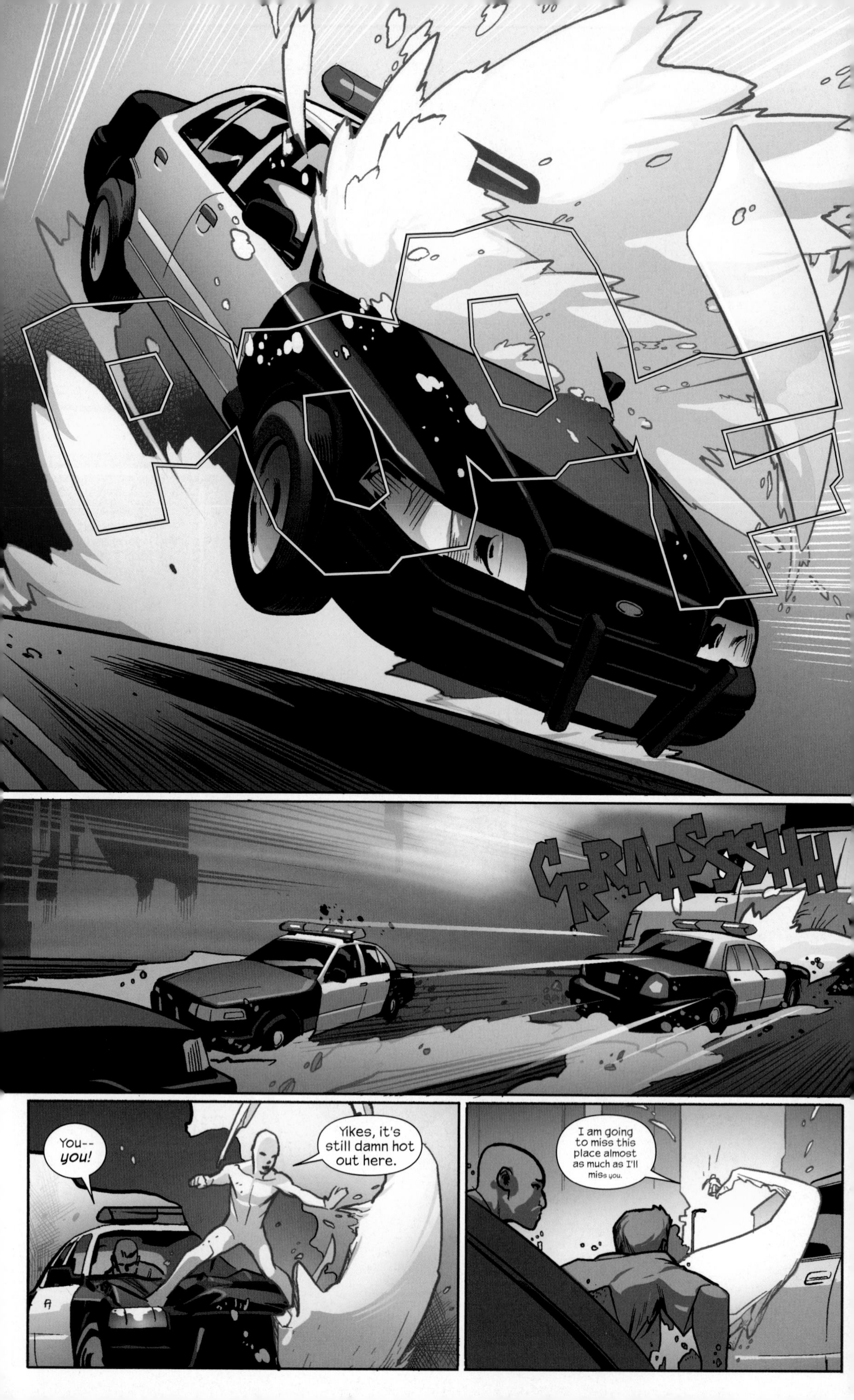
POOF
CRRAASSSHH
You-- *you!*
Yikes, it's still damn hot out here.
I am going to miss this place almost as much as I'll miss you.

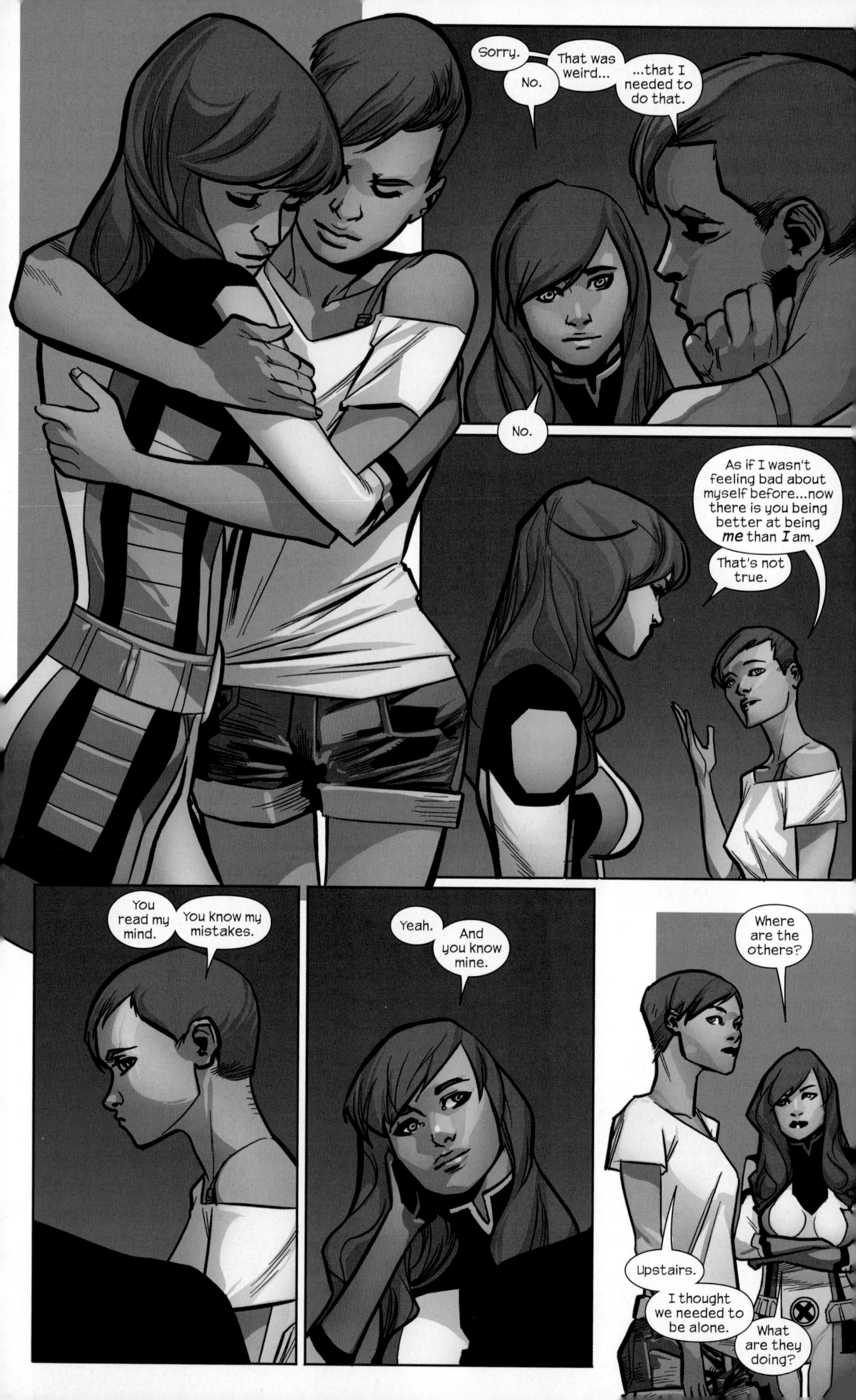
Sorry.
No.
That was weird...
...that I needed to do that.
No.
As if I wasn't feeling bad about myself before...now there is you being better at being *me* than *I* am.
That's not true.
You read my mind.
You know my mistakes.
Yeah.
And you know mine.
Where are the others?
Upstairs.
I thought we needed to be alone.
What are they doing?

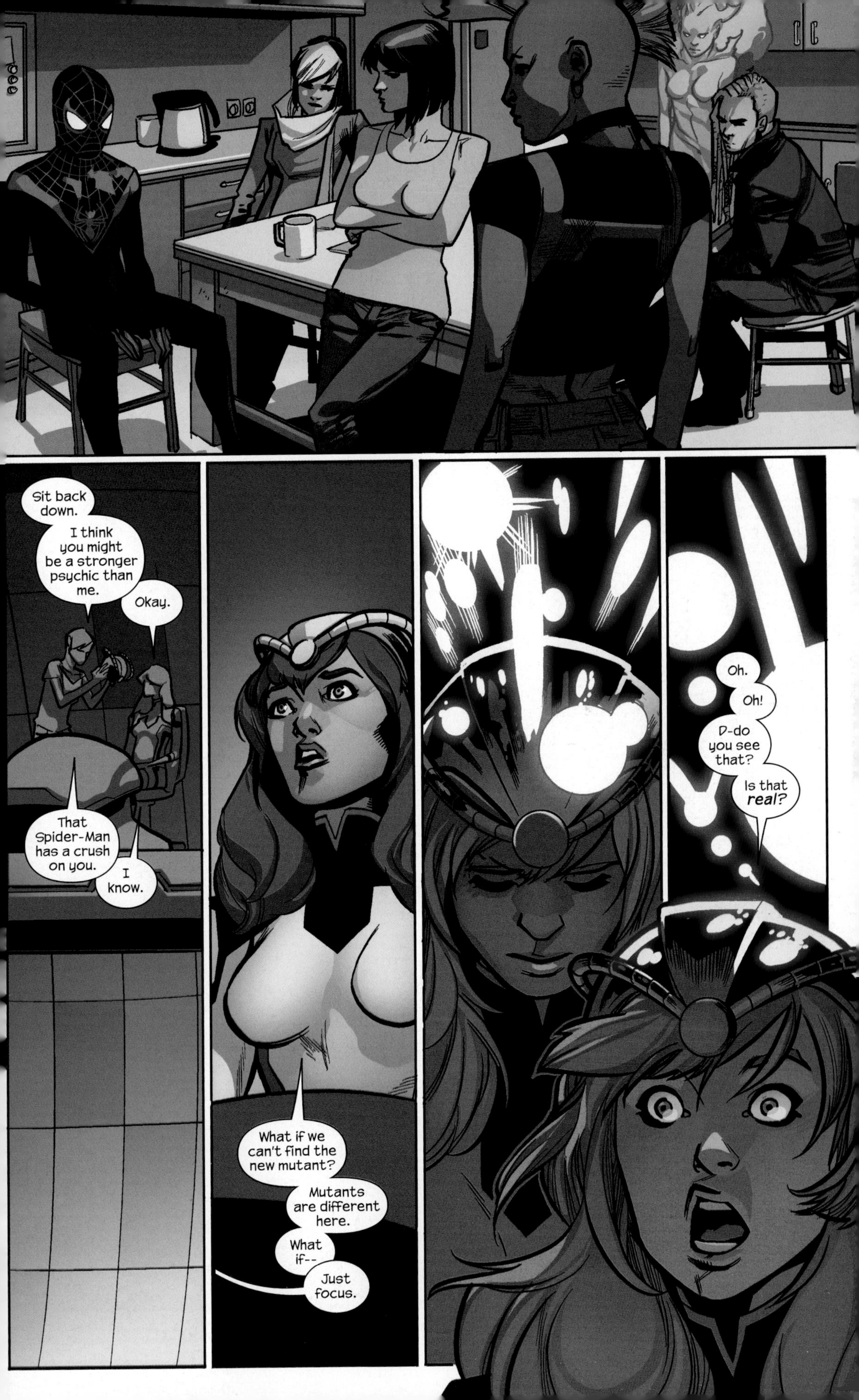

Sit back down.
I think you might be a stronger psychic than me.
Okay.
That Spider-Man has a crush on you.
I know.
What if we can't find the new mutant?
Mutants are different here.
What if--
Just focus.
Oh.
Oh!
D-do you see that?
Is that *real?*

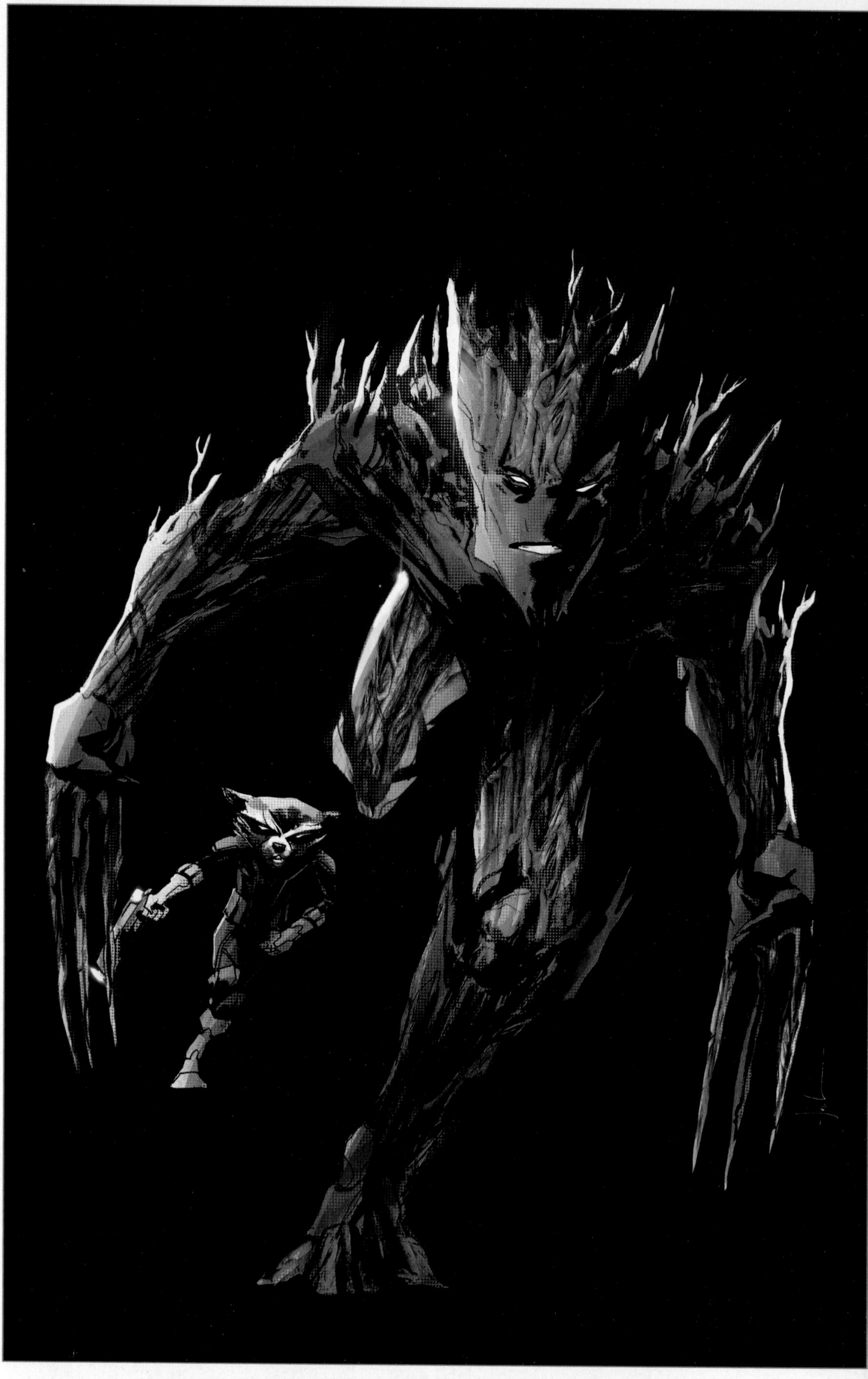

ALL-NEW X-MEN #34 ROCKET RACCOON & GROOT VARIANT
BY JOCK

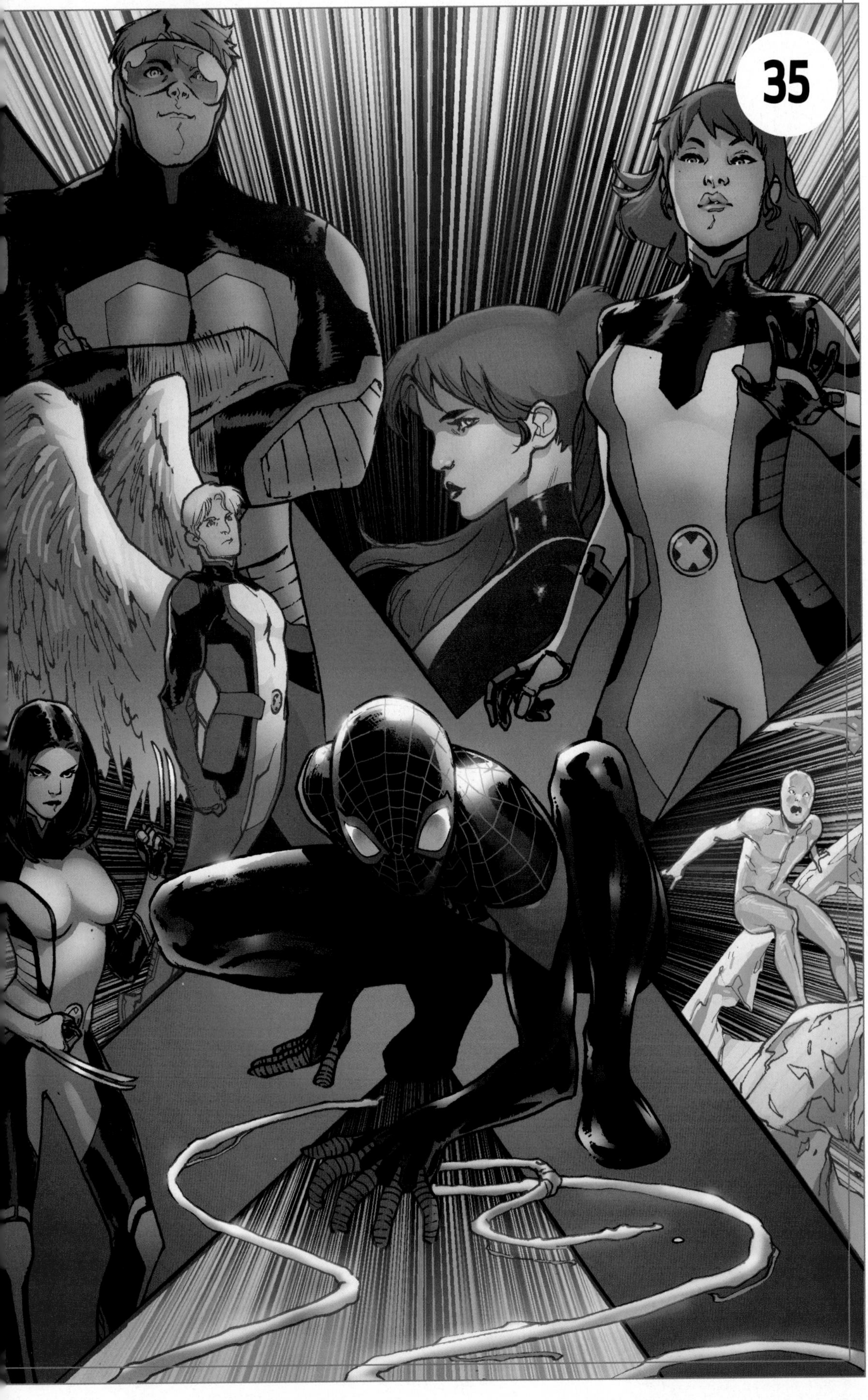
35

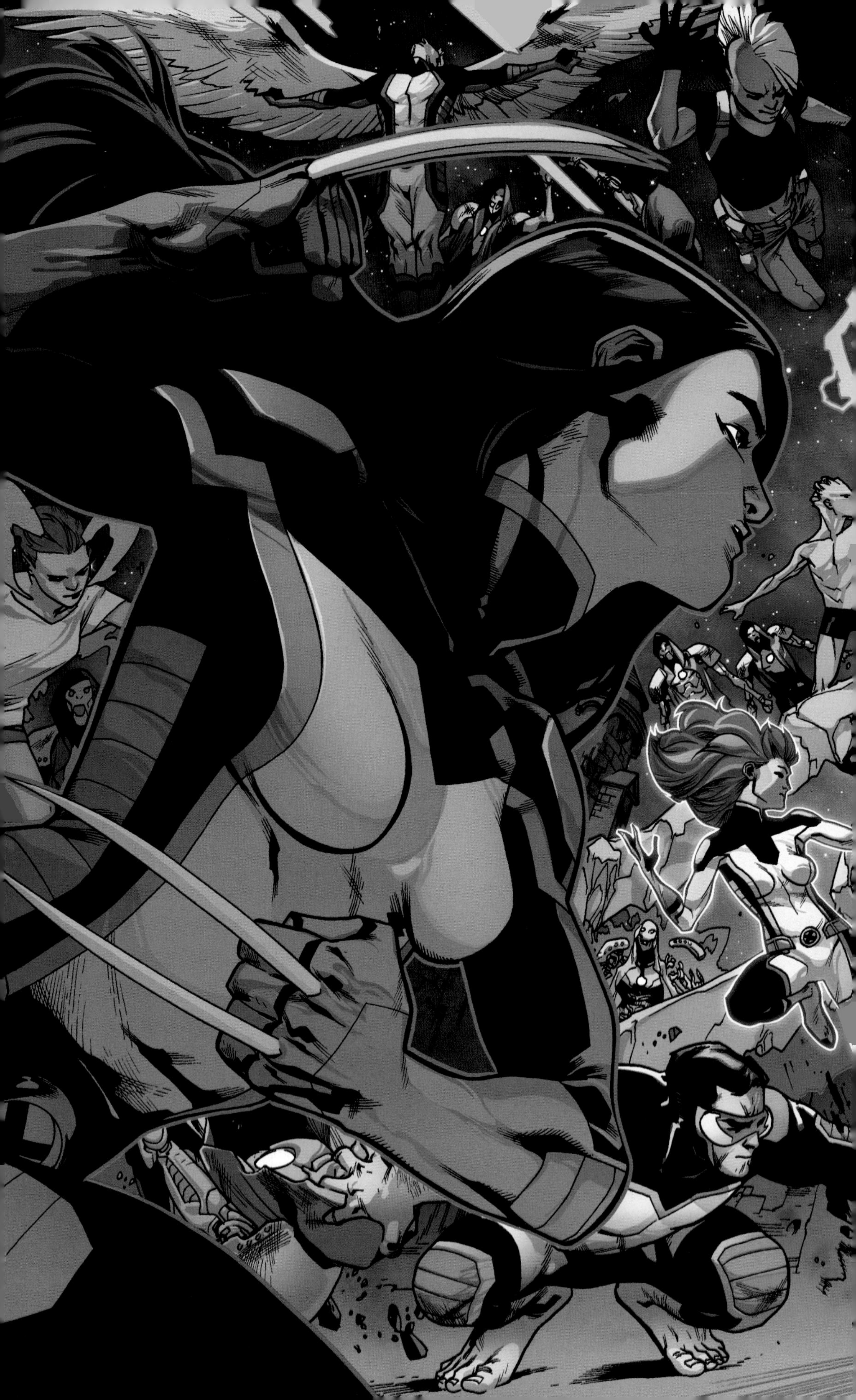

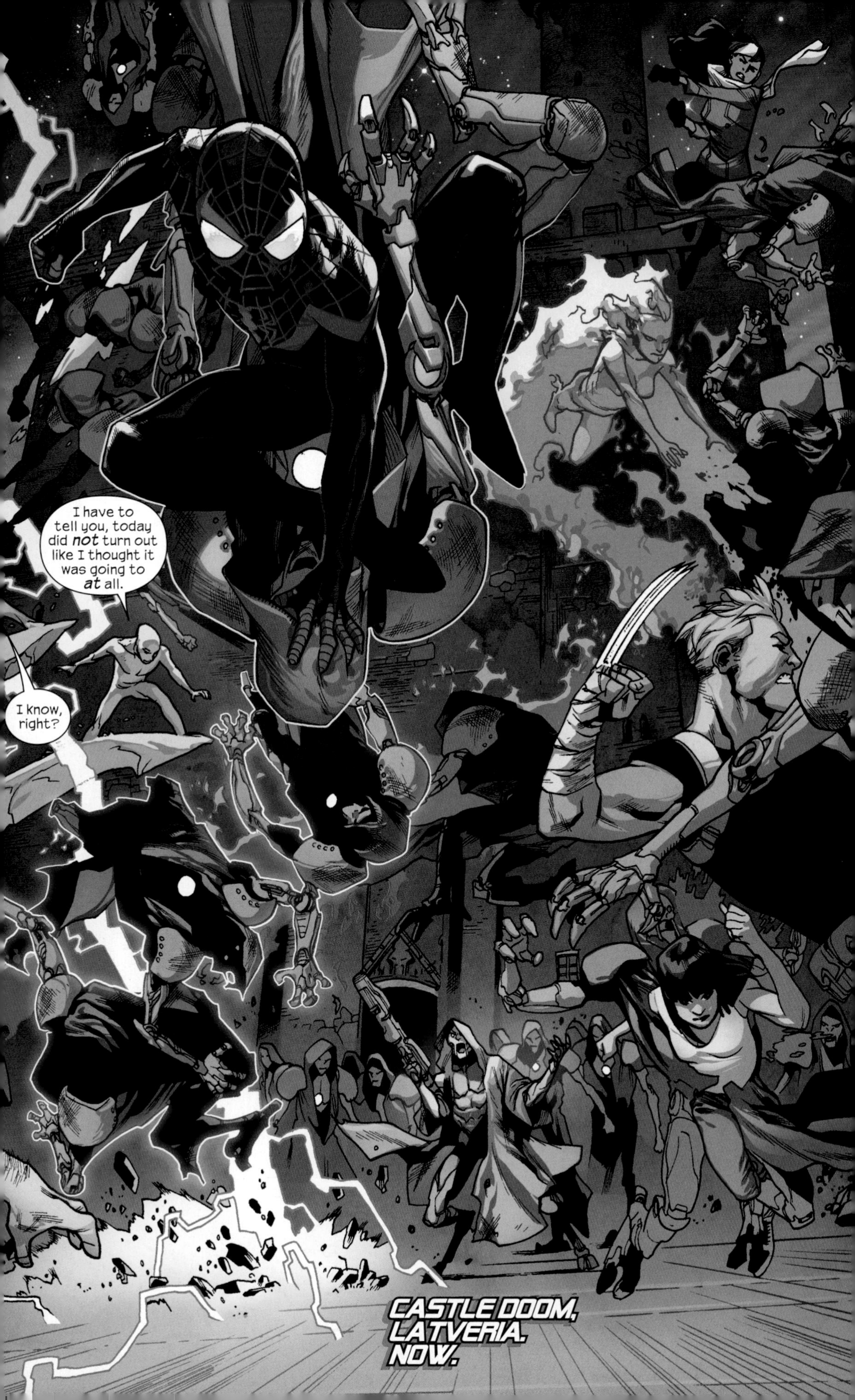
I have to tell you, today did *not* turn out like I thought it was going to *at* all.
I know, right?
CASTLE DOOM, LATVERIA. NOW.

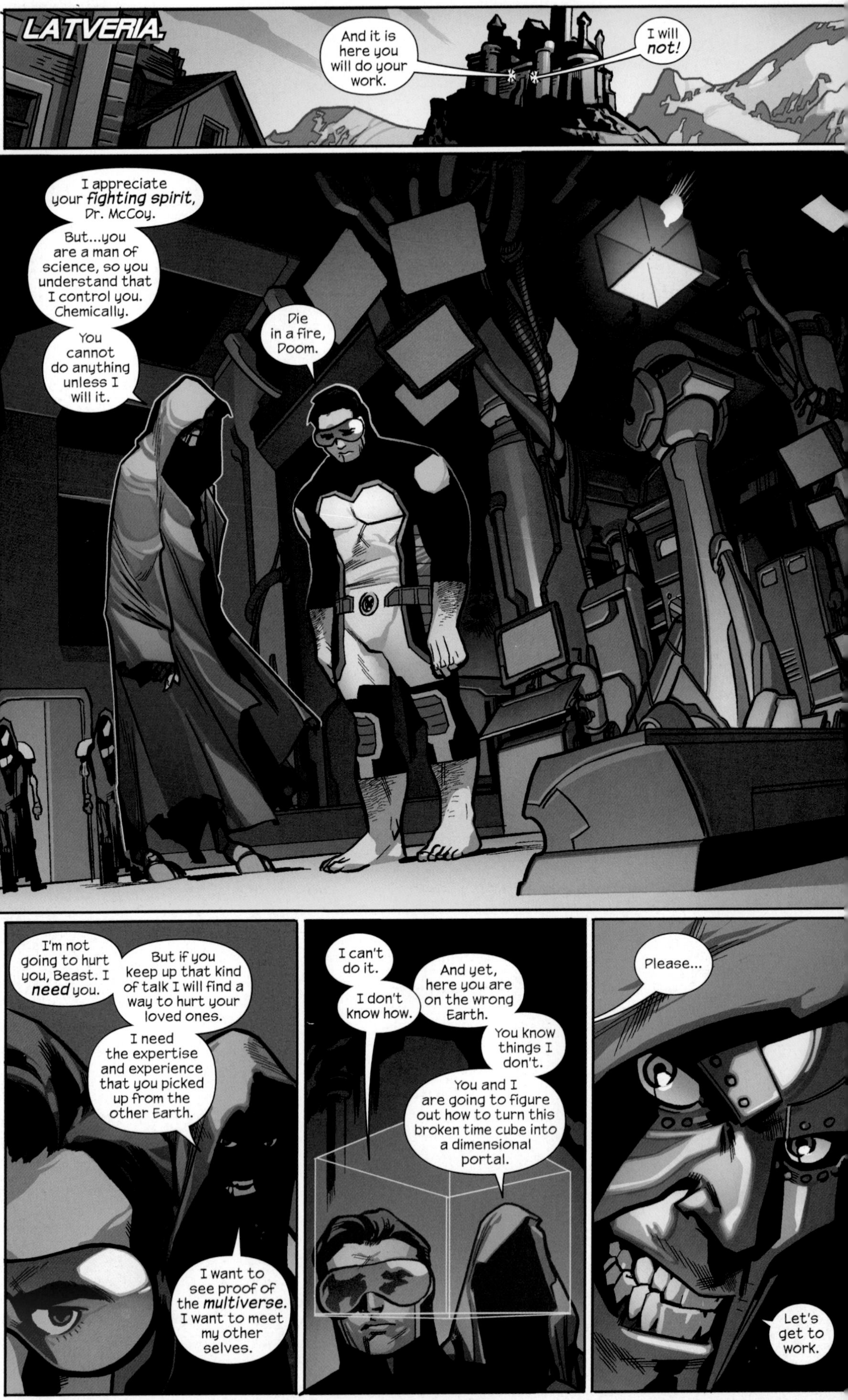
LATVERIA.
And it is here you will do your work.
I will not!
I appreciate your fighting spirit, Dr. McCoy.
But...you are a man of science, so you understand that I control you. Chemically.
You cannot do anything unless I will it.
Die in a fire, Doom.
I'm not going to hurt you, Beast. I need you.
But if you keep up that kind of talk I will find a way to hurt your loved ones.
I need the expertise and experience that you picked up from the other Earth.
I want to see proof of the multiverse. I want to meet my other selves.
I can't do it.
I don't know how.
And yet, here you are on the wrong Earth.
You know things I don't.
You and I are going to figure out how to turn this broken time cube into a dimensional portal.
Please...
Let's get to work.

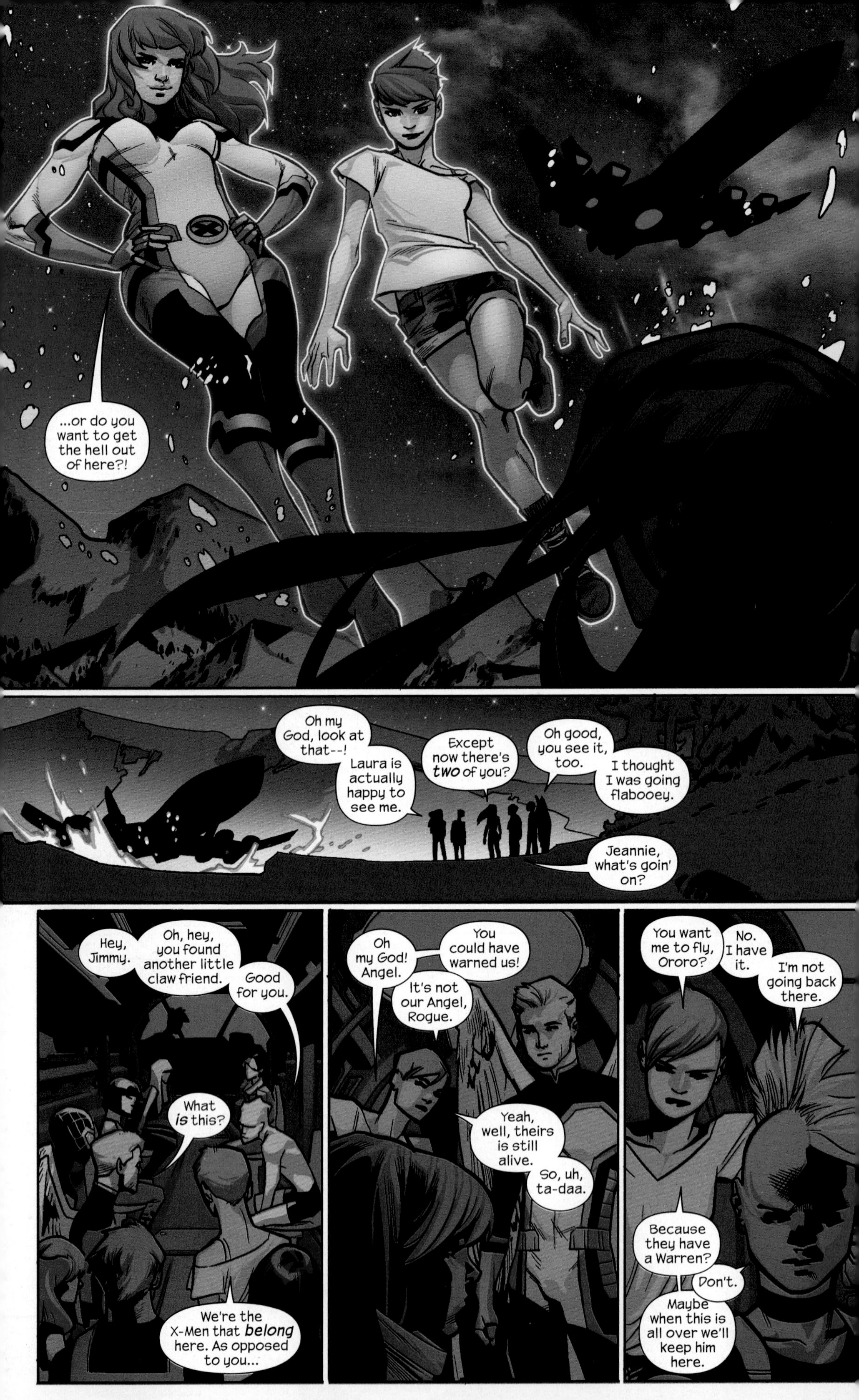
...or do you want to get the hell out of here?!
Oh my God, look at that--!
Laura is actually happy to see me.
Except now there's *two* of you?
Oh good, you see it, too.
I thought I was going flabooey.
Jeannie, what's goin' on?
Hey, Jimmy.
Oh, hey, you found another little claw friend.
Good for you.
What *is* this?
We're the X-Men that *belong* here. As opposed to you...
Oh my God! Angel.
You could have warned us!
It's not our Angel, Rogue.
Yeah, well, theirs is still alive.
So, uh, ta-daa.
You want me to fly, Ororo?
No. I have it.
I'm not going back there.
Because they have a Warren?
Don't.
Maybe when this is all over we'll keep him here.

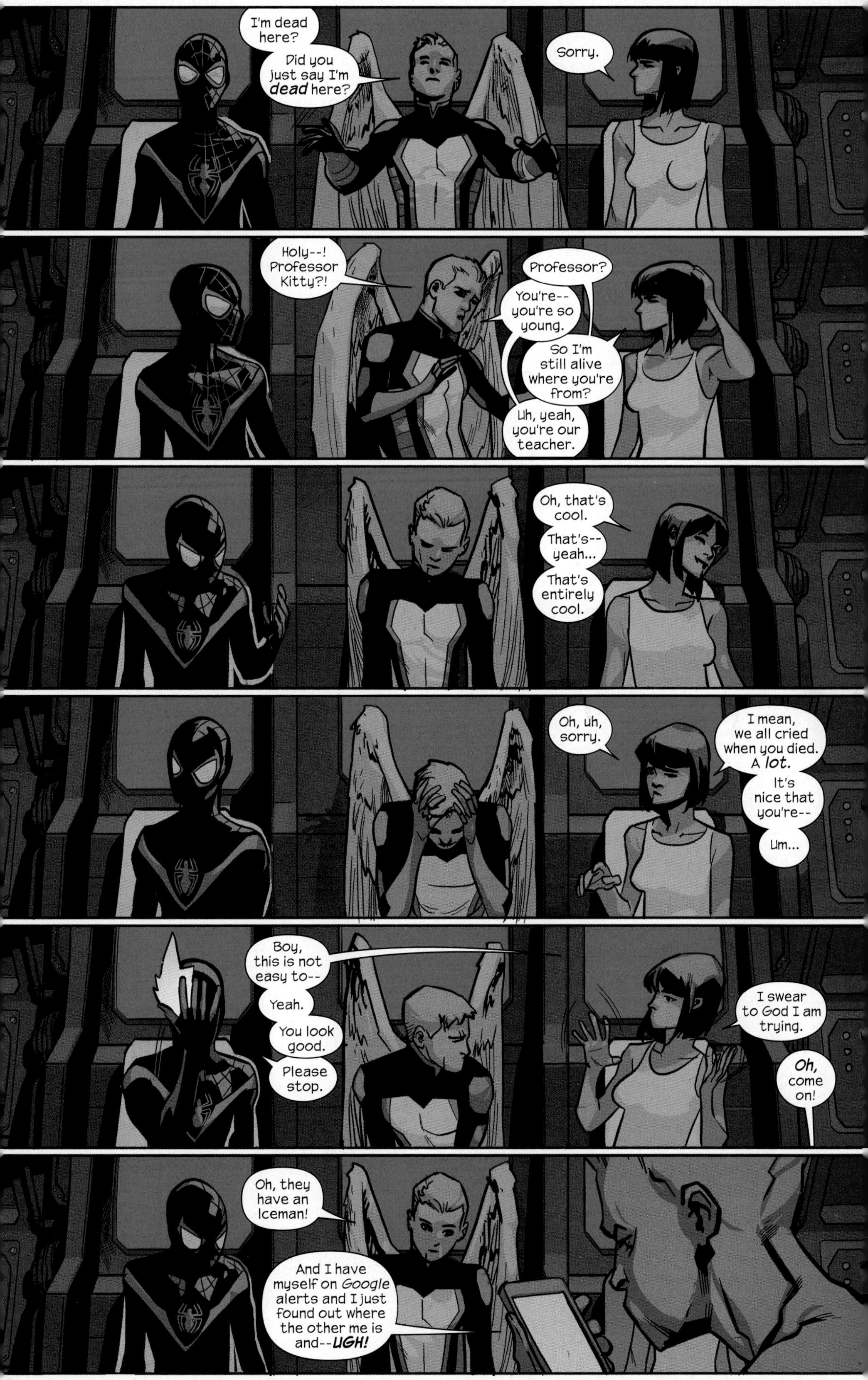

I'm dead here?
Did you just say I'm *dead* here?
Sorry.
Holy--! Professor Kitty?!
Professor?
You're-- you're so young.
So I'm still alive where you're from?
Uh, yeah, you're our teacher.
Oh, that's cool.
That's-- yeah...
That's entirely cool.
Oh, uh, sorry.
I mean, we all cried when you died. A *lot.*
It's nice that you're--
Um...
Boy, this is not easy to--
Yeah.
You look good.
Please stop.
I swear to God I am trying.
Oh, come on!
Oh, they have an Iceman!
And I have myself on *Google* alerts and I just found out where the other me is and--*UGH!*

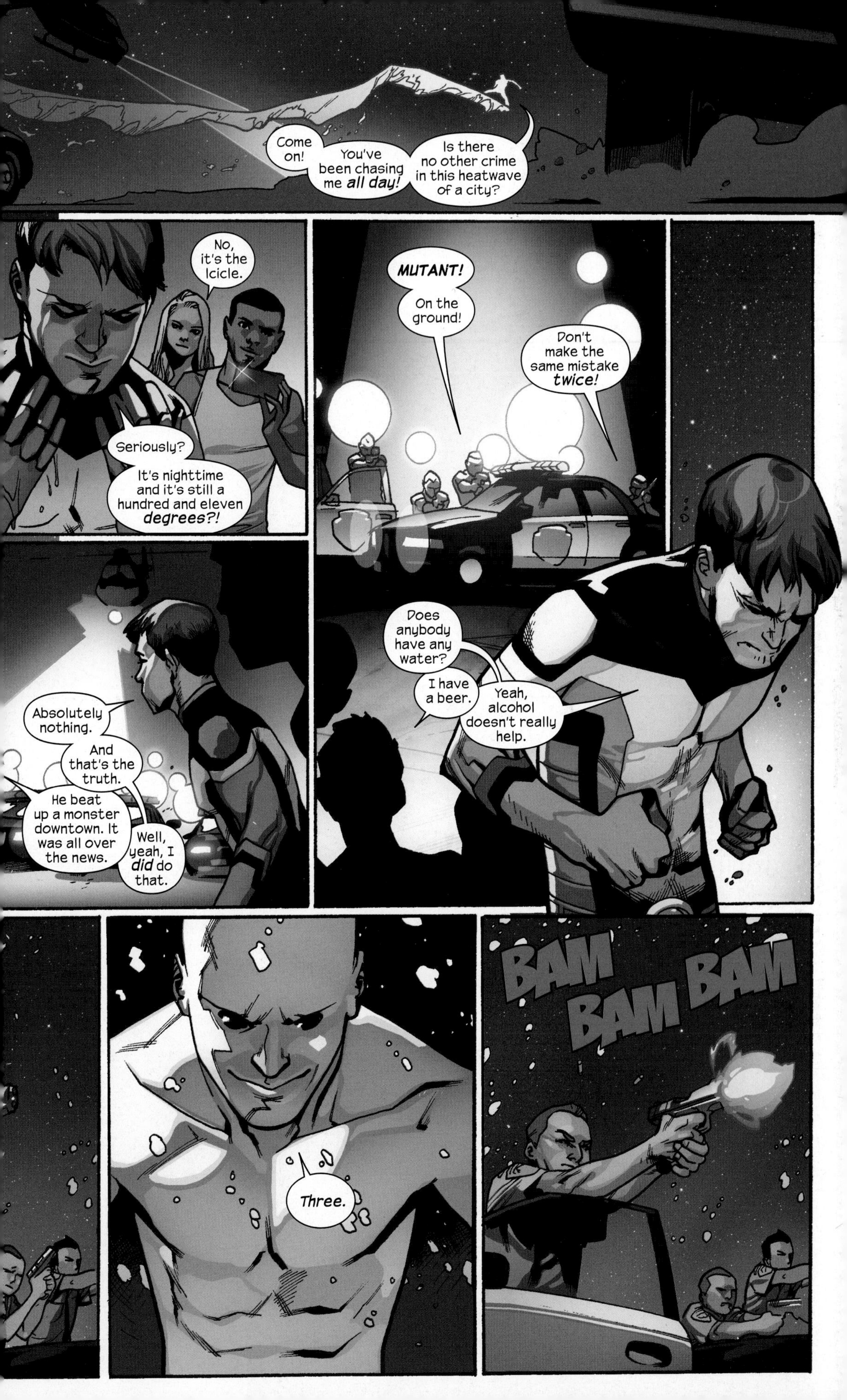
Come on!
You've been chasing me all day!
Is there no other crime in this heatwave of a city?
No, it's the Icicle.
Seriously?
It's nighttime and it's still a hundred and eleven degrees?!
MUTANT!
On the ground!
Don't make the same mistake twice!
Absolutely nothing.
And that's the truth.
He beat up a monster downtown. It was all over the news.
Well, yeah, I did do that.
Does anybody have any water?
I have a beer.
Yeah, alcohol doesn't really help.
Three.
BAM BAM BAM

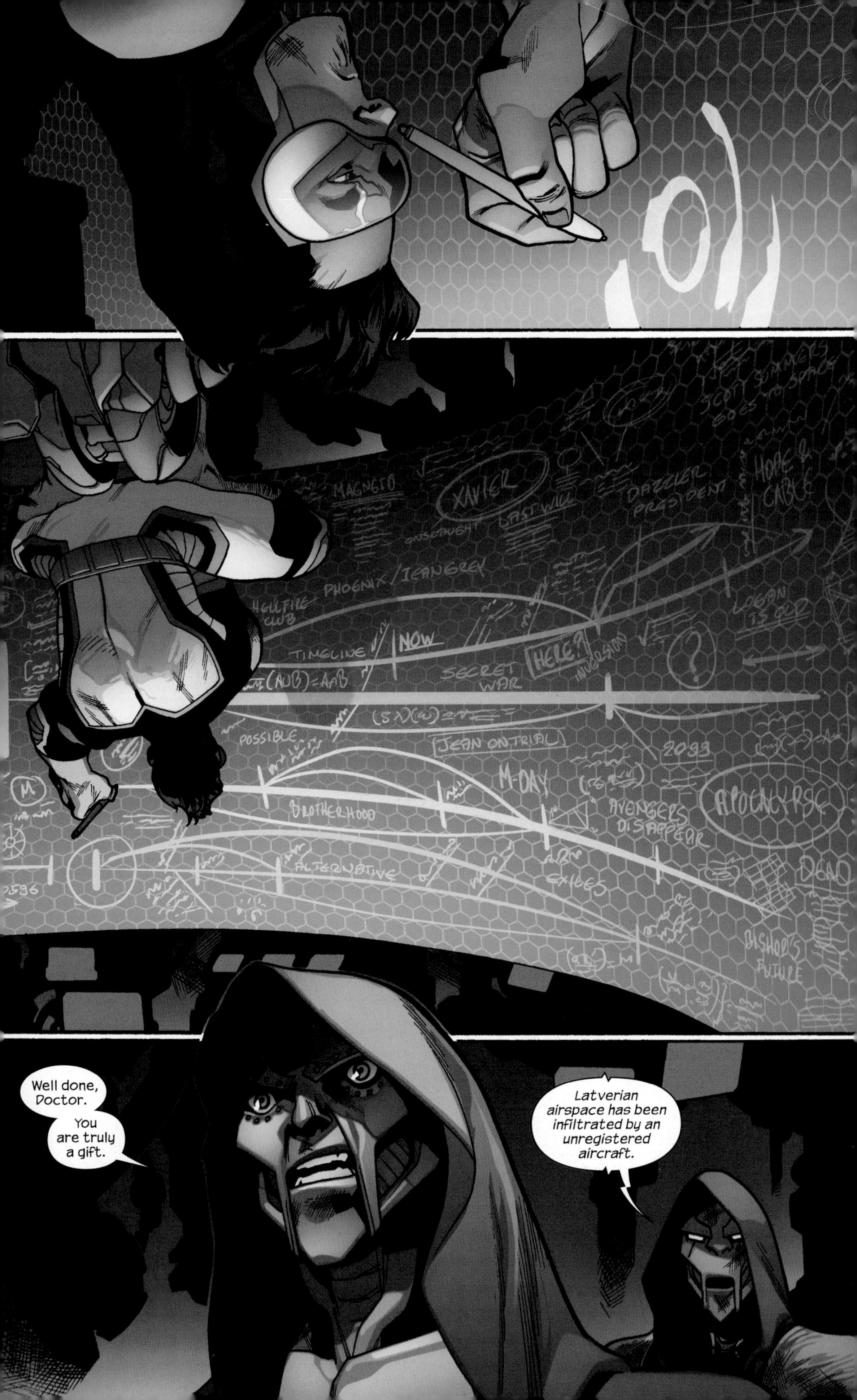

SCOTT SUMMERS GOES TO SPACE
MAGNETO
XAVIER
LAST WILL
DAZZLER PRESIDENT
HOPE & CABLE
ONSLAUGHT
PHOENIX / JEAN GREY
HELLFIRE CLUB
LOGAN IS OLD
TIMELINE
NOW
SECRET WAR
HERE?
INVERSION
POSSIBLE
JEAN ON TRIAL
2099
M-DAY
BROTHERHOOD
AVENGERS DISAPPEAR
APOCALYPSE
ALTERNATIVE
EXILES
BISHOP'S FUTURE
Well done, Doctor.
You are truly a gift.
Latverian airspace has been infiltrated by an unregistered aircraft.

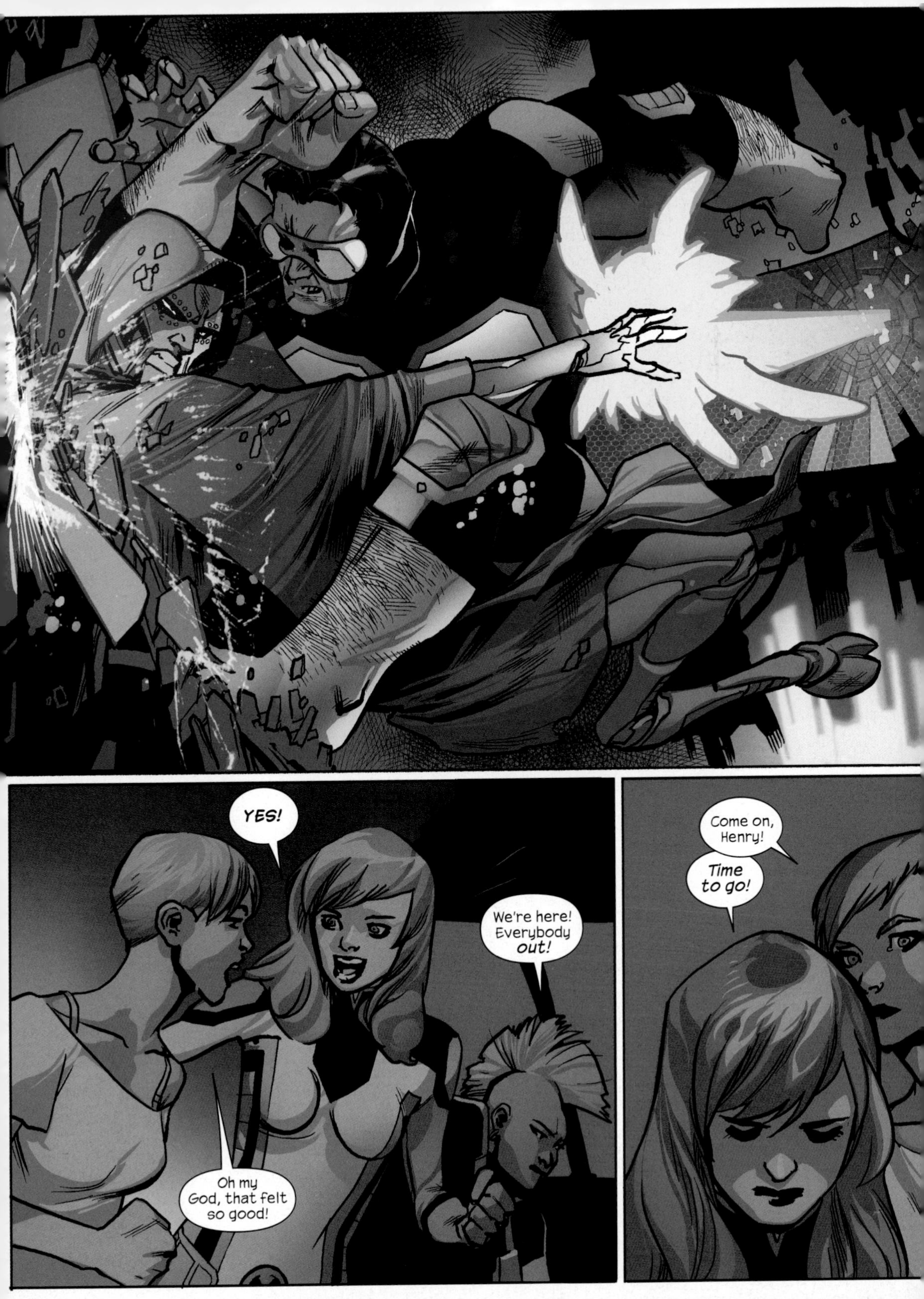
YES!
We're here! Everybody out!
Oh my God, that felt so good!
Come on, Henry!
Time to go!

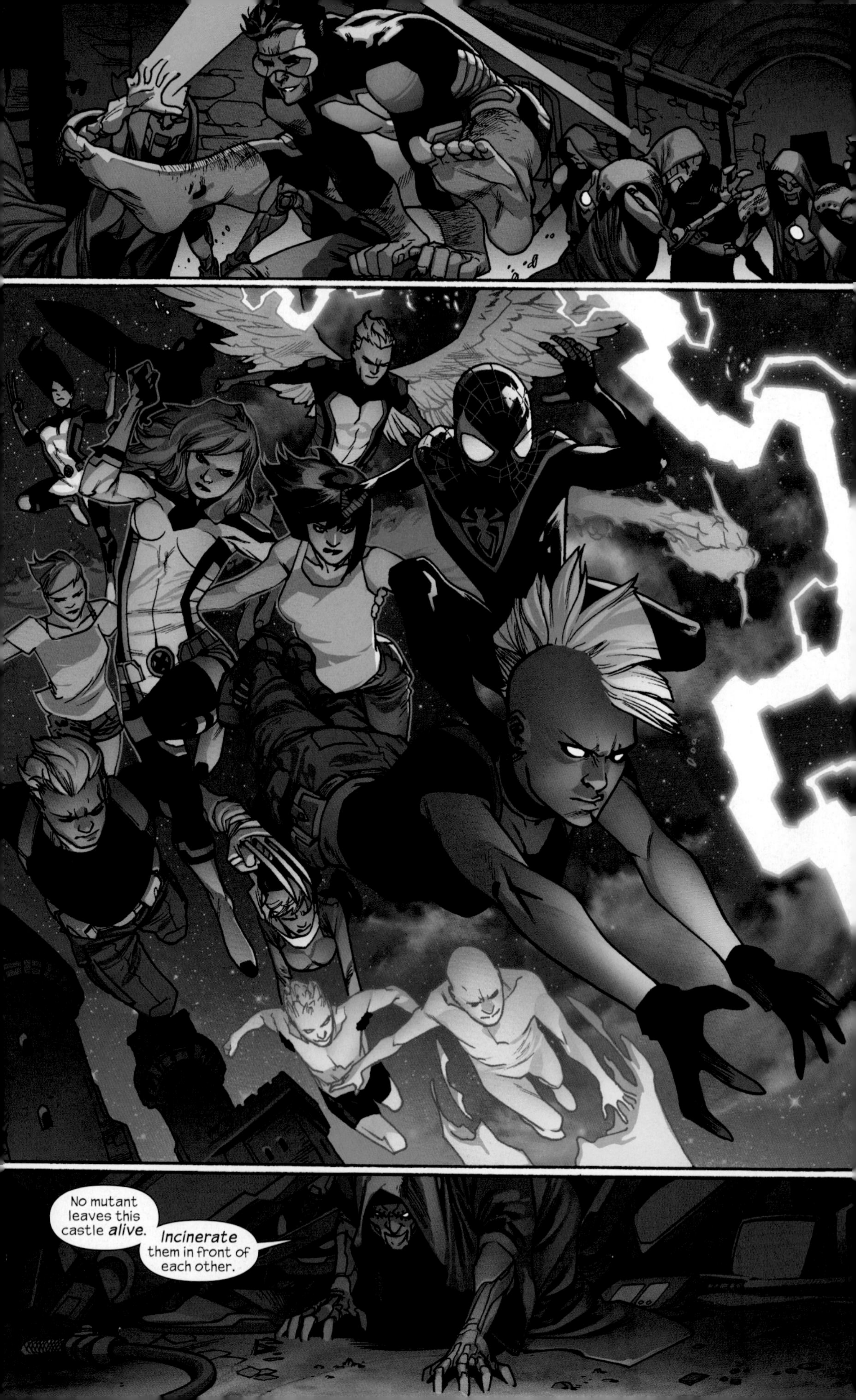
No mutant leaves this castle *alive.*
Incinerate them in front of each other.

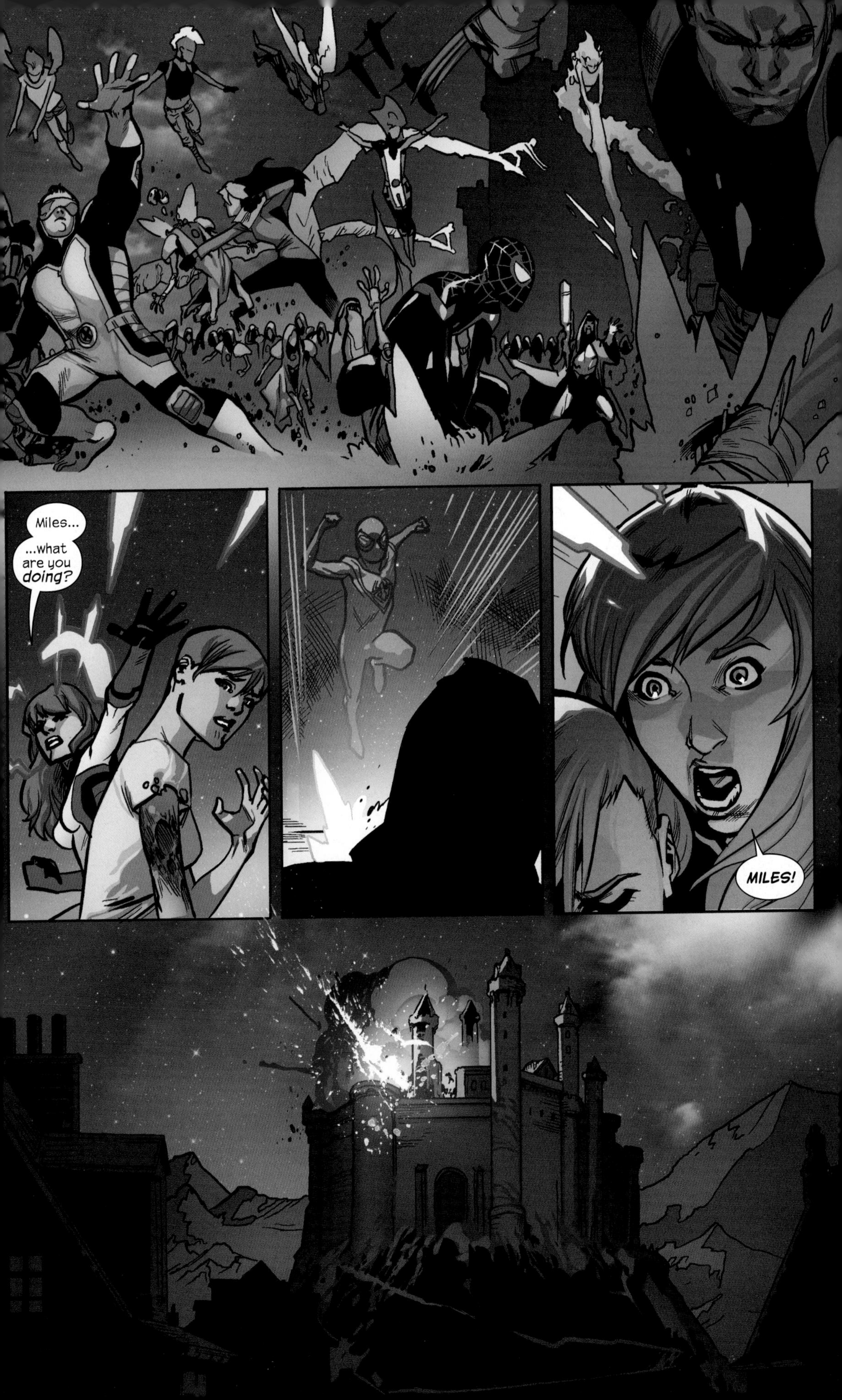
Miles...
...what are you doing?
MILES!

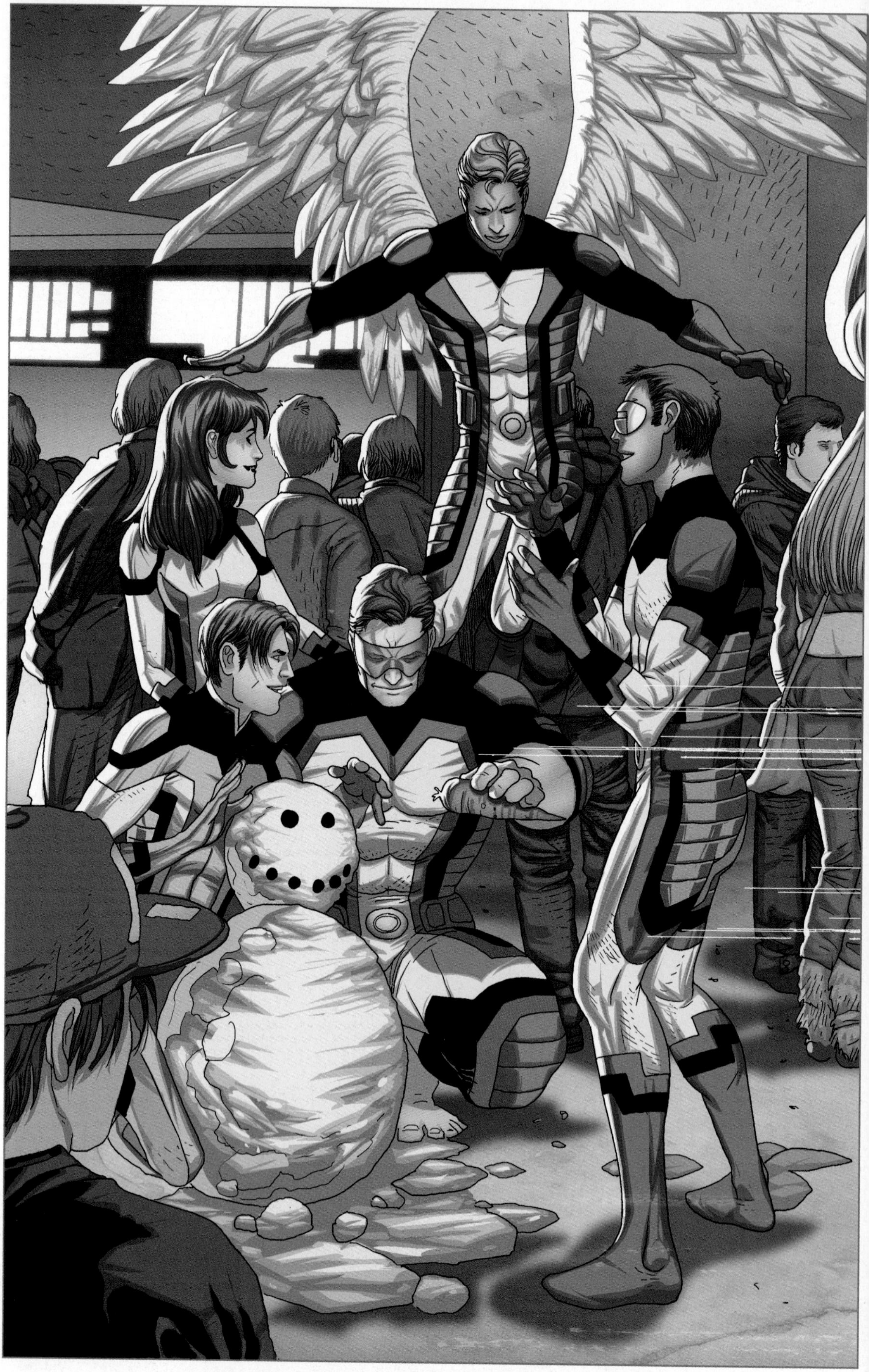

ALL-NEW X-MEN #35 WELCOME HOME VARIANT
BY SALVADOR LARROCA & ISRAEL SILVA

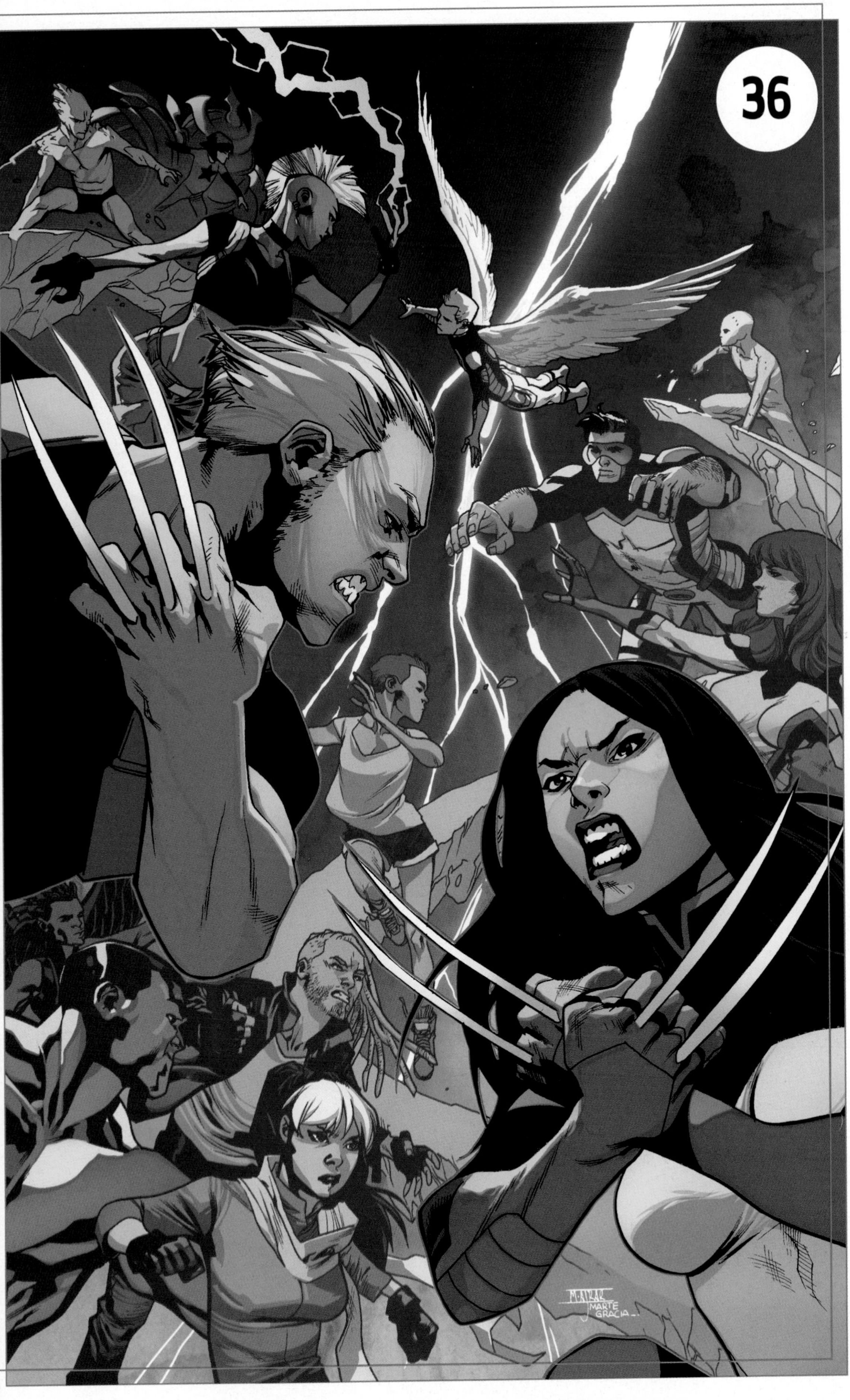
36

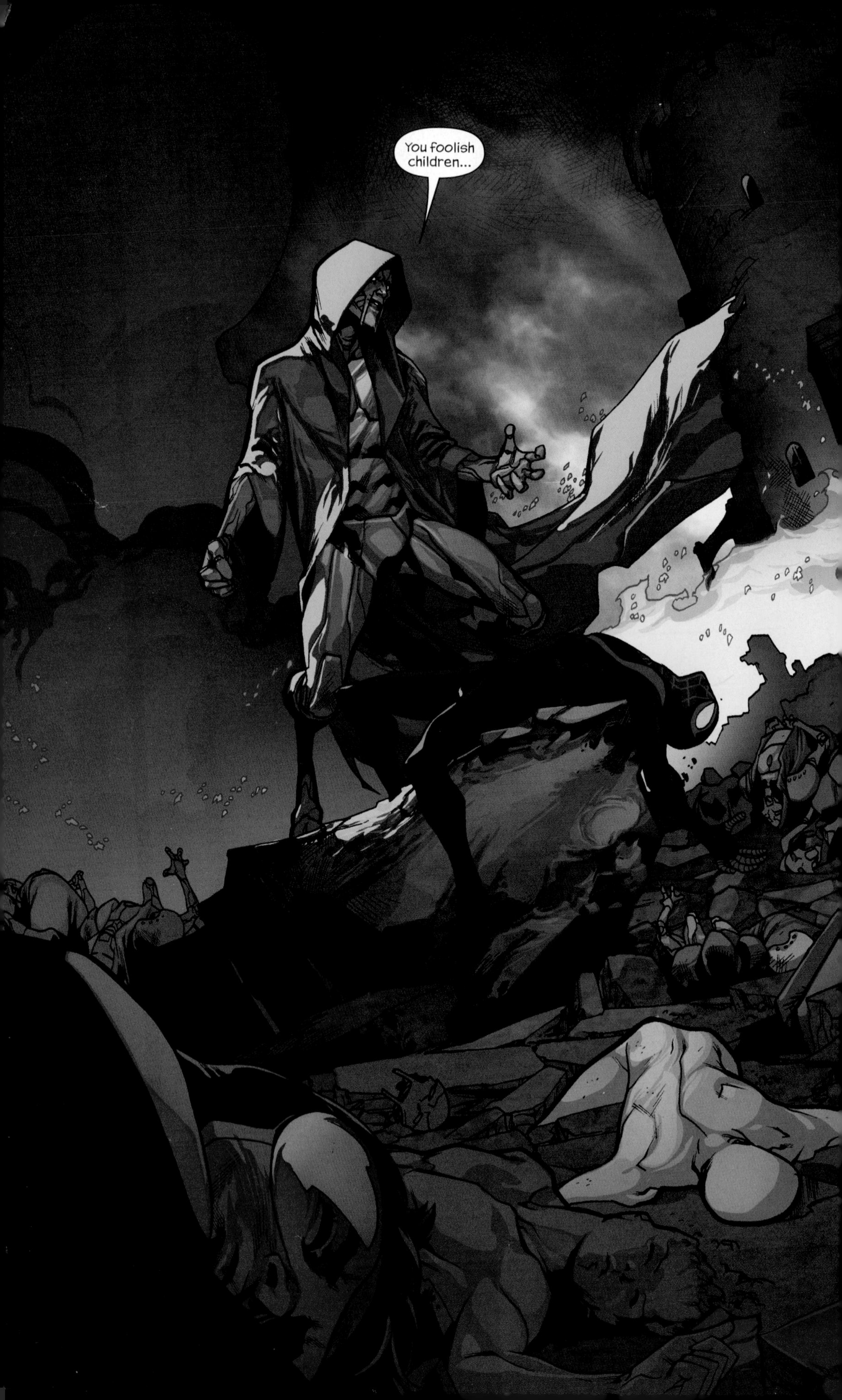
You foolish children...

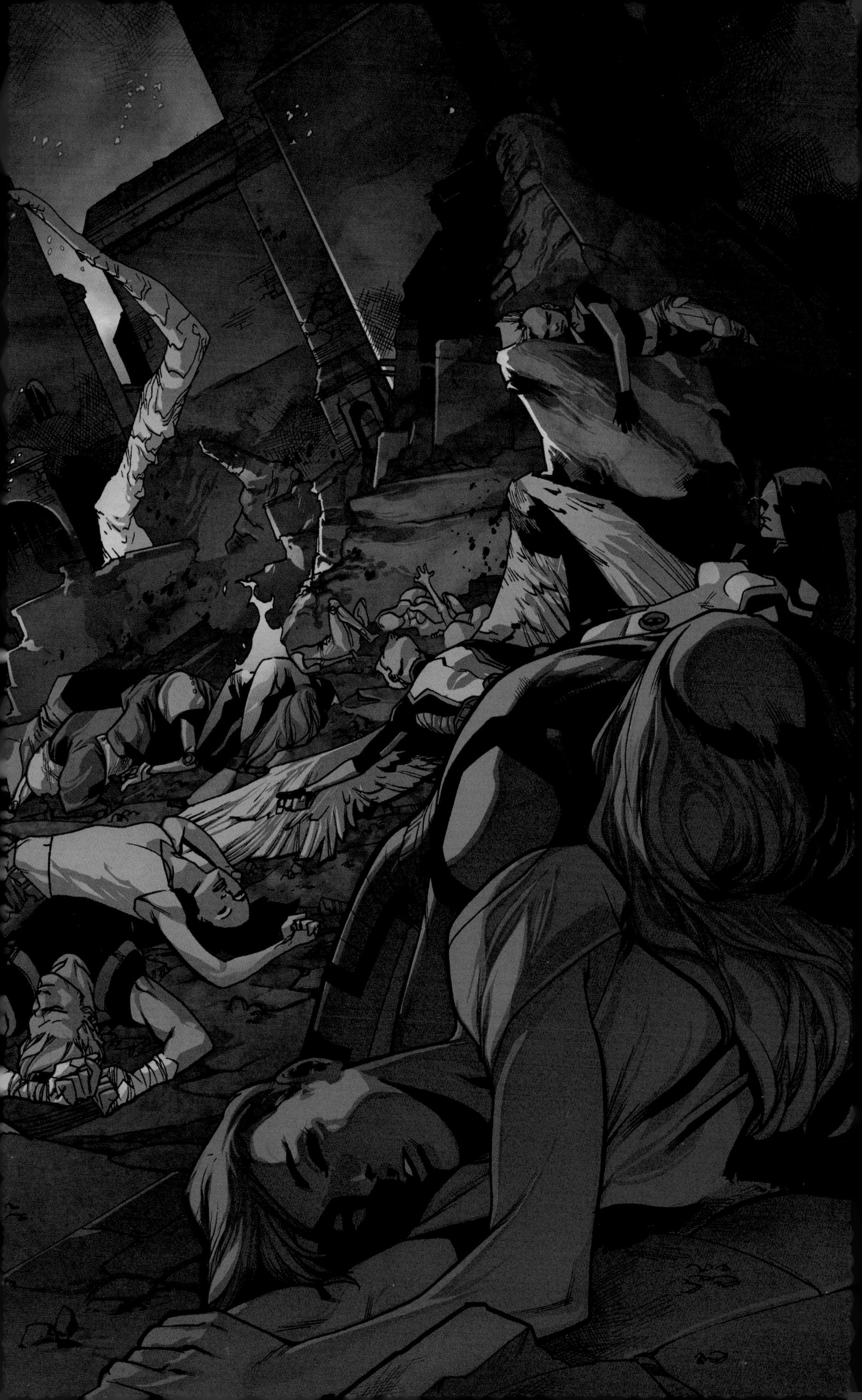

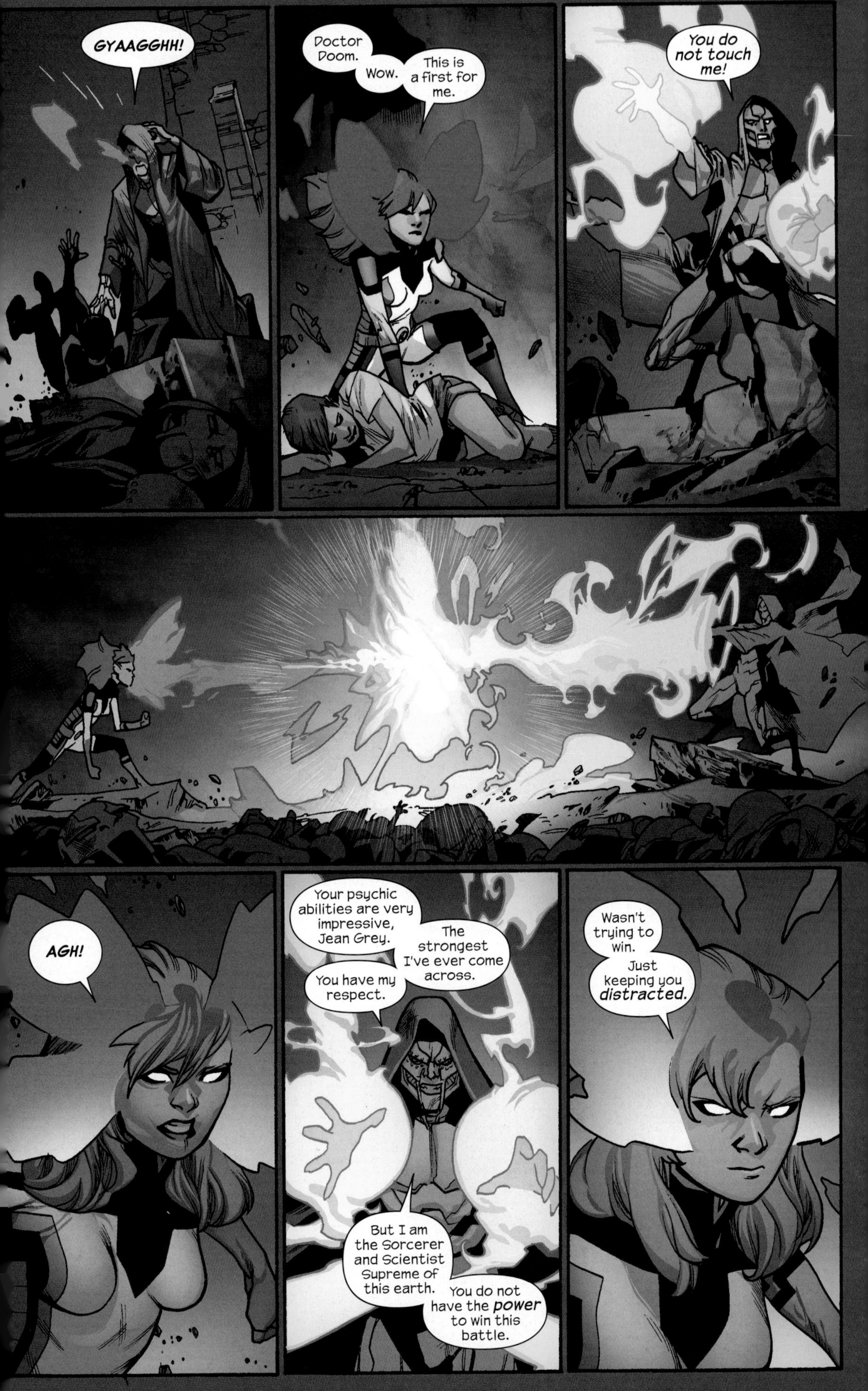
GYAAGGHH!
Doctor Doom.
Wow.
This is a first for me.
You do not touch me!
AGH!
Your psychic abilities are very impressive, Jean Grey.
The strongest I've ever come across.
You have my respect.
But I am the Sorcerer and Scientist Supreme of this earth.
You do not have the power to win this battle.
Wasn't trying to win.
Just keeping you distracted.

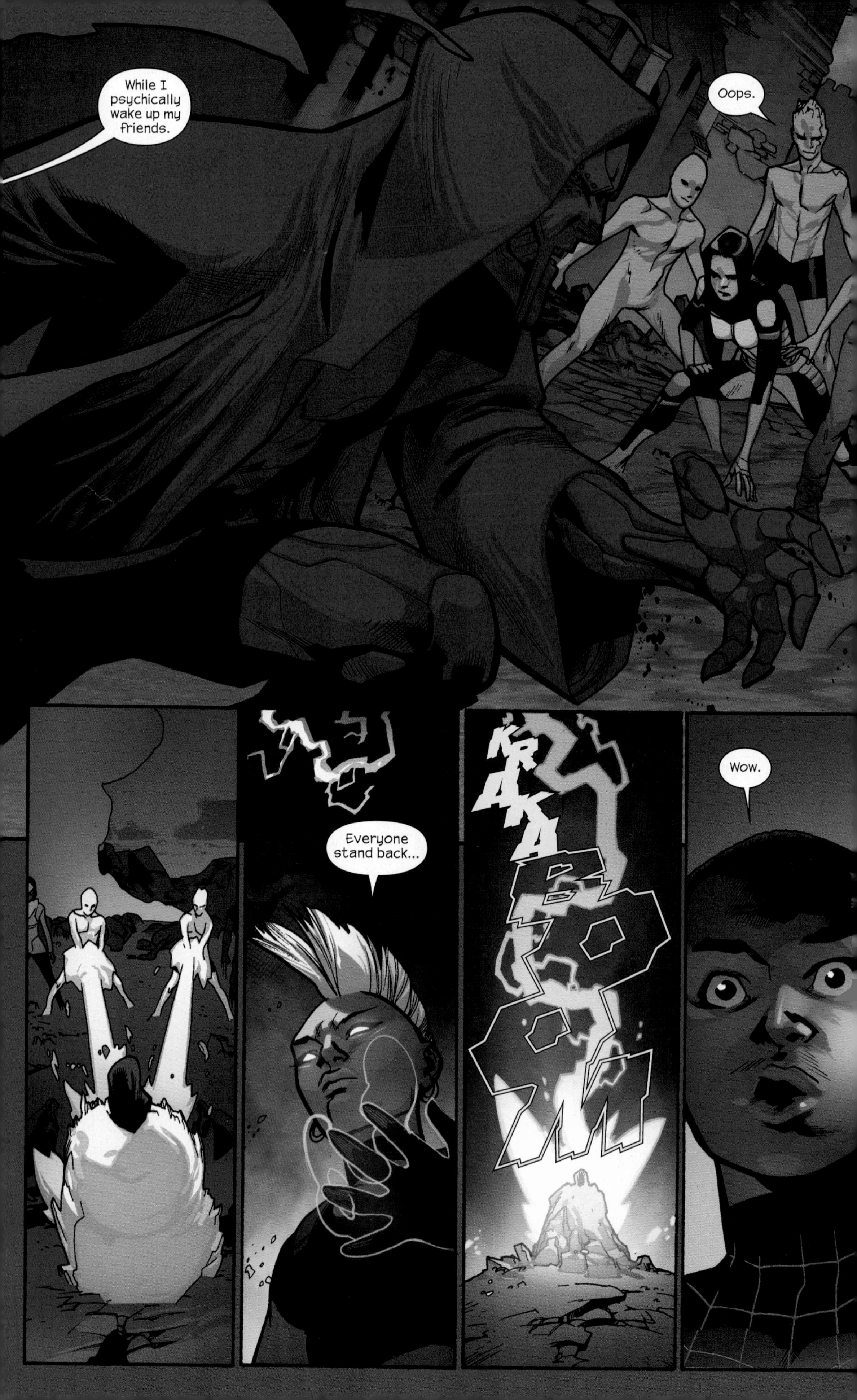
While I psychically wake up my friends.
Oops.
Everyone stand back...
KRAKABOOM
Wow.

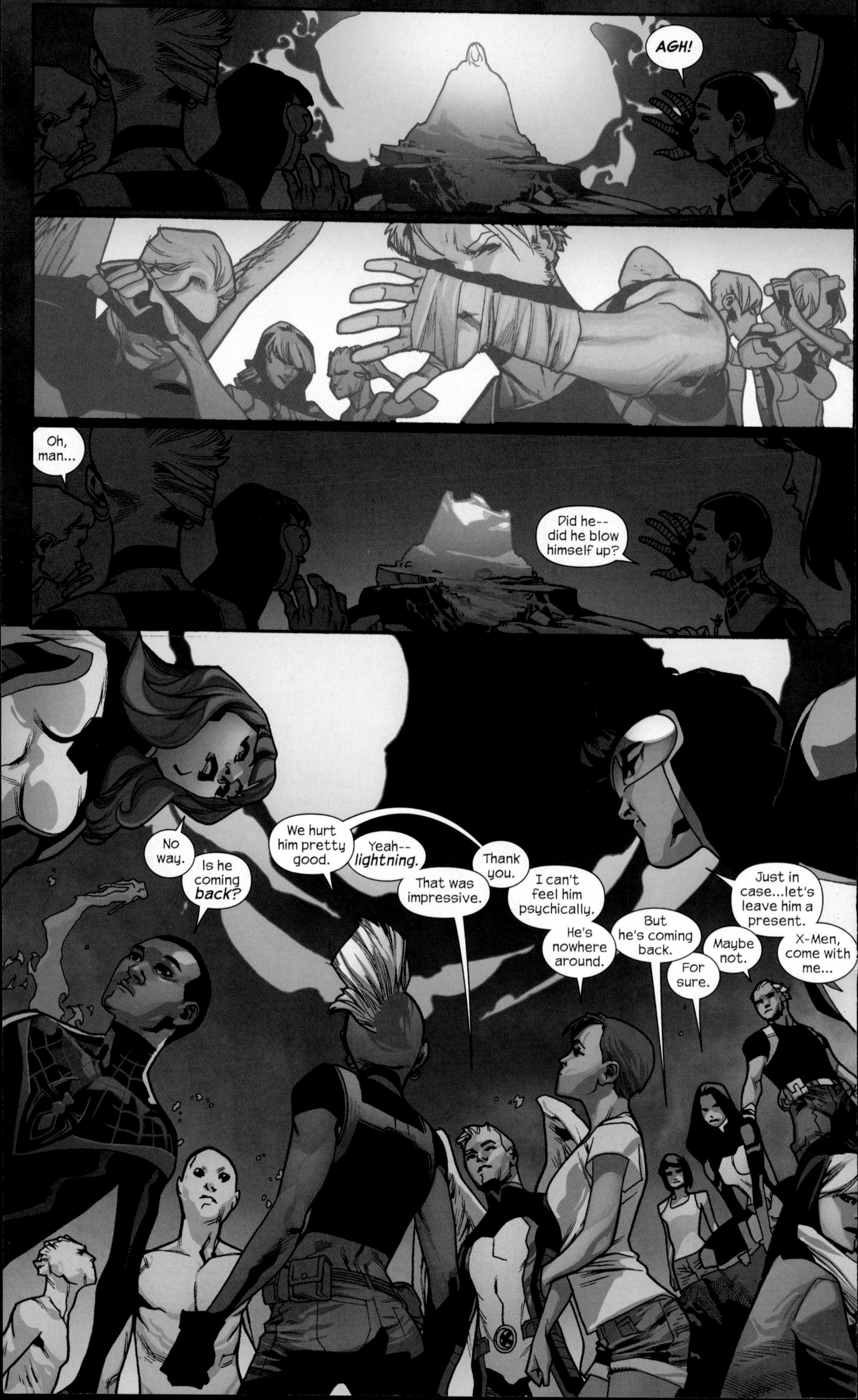
AGH!
Oh, man...
Did he-- did he blow himself up?
No way.
Is he coming back?
We hurt him pretty good.
Yeah-- lightning.
Thank you.
That was impressive.
I can't feel him psychically.
He's nowhere around.
But he's coming back.
For sure.
Maybe not.
Just in case...let's leave him a present.
X-Men, come with me...

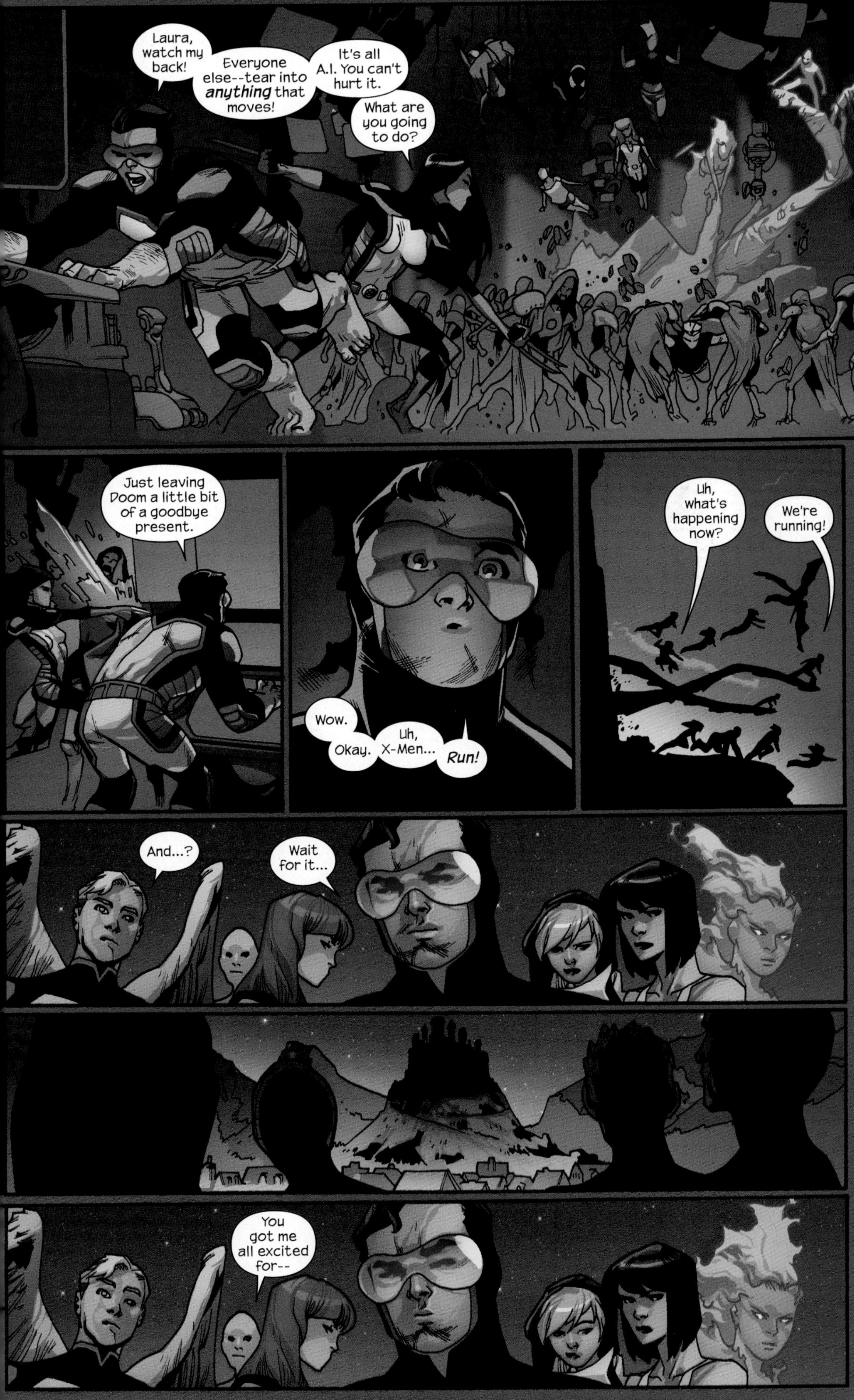
Laura, watch my back!
Everyone else--tear into *anything* that moves!
It's all A.I. You can't hurt it.
What are you going to do?
Just leaving Doom a little bit of a goodbye present.
Wow.
Okay.
Uh, X-Men...
Run!
Uh, what's happening now?
We're running!
And...?
Wait for it...
You got me all excited for--

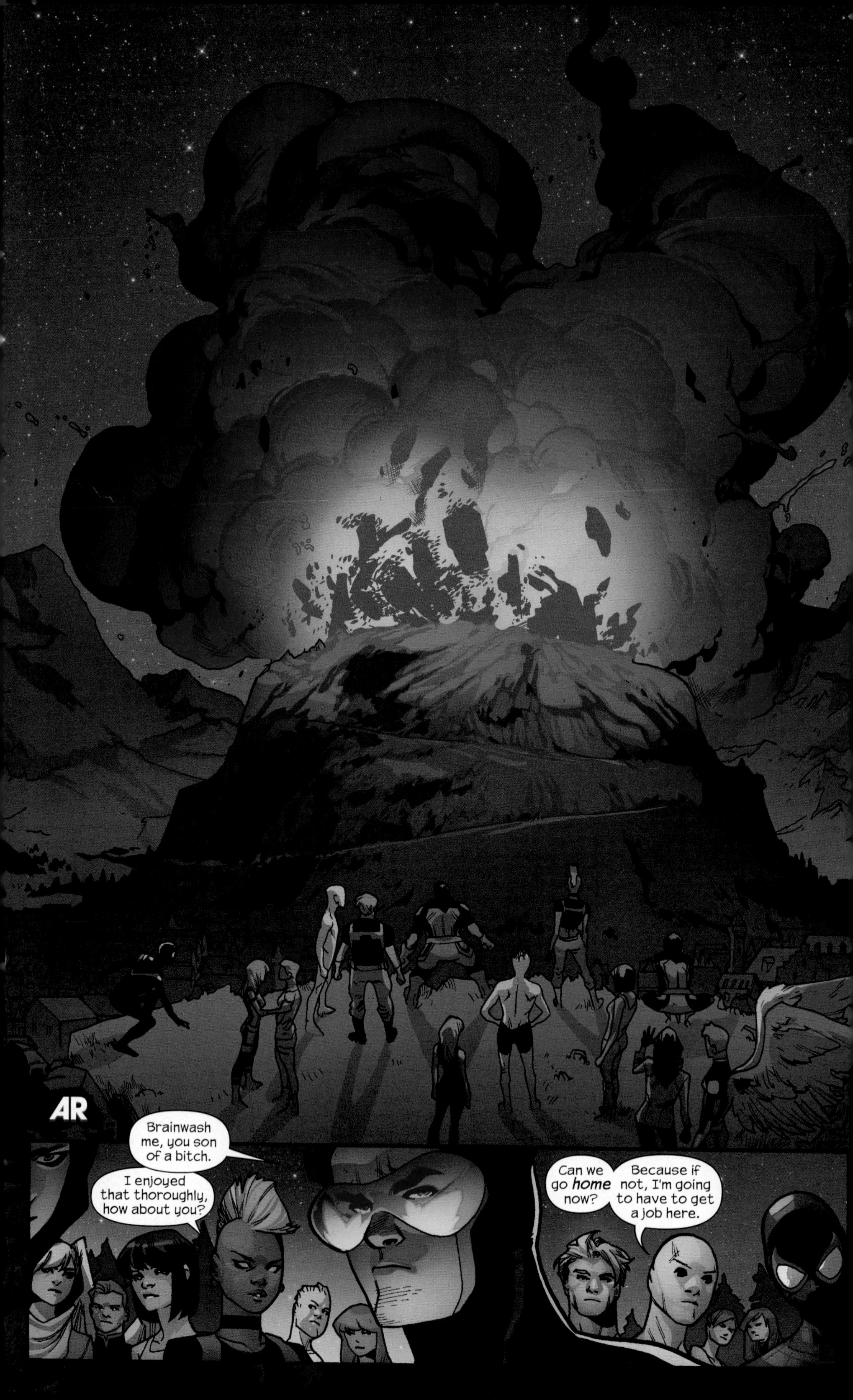

Brainwash me, you son of a bitch.
I enjoyed that thoroughly, how about you?
Can we go *home* now?
Because if not, I'm going to have to get a job here.

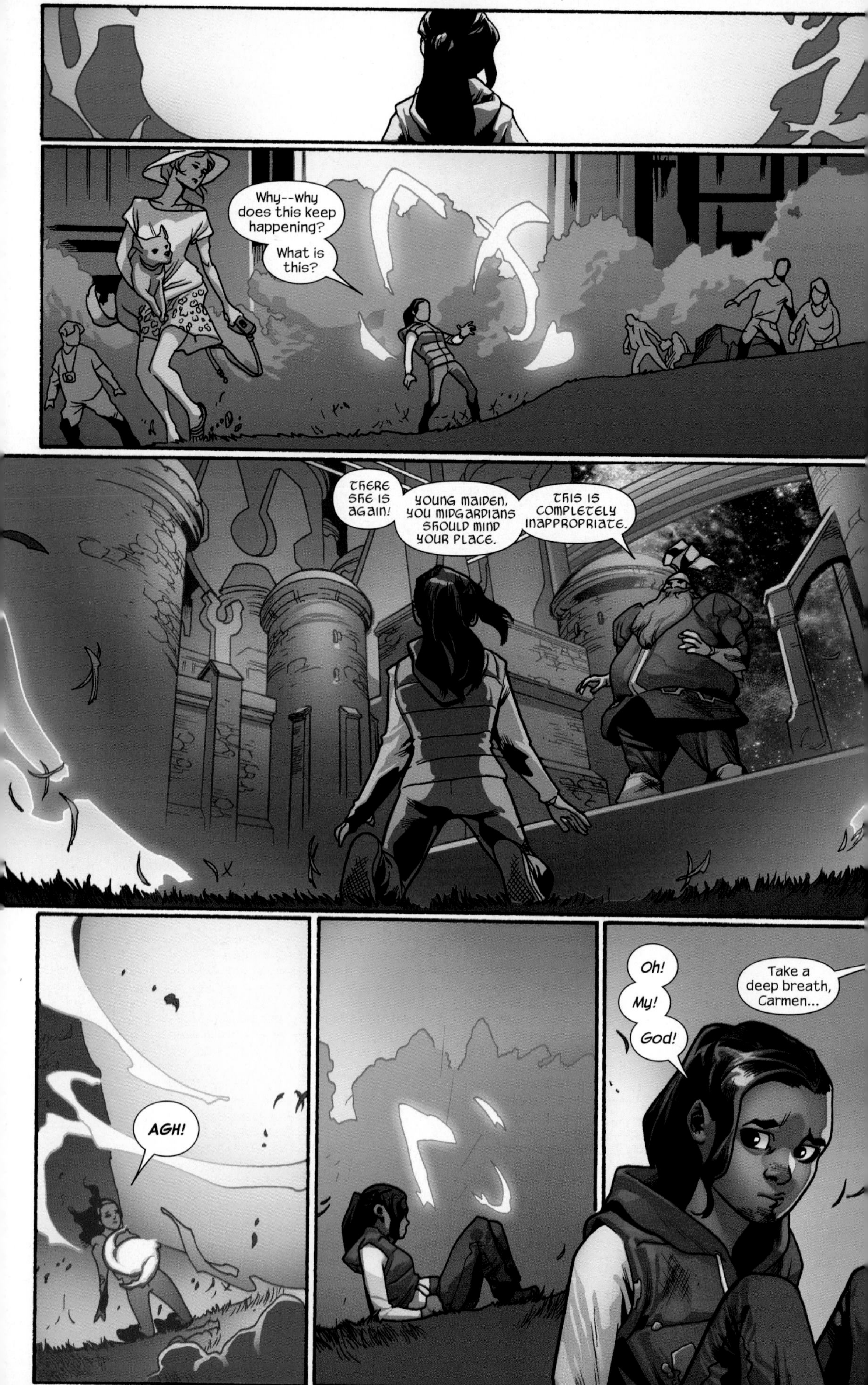
Why--why does this keep happening?
What is this?
THERE SHE IS AGAIN!
YOUNG MAIDEN, YOU MIDGARDIANS SHOULD MIND YOUR PLACE.
THIS IS COMPLETELY INAPPROPRIATE.
AGH!
Oh!
My!
God!
Take a deep breath, Carmen...

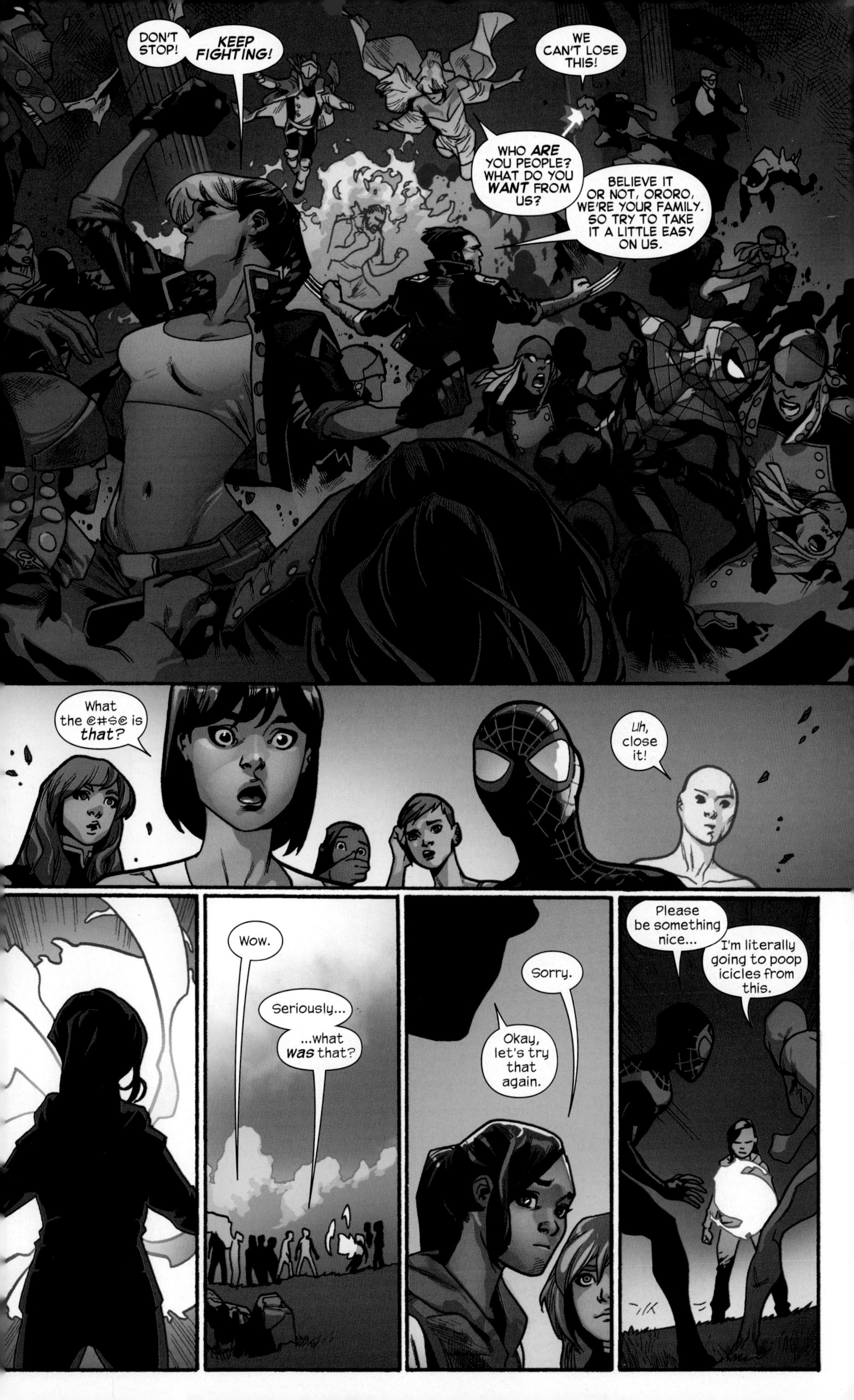
DON'T STOP!
KEEP FIGHTING!
WE CAN'T LOSE THIS!
WHO ARE YOU PEOPLE? WHAT DO YOU WANT FROM US?
BELIEVE IT OR NOT, ORORO, WE'RE YOUR FAMILY. SO TRY TO TAKE IT A LITTLE EASY ON US.
What the @#$@ is that?
Uh, close it!
Wow.
Seriously...
...what was that?
Sorry.
Okay, let's try that again.
Please be something nice...
I'm literally going to poop icicles from this.

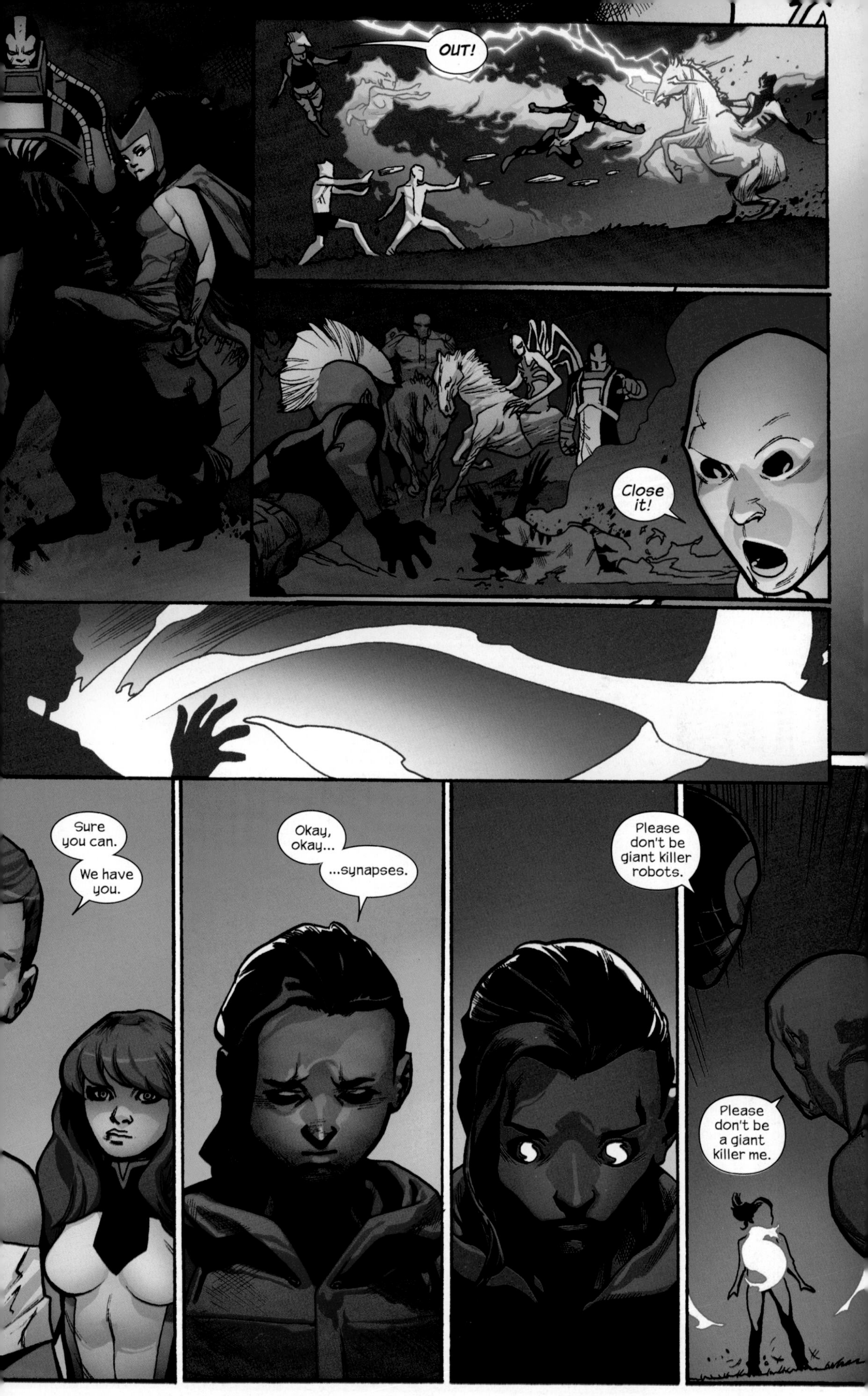
OUT!
Close it!
Sure you can.
We have you.
Okay, okay...
...synapses.
Please don't be giant killer robots.
Please don't be a giant killer me.

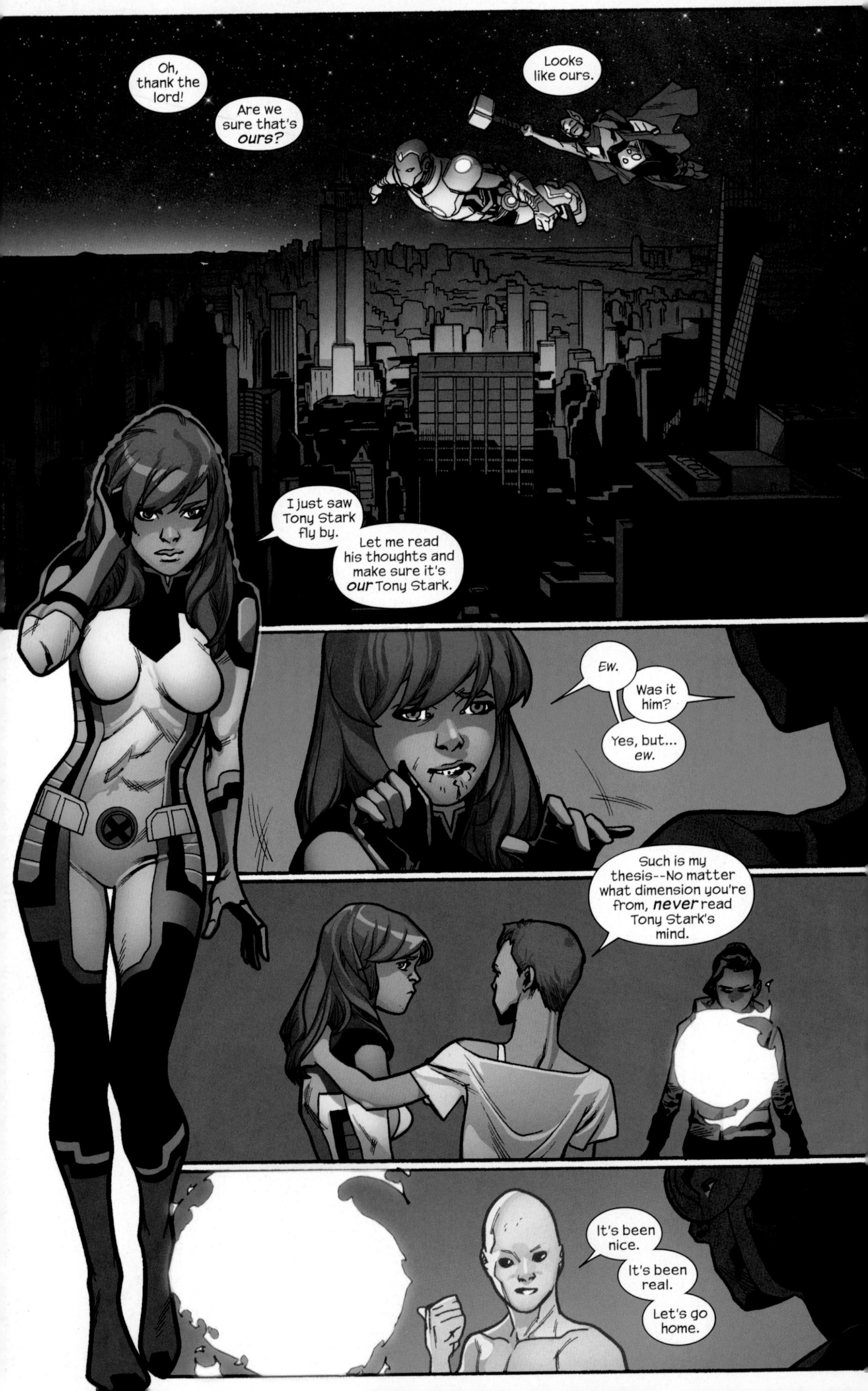

Oh, thank the lord!
Are we sure that's *ours?*
Looks like ours.
I just saw Tony Stark fly by.
Let me read his thoughts and make sure it's ***our*** Tony Stark.
Ew.
Was it him?
Yes, but... *ew.*
Such is my thesis--No matter what dimension you're from, ***never*** read Tony Stark's mind.
It's been nice.
It's been real.
Let's go home.

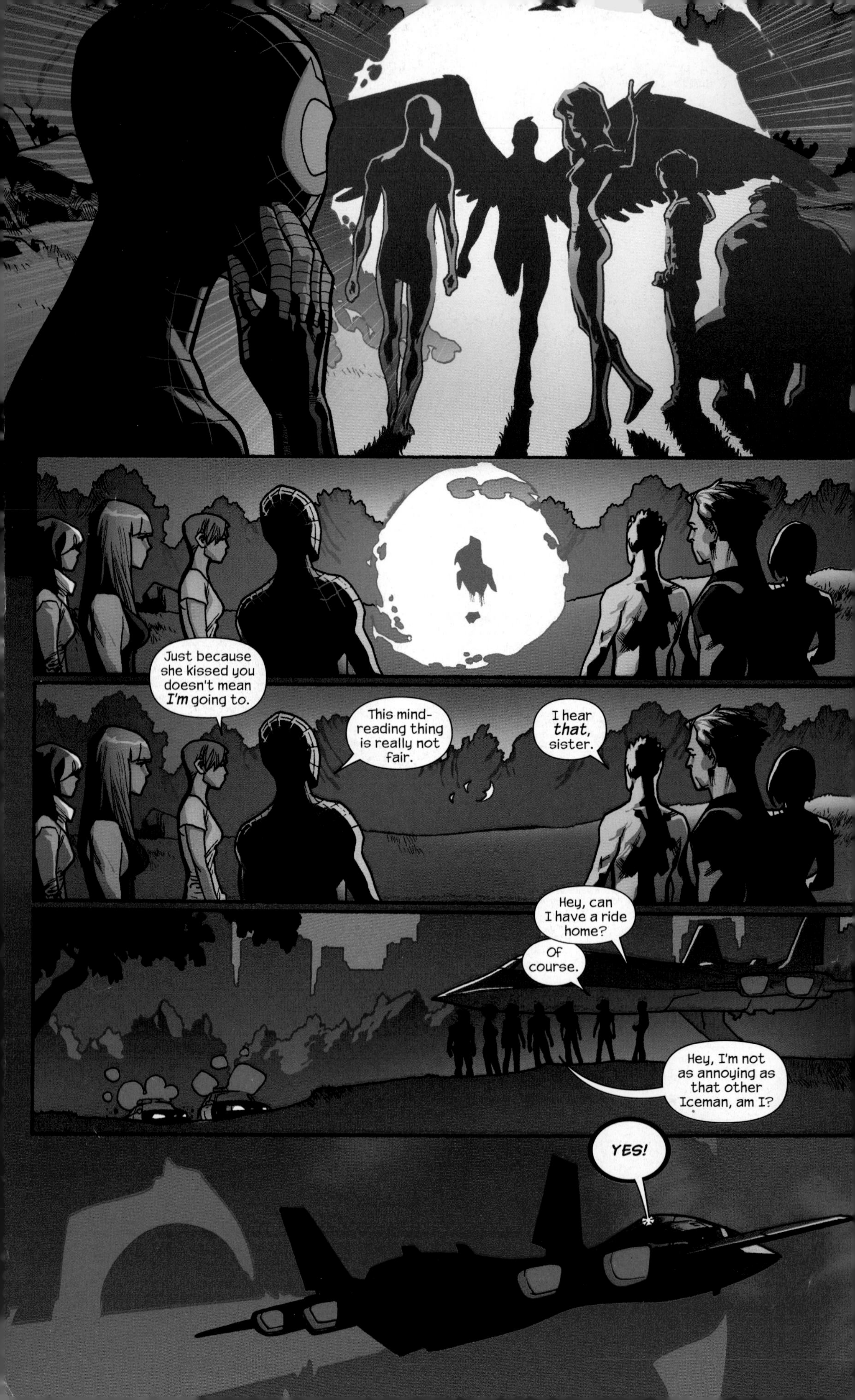
Just because she kissed you doesn't mean I'm going to.
This mind-reading thing is really not fair.
I hear that, sister.
Hey, can I have a ride home?
Of course.
Hey, I'm not as annoying as that other Iceman, am I?
YES!

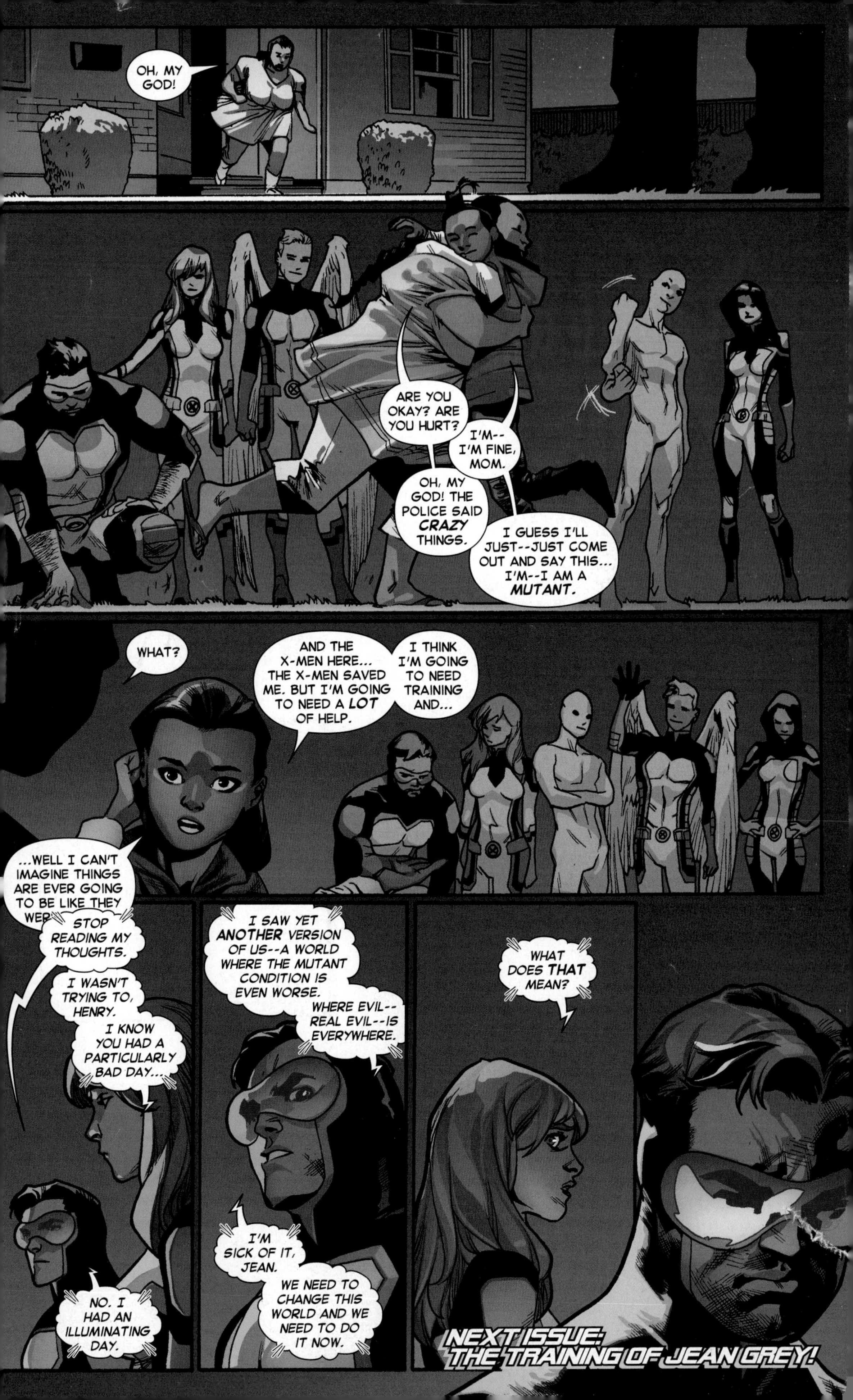

OH, MY GOD!
ARE YOU OKAY? ARE YOU HURT?
I'M-- I'M FINE, MOM.
OH, MY GOD! THE POLICE SAID **CRAZY** THINGS.
I GUESS I'LL JUST--JUST COME OUT AND SAY THIS... I'M--I AM A **MUTANT.**
WHAT?
AND THE X-MEN HERE... THE X-MEN SAVED ME. BUT I'M GOING TO NEED A **LOT** OF HELP.
I THINK I'M GOING TO NEED TRAINING AND...
...WELL I CAN'T IMAGINE THINGS ARE EVER GOING TO BE LIKE THEY WER
STOP READING MY THOUGHTS.
I WASN'T TRYING TO, HENRY.
I KNOW YOU HAD A PARTICULARLY BAD DAY...
NO. I HAD AN ILLUMINATING DAY.
I SAW YET **ANOTHER** VERSION OF US--A WORLD WHERE THE MUTANT CONDITION IS EVEN WORSE.
WHERE EVIL--REAL EVIL--IS EVERYWHERE.
I'M SICK OF IT, JEAN.
WE NEED TO CHANGE THIS WORLD AND WE NEED TO DO IT NOW.
WHAT DOES **THAT** MEAN?
NEXT ISSUE: THE TRAINING OF JEAN GREY!

TO ACCESS THE FREE *MARVEL AUGMENTED REALITY APP* THAT ENHANCES AND CHANGES THE WAY YOU EXPERIENCE COMICS

1. **Download the app for free via marvel.com/ARapp**
2. **Launch the app on your camera-enabled Apple iOS® or Android™ device***
3. **Hold your mobile device's camera over any cover or panel with the AR graphic**
4. **Sit back and see the future of comics in action!**

*Available on most camera-enabled Apple iOS® and Android™ devices. Content subject to change and availability.

ALL-NEW X-MEN

AR INDEX